GREEN NAZIS IN SPACE!

NEW ESSAYS ON LITERATURE, ART, & CULTURE

by

JAMES J. O'MEARA

EDITED BY GREG JOHNSON

Counter-Currents Publishing Ltd.
San Francisco
2015

Copyright © 2015 by James J. O'Meara
All rights reserved

Cover design by Kevin I. Slaughter

Published in the United States by
COUNTER-CURRENTS PUBLISHING LTD.
P.O. Box 22638
San Francisco, CA 94122
USA
http://www.counter-currents.com/

Hardcover ISBN: 978-1-935965-97-8
Paperback ISBN: 978-1-935965-98-5
E-book ISBN: 978-1-935965-99-2

Library of Congress Cataloging-in-Publication Data

O'Meara, James J., 1956- author.
 Green Nazis in space! : new essays on literature, art, & culture / by James J. O'meara ; edited by Greg Johnson.
    pages cm
 Includes index.
 ISBN 978-1-935965-97-8 (hardcover : alk. paper) -- ISBN 978-1-935965-98-5 (pbk. : alk. paper)
 1. Literature and society. 2. Masculinity in literature. 3. Men and literature. I. Johnson, Greg, 1971- editor. II. Title.

PN51.O45 2015
809'.93358--dc23

2015001416

Contents

Preface ❖ iii

1. Green Nazis in Space! ❖ 1
2. Welcome to the Club: The Rise & Fall of the *Männerbund* in Pre-War American Pop Culture ❖ 16
3. The Leaven of the Pharisees: The Judeo as Cuckoo ❖ 44
4. Kafka: Our Racial Comrade ❖ 60
5. Michel Houellebecq's Sexual Anti-Utopia ❖ 70
6. The Fraud of Miss Jean Brodie ❖ 80
7. To Cut Up a Mockingbird: Harper Lee's *Go Set a Watchman* ❖ 88
8. Sour Cream: Michael Nelson's *A Room in Chelsea Square* ❖ 105
9. "The Wild Boys Smile": Reflections on Olaf Stapledon's *Odd John* ❖ 120
10. From Odd John to Strange Love ❖ 162
11. From Ultrasuede to Limelight: Halston & Gatien, Aryan Entrepreneurs in the Dark Age ❖ 178
12. Reflections on Sartorial Fascism ❖ 207

Index ❖ 229

About the Author ❖ 250

This book is for

Jeremy Reed
Poet Laureate of Pop

"But for those who live their dreams, the angel of Death wears black lipstick."

Preface

If I were forced to give it a characterization of some sort—and Mr. Publisher certainly insists that I do so—I would say that this collection continues the themes of my first two collections[1]—most fundamentally, the Aryan *Männerbund* versus Judaic Family Values[2]—but rather than rooting them out in culture high (Henry James) and low (H. P. Lovecraft), here I concentrate on the popular middle ground of prestige Hollywood films, bestselling novels, and the worlds of high fashion and urban nightlife. Seen from that angle, my most recent publication, a small, novella-length[3] collection of mediations on *Mad Men*,[4] serves as a kind of *amuse bouche* preceding the feast that awaits you herein.

Lest it be thought that this move to the study of Pop Culture is turning away from serious, Traditionalist matters in a last, desperate stab at fame and fortune—or only that—let me once more call the reader's attention to the inspirational insight of the archetypal—and archetypical—poet Jeremy Reed: that the hysterical fascination of the pop fan with his idol is not so far removed from the fanaticism of the spiritual devotee and his icon.

And in torch singing, the diva's passionate devotion to unrequired love and the flamboyant gestural vocabulary that ac-

---

[1] *The Homo & the Negro: Masculinist Meditations on Politics & Popular Culture*, ed. Greg Johnson (San Francisco: Counter-Currents, 2012) and *The Eldritch Evola . . . & Others: Traditionalist Meditations on Literature, Art, & Culture*, ed. Greg Johnson (San Francisco: Counter-Currents, 2014).

[2] See *Male Mysteries and the Secret of the Männerbund* by Wulf Grimsson, reviewed in *The Homo & the Negro*, *op. cit.*, and Alisdair Clarke, "*Männerbund*: Aspects of Male Mystery Cults" (published in *New Imperium* magazine March 2006), http://aryanfuturism.blogspot.com/2006/03/mannerbund-and-homosexuality.html.

[3] "The dear, the blessed *nouvelle*!"—Henry James.

[4] *End of an Era:* Mad Men *& the Ordeal of Civility* (San Francisco: Counter-Currents, 2015).

companies the singer's resignation to loss is not so far removed from the poet's desperate realization that only a part of his inner vision will be transmitted to the page.[5]

Please accept these pages, dear Reader, as my own series of flamboyant gestures of passionate devotion and desperate resignation. Enjoy!

As per usual, my thanks to Dr. Greg Johnson, for all his efforts on behalf of myself and our race; to Mr. Kevin I. Slaughter, for cobbling together another outstanding original cover design out of my mute, inglorious gestures; to Dr. Kevin MacDonald, who accepted an earlier version of Chapter Two that was greatly improved for publication by his critical comments; and above all to the small, distinctly disturbed band of Constant Readers at Counter-Currents.com, for whom most of these small patterns of white and black were first composed.

Rust Belt, USA
December 23, 2015

---

[5] Jeremy Reed: "Poetry, Madness and Masturbation," in *Angels, Demons and Blacklisted Heroes* (London: Peter Owen, 1999), p. 133.

Green Nazis in Space!

Green Lantern (2011); 114 min.
Director: Martin Campbell
Ryan Reynolds as Hal Jordan/Green Lantern; Mark Strong as Sinestro; Peter Sarsgaard as Hector Hammond

"In brightest day, in blackest night,
No evil shall escape my sight,
Let those who worship evil's might,
Beware my power, Green Lantern's light."

"I pledge allegiance to a lantern, given to me by a dying purple alien."
— Hal Jordan

When I was growing up in Detroit in the 1960s and '70s, comic books weren't that big a deal—contra Boomer and Hipster rebooting of pop culture as comic-centric. But during the few years I paid attention to them, comics were a DC joint, if only by default. I occasionally noticed a Marvel "mag" as they would say, but a quick glance revealed them to be not really the soul-feeding material I was looking for; in fact, they seemed—cover your eyes, fanboys with Stan Lee boy-crushes!—well, creepy and weird; for losers, like Disneyland or the Beatles.[1]

Today, of course, I recognize what the problem was—they were the second wave of Judaic culture, in which the mask slipped a bit and a little more of the reality was exposed, deliberately or not.[2]

---

[1] And not the good kind, like Iggy Pop.

[2] At the same time, a similar process, thanks to the Civil Rights Movement, was unfolding amongst the American Negro, who, no longer expected to "act white" and in fact encouraged to "express himself" was embarking on the slow devolution from Cab Calloway to Fitty; and what you lookin' at? Correspondingly, the Judaics have become yet more pushy and vulgar, a Third Wave in which schlubby

Yes, of course, I know that comic books *per se* are a Judaic invention, but the initial, first wave—like Hollywood—was rather sedate, almost entirely Aryan in look and feel (I mean, whatever the "hidden meanings," come on, *Superman*?), while Marvel gave off, quite deliberately I gather, an unmistakable whiff of the *foetor judaicus*.[3]

That would be all the elements the fanboys love: "conflicted" heroes, moral "ambiguity," stopped-up kitchen sink "realism," relentless concentration on "urban" and "only in New York, folks!" settings and "in your face" attitudes, etc. In short, what I've called the Cockroach Culture.[4]

At least I wasn't scarred for life like this poor contemporary of your author:

> **Amazing Spider-Man #5;** October 1963. My first Marvel comic ever, bought off the rack when I was six years old. *This was the most totally shocking comic I had ever read*! Why? As a DC Universe fan, *I was shocked to see the heroes in this book constantly fighting with each other*. It was so bad *I wasn't even sure who the HEROES were supposed to be*.[5]

"Heroes" constantly fighting each other? Divide and conquer bitchez!

The book's star, Spidey, seemed to come off pretty badly

George Costanza is replaced by the in-your-face Sandra Bernhard or Sarah Silverman.

[3] See Jay Geller's "(G)nos(e)ology: The Cultural Construction of the Other" in *People of the Body: Jews and Judaism from an Embodied Perspective*, ed. Howard Eilberg-Schwartz (Albany: SUNY Press, 1992), who notes that Schopenhauer was "perhaps the most celebrated modern disseminator" of the notion.

[4] The more anodyne way of expressing the DC/Marvel difference, is that DC is "plot driven" while Marvel is "character driven." This is fine as far as it goes, but every Marvel "hero" is a pathetic loser; every origin story could be summarized this way: "As Gregor Samsa awoke one morning from unruly dreams, he found himself transformed in his own bed into a monstrous cockroach."

[5] http://www.dialbforblog.com/archives/594/

almost all the time. He wasn't famous and respected, like Superman. And the people and heroes in this book didn't look anything like the people drawn by Curt Swan. They were all weird and . . . Spidery! I didn't know why at the time, as a kid, but of course now we all know why: STEVE DITKO. *Reading this book was like opening the door to another universe*: the MARVEL Universe. *I was hooked* . . .

Hooked indeed! And "bought off the rack". . . they weren't Walt White enough to make the first one free.

With the triumph of this Judaic element in our culture, it's no surprise that this fairly straightforward screen adaptation of the Silver Age Good Guy living in Coast City, CA, would be met with howls of execration.

For example, a blunt judgment from DVD Verdict Jury Room, "*Green Lantern* or Douchebag in Space": "Hal Jordan (Ryan Reynolds) . . . is probably the worst superhero ever portrayed on screen."[6] Or from Amazon:

> [T]oday's movie superhero fans expect a guy in a cloak that's just like you and me without any of the world-spanning baggage. Green Lantern's guilty of being true to Green Lantern, spandex, mask, ring and all. For those who find it implausible, maybe a superhero powered by a jade-colored light source isn't for them.

Indeed. Just like us — a cockroach in a cloak.

Since no one saw the film, here you go, from our friends at DVD Verdict:

> Hal Jordan (Ryan Reynolds, *Buried*) is a cocky test pilot with a troubled past and disdain for authority. His reckless ways in the air land him in trouble with his employers and his on-again-off-again love interest Carol Ferris (Blake Lively, *The Town*). That's the least of his worries, though, after an alien spacecraft crash lands on Earth and its dying

---

[6] http://www.dvdverdict.com/juryroom/viewtopic.php?t=5195%20\%20p66521

pilot, Abin Sur (Temura Morrison, *Star Wars Episode II: Attack of the Clones*) gives him a powerful ring and lantern, telling Hal that he is a Green Lantern.[7]

What's a Green Lantern? That's what Hal learns as he's whisked off into space, to the planet Oa, where he discovers he's the newest member of an intergalactic peacekeeping force. There, he meets his trainers, Tomar-Re (Geoffrey Rush, *The King's Speech*) and Kilowog (Michael Clark Duncan, *Daredevil*), along with the esteemed Sinestro (Mark Strong, *Sherlock Holmes*), who has some radical ideas about how the Green Lantern Corps is to be run.[8]

Back on Earth, quirky scientist Hector Hammond (Peter Sarsgaard, *Orphan*) becomes infected with a piece of Parallax, the alien who killed Abin Sur. Now Hector is getting smarter, more grotesque, and more bloodthirsty. In conjunction with this, Parallax itself is headed straight for Earth. Is Hal Jordan's will strong enough to conquer his fears, save the world, and prove himself worthy of the Green Lantern name?

I don't have much memory of Green Lantern, and I gather the film is in fact rather unfaithful in several aspects of the Silver Age version; this Sinestro chap is actually supposed to be a super-villain, not a mentor, and GL actually becomes this Parallax guy, etc., but for the reasons already given, I never read a comic book after about age 12 and never will have the patience to work through the several decades of ret-cons and rebooting that DC has gone through in a fruitless attempt to "marvelize" itself as part of its surrender to the Cockroach Culture.[9] Let's just take the movie as it is.

---

[7] http://www.dvdverdict.com/printer/greenlanternbluray.php

[8] And who, in addition to playing the chrome-domed villain in every single movie—*Kick Ass, Sherlock Holmes, Robin Hood, Green Lantern, John Carter*—shares the cutest little snaggle-toothed smile with your humble author.

[9] Or, to some, a "rich mythology that has developed around the Emerald Knight over the course of more than seven decades," http://www.geeksofdoom.com/2011/06/20/green-lantern-was-almost-a-jack-black-comedy

Of course, a lot of that might have been added or explained away if the movie hadn't bombed and the producers, drunk on visions of another comic book franchise, had had the chance to produce the trilogy that seemed to be their ultimate goal. As it is, it looks like they stirred in plenty of *Lord of the Rings* stuff for luck. There's the usual "humans are too dumb/primitive to help." Oa looks like a Lovecraftian version of Rivendell, while Sinestro seemed to be doing a lot of Hugo Weaving-ing. On the other hand, he even forges another ring to supposedly fight the Bad Guy with his own Evil Power, as Gandalf advised against, though as far as I remember that subplot simply disappeared. If the Council of Elrond was the UN Security Council, the meet-up of all the alien Green Lanterns went one better in size and variety of species, sort of like the General Assembly.[10] Of course, like the UN, bigger does not mean better.[11]

But really the problem lies with the most basic decision that the producers made: imposing the same old "superhero movie" template on far more interesting material. A reviewer at Amazon is perceptive enough to deserve quoting at some length; after Hal arrives on the aforementioned Oa:

---

[10] Reviewing Arie Kaplan's *From Krakow to Krypton: Jews and Comic Books* (Philadelphia: Jewish Publication Society, 2008) on Counter-Currents, Ted Sallis notes, "The same thing was going on at DC comics. Kaplan writes: 'And the fact that Broome and Kane were "members of the Tribe" meant that occasional Jewish signifiers filtered into the stories . . . The intergalactic diversity of the Green Lantern Corps is a metaphor for the ethnic diversity Broome wished for all peoples.' *All* peoples? Including Israel?" http://www.counter-currents.com/2011/10/from-krakow-to-krypton-jews-and-comic-books/

[11] And it could have been worse; as the aforementioned Geeks of Doom report, the original idea was *a comedy starring Jack Black*. "It's indicative of Hollywood's simmering contempt for comic book properties and sadistic desire to milk every last cent they can out of them that they were willing to transform an iconic superhero like the Green Lantern into a one-note comic buffoon in the desperate hope their devious effort would make them a profit." For a review of the similar attempt to re-boot the Green Hornet as Seth Rogan, see my Counter-Currents review "The Green Cockroach," http://www.counter-currents.com/2011/01/the-green-cockroach/

At this point I excitedly waited for the film to really take off. Until now there had been some exciting action and nice character work. Hal had been firmly established as a screw-up, adrift in life, hoping for something bigger, and now that fate has handed him the chance to join the Green Lantern Corps, he presumably has a chance to right his course in life. But in an incredibly contrived moment, he decides that he's not up to snuff, quits the corps, and returns to Earth (although, strangely enough, he is allowed to keep the ring). Instead of the epic space opera I was expecting, the filmmaker decides on something far more quotidian: a superhero movie. The rest of the film goes through the usual superhero motions . . .

Green Lantern is a decidedly schizophrenic movie. Where the first half of the film provides the perfect setup for the "hero's journey," a story about one character being plucked from the mundane world and lifted into an exciting realm of adventure, the second half of the film seems content on playing superhero connect the dots. . . .

Unlike Batman, Spider-Man, or even Superman, the Green Lantern Corps lends itself to interplanetary superheroics more in the vein of *Star Wars* and Flash Gordon than Iron Man. But this is also what makes the character exciting. Where we have seen the basic outline of a superhero movie time and again, *Green Lantern* offers the chance of more science fiction tropes, which could potentially differentiate him from the glut of other superhero movies. Instead of shying away from the imaginatively bizarre, the filmmakers should have embraced the alien aspects of the Green Lantern mythos. Perhaps the most frustrating aspect of *Green Lantern* is that it represents a missed opportunity. . . . Trying to make *Green Lantern* like *Iron Man* was a grievous error in judgment. I expected more from Martin Campbell.[12]

This, I think, is why the second half is not only uninvolving

---

[12] Who directed the rather successful Bond re-boot, *Casino Royale*, which indeed is more of a "hero's quest" showing how Bond becomes Bond rather than super-agent heroics.

but wrong-headed. I'm no more interested in "space operatics" than "super-heroics," but what this reviewer has tumbled on is that the basic Green Lantern story — both how an individual deals with his fate and the creation of an Order of such men — is much more than "the usual superhero motions": an actual Traditionalist myth — or *mythos*, for you Lovecraftians.

While Superman just falls ass over teakettle into superpowers, and Batman struggles to become, really, just a vigilante in need of psychiatric help, the third-string player on DC's roster is far more interesting: he is offered the chance to remake himself, become his own creator. It is a hermetic if not heroic quest.[13]

As IronFanofSteelofThunder (sheesh!) recently noted:

> The difference is this: Green Lantern is the one guy who not only had some really cool powers and adventures thrust upon him, *he was required to be actively responsible as well.* Superman could've just stayed a farmer. Batman could've been a normal person and gone through some therapy rather than becoming the world's finest ninja. Billy Batson could've been Batman. Bilbo could've stayed in his hole! *The difference between Green Lantern and those other guys is they didn't really have a choice and because his power chose him in spite of him.* . . . Green Lantern is kind of a loser, *but can conquer his own fears.* That's what makes him a winner. Because he doesn't really have a choice. I mean . . . he does. But does he?[14]

Well, it is hard to tell, when it's a man and his fate. Does he choose it, or does it choose him?[15]

---

[13] See my "Evola on Wheels: Psychomania as Hermetic Initiation," http://www.counter-currents.com/2013/10/evola-on-wheels-psychomania-as-a-hermetic-initiation/

[14] IronFanofSteelofThunder; "What Makes Green Lantern Great: A comparison with Lord of the Rings, Batman, CAPTAIN MARVEL, and Superman," September 10, 2013, http://www.comicvine.com/profile/ironfanofsteelofthunder/blog/what-makes-green-lantern-great-a-comparison-with-1/93656/

[15] Evola discusses the various theories of pre-natal choice, and

"The ring chooses you."[16]

He, like us, doesn't really have a choice, if he wants to be a real man.

Jef Costello recently made use of a couple of D. H. Lawrence quotes he picked up from Derek Hawthorne, and I'll use them here too:

> "It is the desire of the human male to build a world: not 'to build a world for you, dear'; but to build up *out of his own self and his own belief and his own effort* something wonderful. Not merely something useful. Something wonderful" (*Fantasia of the Unconscious*, p. 18).

And:

> "Primarily and supremely man is always the pioneer of life, adventuring onward into the unknown, alone with his own temerarious, dauntless soul. *Woman for him exists only in the twilight, by the camp fire, when day has departed.* Evening and the night are hers" (*Ibid.* p. 109).

Whereas, of course, the superhero is the far more conventional figure, saving the innocent and winning the girl, living happily ever after.[17]

This dichotomy, as Lawrence postulates it, is in harmony with the division Baron Evola makes between society, the realm of women and family values, and the State, the realm of war and men.[18]

---

their implications, in the discussion of suicide in *Ride the Tiger: A Survival Manual for Aristocrats of the Soul*, trans. Joscelyn Godwin and Constance Fontana (Rochester, Vt.: Inner Traditions, 2003).

[16] Despite several repetitions in appropriately awed tones, I never shook off the feeling that his was from a Yaakov Smirnoff routine: "In America, you choose ring; in Soviet Union, ring chooses you!"

[17] Of course, Christopher Nolan's Batman series has succeeded, by choice or not, in highlighting hermetic and Traditionalist elements, even questioning the validity of the whole "saving Gotham" motive.

[18] See his *Men Among the Ruins*, trans. Guido Stucco, ed. Michael

In that light, here's IronFanofSteelofThunder's summary of what we've been calling the Green Lantern Mythos:

> Fearless adrenaline junkie, Hal Jordan, suddenly has the most powerful weapon in the galaxy, the Green Lantern's ring, forced upon him. He goes to the home planet of the Green Lantern Corps, Oa, and finds out that he is a member of an exclusive force of super space cops.

Now, that's a movie![19]

I think in general we can say that tempting as it is to see the "superhero" genre, either as comic book or movie, as one of the last locations for manly heroism, it represents a corruption—a rendering ineffective—of the Aryan Hermetic Quest; the Hero is constantly expected to put his self-actualizing on hold while saving *Untermenschen* and pining away for some female. Back to the campfire, in short.

OK, for now, let's get back to *Green Lantern*. The basic idea, here, is that Hal Jordan is chosen by the Ring because he is without fear; actually, because *his will is powerful enough* to overcome his fear. The Ring then will enable him to fully exteriorize what he wills; this is his only "superpower."[20]

Moynihan (Rochester, Vt.: Inner Traditions, 2002).

[19] Paris: "Wealthy, good-looking hedonistic heir to billion dollar multi-national media conglomerate moves to London and spends nights pining away for his college girlfriend—who's watching that movie?" The Gilmore Girls, "The Long Morrow."

[20] We see a similar set-up in the equally white movie *Dune*, where Paul Atreides shows his chosen-ness by conquering fear, although this is only a prelude to his actually transformation through the spice. There's even a little oath, just like Hal's:

> *I must not fear.*
> Fear is the mind-killer.
> Fear is the little-death that brings total obliteration.
> I will face my fear.
> I will permit it to pass over me and through me.
> And when it has gone past I will turn the inner eye to see its path.
> Where the fear has gone there will be nothing.

The ring that gives Hal his powers, or rather, allows him to wield them, is obviously once again the Hermetic Stone. Apart from its green color, its Luciferian origin is even more obvious than in *Psychomania*: as the Grail was made from, or held, a green stone that had been mounted on Lucifer's crown, or his forehead—Shiva's Third Eye—so this ring falls from the hand of Abin Sur who literally falls from the sky—in his escape pod[21]— after being mortally wounded by Parallax. His vaguely Arabic name jibes with the Arabic origin of this tale,[22] and his Luciferian nature—bearing the Light of the Green Lantern—is rubbed in by his red color. The latter is not exactly a pigment but rather results—an odd fact we learn from the alien autopsy— from his transparent skin, which reveals his musculature. A rather odd evolutionary detour, but it reminds us of how the Realized Man literally reconstructs his body from the inside out, of new, immortal materials, through his realized Will. Not that it helps ol' Abin Sur . . .

So man—or at least a man, Hal—receives from Lucifer—the Light Bearer—the tool with which to develop himself and, ultimately, defeat the malign Abrahamic God. That tool, symbol-

---

Only I will remain.

[21] The Gnostics, some of whom did venerate Lucifer, called their Redeemer "The Alien God." Alien, that is, from the world created by the false, deluded and deluding god, YHVH, whom they, like Blake, liked to call Nobodaddy or The Exterminator; appropriate names for Parallax. If Sur is Lucifer, then his enemy Parallax is the Abrahamic God, or rather, the false, deluded and deluding YHVH. An amorphous, cloudlike being, like Cthulhu, but animated by a malign intelligence. The Church of the Sub-genius returned the favor by designating its nemesis as "the orbital alien space-god, JHVH-1."

[22] Thus, the desert world of Dune is obviously crypto-Arabic; we note also the Ra's al Ghul—"Demon's Head"—in Nolan's *Batman Begins*. Since the Templars—who reportedly worshiped a head, Bathomet—presumably Lucifer's—The Arab has functioned as a symbolic proxy for the Aryan Tradition, perhaps due to it seeming a more manly, thus more Aryan, version of the Abrahamic religion (as Evola thought; see *Revolt Against the Modern World*); or perhaps "the enemy of my enemy"?

ized by the Ring which is charged by the light from the Lamp—is simply this instruction: so strengthen your will so as to be able to create what it wills—become as God.[23]

As I noted in my review of *Psychomania*, this notion, though arcane and hermetic, has more than a little in common with our very familiar American school of "New Thought" or "Mind Science."

For example, here's Wallace D. Wattles giving away The Secret in his classic *The Science of Getting Rich* (an American title if ever there was one):

> *There is a thinking stuff from which all things are made, and which, in its original state, permeates, penetrates, and fills the interspaces of the universe.*
>
> *A thought, in this Substance, produces the thing that is imaged by the thought.*
>
> *Man can form things in his thought, and, by impressing his thought upon formless substance, can cause the thing he thinks about to be created.*[24]

The American proponents of New Thought, such as Wattles—who bore a disconcerting likeness to Percy Kilbride of "Pa Kettle" fame—took their ideas from Emerson, but Emerson was quite clear about taking *his* ideas from Hegel, Plotinus, and ultimately from both Plato and Hinduism.[25] Thus, "New Thought" was "new" only in the American, or Christianized Aryan context; it is, however banalized by New Thought[26] or *Green Lantern*, the transcendent and primordial Tradition.[27] As such, of course, it is also present in the Abrahamic and Christianized Ar-

---

[23] "If one does as God does enough times, one will become as God is."—Hannibal Lecter, *Manhunter*.

[24] New York: Tarcher, 2007; first published 1910; pp. 22–23.

[25] See Anderson and Whitehouse, *New Thought: A Practical American Spirituality* (Bloomington, Ind.: Authorhouse, 2012).

[26] At the beginning of the MST3k version of *Devil Doll*, the possessed dummy, seated in the back of a London taxi, gloats, "I'm driving . . . *with my mind!*"

[27] See Maya D'Oust and Adam Parfrey, *The Secret Source* (Port Townsend, Wash.: Feral House, 2012).

yan religion in the occluded form of "original sin" and "Luciferian pride."[28]

What's really missing from the film is the Green Lantern Corps; even the fanboys complained about how totally wasted the whole idea of the Corps is. It is, of course, a *Männerbund* or rather, its more modern equivalent—a Lodge or Order devoted to preserving Order in the universe.[29]

The Guardians of the Universe are the immortal founders and leaders of the Green Lantern Corps. Resident on Oa, they resemble a mash-up of those Star Trek aliens with the big foreheads with the creepy pulsating vein and the invaders of *Mars Attacks!*, although they seem to be true to the comic book original. They are ensconced atop several gigantically tall but narrow pillars, and seem pretty immobile—the heads seem to move now and then, though that could be a CGI mistake—hence the need of the Corps (though if they are masters of will . . .)[30] They are altogether reminiscent of the stones that the motorcycle gang become at the end of *Psychomania*, although since this is a positive version of the myth it is presumably the immobility of those who have achieved the Center rather than a punishment.

At the climax of the Oa scenes the Corps sends their ring lights skyward in unison, and the effect is reminiscent of the "Cathedral of Light" at that Nuremberg rally . . . say, wasn't that movie called *Triumph of the Will*? And who else had cool rings, too?

But, as we've seen, just when you think it's going to be a cool movie about Green Nazis imposing their irresistible Wills upon the universe, Hal gets homesick or something and returns to Earth, and the whole thing become just another super-

---

[28] See Evola, *The Hermetic Tradition: Symbols and Teachings of the Royal Art*, trans. E. E. Rehmus (Rochester, Vt.: Inner Traditions, 1995), ch. 1.

[29] It's hard to tell if any of the countless aliens are female, though Tomar-Re seemed androgynous enough to remind one of Michael Manning; see my "The Hermetic Environment and Hermetic Incest: The True Androgyne and the 'Ambiguous Wisdom of the Female'," http://jamesjomeara.blogspot.com/search?q=michael+manning

[30] And why don't they recognize Parallax's name in the first place, and? . . . It's just a movie, I should really just relax.

hero soap opera.
From IMDb:

> Superman's first appearance on Earth in the Donner version had you cheering, as Superman saves our feisty, likable damsel in distress Lois Lane, from a nasty helicopter crash, in front of a diverse social cross section of the good people of Metropolis.
>
> Green Lantern's first appearance on Earth leaves you cold, as he saves an already established grease ball politician, from a nasty helicopter crash, in front of a gathering of over-achievers and posh-knobs who frankly you couldn't give a tinker's cuss about.
>
> The script had no character development. *What seemed to be a story about fear and will power turns out to be about fighting a giant tumor and a giant fart.*
>
> The villains were an insult to both the general public and comic book fans intelligence. When will writers learn that smoke doesn't work as a villain? First they did this to Galactus in the equally bad Fantastic Four sequel and now to Parallax.
>
> Did Peter Sarsgaard really think his character could be taken seriously? Not enough with giving one of the most dull performances of all time in the first half of the movie, after he becomes a giant tumor he decides to reach levels of overacting that made him unwatchable.

Peter Sarsgaard plays Hal's nerdy failed romantic rival Hector Hammond (Harry Haller? Hermann Hesse? Heinrich Himmler?) as an unlikeable geek and then as essentially a giant, insane tumor.[31]

Infected by a little bit of Parallax, his color is, like Parallax, yellow; not the true yellow of the Sun, Lion, and indeed, Fear-

---

[31] At times I thought I had fallen asleep and woken up to a repeat of *Spawn*, "in which a vengeful mutant roams the Earth accompanied by an insane farting clown from hell. — "Review: Fascist 'Starship' troops lacking in irony" by Paul Tatara, November 11, 1997, http://www.cnn.com/SHOWBIZ/9711/11/review.starship.troopers/

lessness, but its earthly or demonic counterfeit, the yellow of gold, money, filthy lucre. He is, in short—short!—Alberich, especially in his misshapen mutated form. It's as if we moved from Valhalla to Nibelungland, but never found our way back.

True to form, just as Alberich "rationalizes" and regiments the Nibelung workers, so Hector devises some kind of serum which, when injected, will produce the same mutation. We see here the typical non-Aryan who thinks that elite status can be achieved by some artificial, mechanical method, without either character development or the proper racial background. "Dress British, think Yiddish" as they used to say on Wall Street.

Hector's true status is revealed by his basic goal of stealing Hal's gal. Although we might think of today's peddlers of "The Secret" as Reaganite yuppies, the original New Thinkers were resolutely opposed to the Social Darwinists, Robber Barons, and Trusts of their day; several had emerged from the Social Gospel or Christian Socialist movements, though they also abjured equally crude methods such as state control or revolution.

Instead, they exhorted their readers to "rise from the competitive to the creative plane."[32] The idea was to have the faith that one could *will more*, not use the will to take a limited supply from another. To think otherwise was to accept the idea—what we or the Gnostics would recognize as essentially Judaic—that "God has finished his work."[33] Wallace's phrase irresistibly brings to mind the Biblical creation story, in which Creation is finished and Man is tasked to sweep up occasionally. But then something green appears . . .

Hal is thus able to trick the unfit Hector at the climax by offering him the ring (sound familiar?). Hector thinks he can just take it and redouble his power, but as we know, "The ring chooses you." Hector's powers rebound against him and destroy him—just as happens to someone who attempts initiation without the proper qualifications and predisposition.

Speaking of race—although the movie starts on the right, white note by making Hal a test pilot (a notably white occupation), the later Earth scenes work in all the usual anti-white

---

[32] Wallace, *op. cit.*, p. 38.
[33] Wallace, *op. cit.*, p. 43.

tropes, from the evil blond Senator/father to the black female scientist; in the climax, Hal needs to rescue both her and a generic sassy black female character; in a more Traditional film, their predicaments would have been played for laughs.[34]

Apart from the racial undertones of the climactic battle between Hal and Hector, there is one interesting scene when the evil Senator[35] mocks his son, pre-mutant Hector, as a mere thinker and praises Hal as someone who gets out there and does things. Hal, displaying Aryan modesty and loyalty to his friend, points out that what really matters is the ability to do both.

Plot-wise he's taking his hopeless and ultimately treacherous friend's side against his mean father; but actually, if you listen closely and think a bit, he's enunciating a more nuanced view than either; what our culture must develop are not pale, abstract "thinkers" and rootless, cosmopolitan "critics," nor dusky savages of mere "action" (most likely under the more or less surreptitious control of the former, of course) but men who can think and then act; the man who can *realize his Will*.

Now that would make a great movie! No wonder They didn't want it made. Who has the Will to make it real?

> "His actions are a reminder of why the ring chose each of us—to overcome fear, and destroy evil wherever it may hide. As Lanterns we must fight with all our will. Our wills have not always been united. It's time they were." — Sinestro!

Counter-Currents/*North American New Right*
January 23, 2011

---

[34] "Feets don't fail me now" etc. The post-9/11 behavior of the crowds is decidedly odd: when Parallax hovers above the city, blotting out the sky, they just wander about, "Hey, looky there" and all; only when the buildings start to fall do they reach the level of panic any Tokyo crowd would have exhibited in a classic Godzilla movie right from the start. Poor direction or a comment on our narcotized masses?

[35] Played by an unrecognizable Tim Roth, who seems to be channeling Greg Kinnear's super-douchebag from *Mystery Men*, an earlier Judaic belittling of the Hero myth.

WELCOME TO THE CLUB:
THE RISE AND FALL OF THE *MÄNNERBUND* IN PRE-WAR AMERICAN POP CULTURE

Jeffrey P. Dennis
We Boys Together: Teenagers in Love before Girl-Craziness
Nashville, Tenn.: Vanderbilt University Press, 2007

> "I, state name here, [but everyone just repeats Stymie's name], a member of good standing of the He-Man Woman-Haters Club, do solemnly swear to be a he-man and hate women and not play with them or touch them unless I have to and especially never fall in love and, if I do, may I die slowly and painfully and suffer for hours or until I scream bloody murder."
> — *The Little Rascals*[1]

> "Wherever love and sex prevail, women will command sooner or later."
> —Julius Evola, *L'Arco e la Clava*

> "If you let Andy [Hardy] get too crazy about girls, you lose your audience!"
> —Louie B. Mayer[2]

You know I gotta love any book that not only discusses pre-'60s, or in this case, pre-'40s pop culture, especially the truly popular, beneath critical contempt "B" films or pulp fiction, but also does so with an eye for the archetype of the Wild Boy, who forms the *Männerbund* from which Aryan culture uniquely derives—an interest that unites such disparate observers as Baron

---

[1] Text obtained from http://ourgang.wikia.com/wiki/He-Man_Woman-Haters_Club. This 1994 movie recycles plot elements from the original *Our Gang/Little Rascals* shorts.

[2] Bosley Crother, *Hollywood Raja: The Life and Times of Louis B. Mayer* (New York: Henry Holt, 1960), p. 239.

Evola and William Burroughs.³

Unfortunately, this isn't that book; like most things, it turns out to be more interesting in the planning than in the execution. Although reading the book—or just checking out your favorite old boys' book or movie serial—is well worth it, the caveats I have about the book itself are relevant to more general issues in the Alt-Right area, and thus should be of some interest to Counter-Currents readers.

1. POP CULTURE & "THE CONSERVATIVE"

Before addressing these, and the book itself, I may first need to answer the reader who demands to know what all this has to do with the Alt-Right; who cares about these old movies, comic strips, and penny-dreadfuls anyway?⁴ The answer is, to prevent ourselves from falling from the bright light of the Alt-Right into the error of "conservatism." A "conservative" might be defined as someone who, sensing correctly, but more or less vaguely, that Something is Wrong in modern society, but, lacking Traditional data, as Guénon would say,⁵ looks not *up* to metaphysical principles but *back* to some favorite period of their own past, which becomes their touchstone for "traditional" values.⁶

---

³ See the various True Right cultural figures designated as Wild Boys in *The Homo & the Negro* (San Francisco: Counter-Currents, 2012) and *The Eldritch Evola . . . & Others* (San Francisco: Counter-Currents, 2014) as well as my occasional blog, *Where the Wild Boys Are*. On the *Männerbund* in general see the work of Wulf Grimsson, as well as my "A Band Apart: Wulf Grimsson's *Loki's Way: The Path of the Sorcerer in the Age of Iron*" in *The Homo & the Negro*.

⁴ Although, as we'll see, some of the figures to be discussed here, such as Lovecraft and Robert E. Howard, are already of interest on the Right. See the works cited in note 3 above, as well as Jonathan Bowden, "Robert E. Howard and the Heroic" (http://www.counter-currents.com/2013/05/robert-e-howard-and-the-heroic/) and Kerry Bolton's *Artists of the Right* (San Francisco: Counter-Currents, 2012).

⁵ Or, failing to rise to the level of "the seriousness of the Concept," as Hegel would say; see G. W. F. Hegel, *Hegel: Texts and Commentary*, trans. and ed. Walter Kaufmann (Garden City, N.Y.: Anchor Books, 1966), p. 8.

⁶ See Matt Parrott's "Ten Reasons for White Nationalists to Cheer

A darkly amusing example from current politics can be found amongst those "conservatives" who, lamenting the almost complete negrofication of American society—what Paul Kersey calls BRA (Black Run America)[7]—can find nothing more to oppose to it than laments for "abandoning the blessed ideals of the Rev. Dr. Martin Luther King."

The "conservative" perversely argues over where precisely the clock should be set back to, while what needs to be done is to smash the clock—the original emblem and engine of cyclical futility itself.[8]

Up" (http://www.counter-currents.com/2014/02/ten-reasons-for-white-nationalists-to-cheer-up/); #7 calls conservatives "yesterday's liberals."

[7] Defined by Larry Auster thus: "In my understanding, Paul Kersey's term 'Black-Run America' obviously does not mean that America is literally run by blacks. It means that with regard to issues touching on black interests, black self-esteem, black advancement, the truth about black intelligence, the reporting of black crime and so on, the country is, to a very large extent, run for the benefit of blacks. Not totally, not in every instance, of course not. But the bias favoring blacks is systematic and overwhelming. Thus, to take one example out of thousands, when McCain in 2008 prohibited Republican criticism of Obama over his twenty-year membership in Rev. Wright's anti-white anti-American church that was Black-Run America at work." (http://www.amnation.com/vfr/archives/020455.html).

[8] "Indeed, setting the clock back is never something to be desired—it would merely cause us to repeat events and end up back where we are now. The idea held by some that we can 'return to a Christian Europe/America/Canada/West' is unlikely even those few times when it is correctly understood and not born of a fundamentalism that takes as its standard the crassest and most base forms of the religion, many of which do not remotely resemble the faith which animated the old world." "Eyes Fixed on Eternity: The True Right," http://thisroughbeast.wordpress.com/2013/08/19/eyes-fixed-on-eternity-the-true-right/. This inability to rise above history to new levels, but instead only repeating the same cycle over and over, is a product of the same metaphysical blindness—a defining characteristic of modernity—that leads to such absurd ideas as literal reincarnation, offered as a "superior" concept to the admittedly historicist idea of Christian one-time salvation.

To see the real effect of these blinders, you must realize that an essential part of this mentality is proceeding to read back into the past the assumptions of the not-so-distant past, thus distorting and limiting the availability of the past.[9] Thus, as I noted in *The Homo & the Negro*,[10] both the "progressive" and the "conservative" assume the same distorted idea of "The Homosexual" (itself a 19th-century construct) and thus, when met with evidence that some historical figure or culture was not entirely straight, imagine them mincing around in pink togas and lisping like Monty Python's Biggus Dickus. And so the Conservative denies they could possibly be "gay" (and, in that sense, they certainly weren't) while the Liberal thinks *it's wonderful!* that they were, and neither can truly break out of the Liberal Mindset.

Now, the great thing about pop culture is that, within certain limits, it lets us in on what people were taking for granted, back in Ye Olden Dayes, or at least what didn't strike them as absurd or impossible. "B" movies and pulp writing are particularly valuable, since these are made quickly, to please as large a crowd as possible, with location shooting rather than expensive sets (thus documenting the physical past), and above all without the meddling of smarty-pants Hollywood screenwriting "innerlekshuls" seeking to inject some party line, or that Barton Fink Feeling.[11]

---

[9] A related case, the need for Bible-thumping Christians to find some differences between the Talmud and the Old Testament, so as to privilege the latter over the former, and continue their judeophilia. See, most recently, Michael Hoffman's "Is the Talmud the Direct Descendent of the Old Testament?," http://revisionistreview.blogspot.com/2014/02/is-talmud-direct-descendant-of-old.html; "One of the most virulent hoaxes of history is the one put forth by Douglas Reed, and before him, the Nazi leadership, that rabbinic Judaism is an Old Testament religion. It is in fact the quintessential *anti*-Old Testament religion." Here anti-Talmudist Hoffman joins hands with the ADL and denounces those crazy, irrational, *other* Jew-haters. It's like SNL's shyster Nathan Thurm; "not just different, but so different, it's funny to me that you would think. . . . Is it me, or is it him? It's him, right?"

[10] See note 2 above.

[11] As the screenwriter of *Kiss Me Deadly* put it, "I wrote it fast because I had contempt for it. It was automatic writing. Things were in the air and I put them in it." On the far from intended results, see my

2. THE ARYAN ARCADIA OF BROMANCE

The author of the book under review—thought I'd forgotten about that, eh?—describes on his blog exactly this liberating experience of encountering the cultural Wholly Other, while living in a small town so small-time it even had second rate newspaper comics:

> When I was a kid in the 1960s, I was jealous of the comics they got across the river in Davenport, Iowa. They got *Peanuts*, we got *Winthrop*. They got *The Wizard of Id*, we got *Apartment 3-G*. I sort of liked *Alley Oop* and *Prince Valiant*, but what was up with the single-panel strip, *Out Our Way*? [...]
>
> Boys in my world were expected to groan with longing over the girls who walked in slow-motion across the schoolyard, their long hair blowing in the wind. They were expected to evaluate the hotness of actresses on tv, discuss breasts and bras, and claim innumerable sexual conquests. *But boys in Out Our Way never displayed the slightest heterosexual interest. Instead, they consistently mocked the silliness of heterosexual romance.* What sort of world was this? Many years later, I found that *the comics I read in the 1960s were reruns from the 1930s and 1940s, and even then, many had been nostalgic,* evoking the author J. R. Williams' childhood at the turn of the century. *I was gazing into a time capsule, into an era when heterosexual desire was expected to appear at the end of adolescence, not at the beginning,* so teenage boys were free from the "What girl do you like?" chant.[12]

Cross-dressing and polygamy; perfectly normal teenage behavior "out our way"

"Mike Hammer, Occult Dick" in *The Eldritch Evola*.

[12] "Out Our Way: Teenagers Before Girl-Craziness" (http://everydayheterosexism.blogspot.com/2013/01/out-our-way-teenagers-before-girl.html) at the author's blog *Boomer Beefcake and Bonding*, January 11, 2013.

In his subsequent book, *We Boys Together*, Dennis extends that *frisson* of cultural weirdness (akin to the effect of Lovecraftian weird fiction) into an exhaustive (and, frankly, exhausting) study of how pop culture from roughly the first half of the 20th century differs radically from what "we all know" today. Here's a pretty good summary of Dennis's data and conclusions:

> For decades adults and adolescents have assumed that when boys reach puberty their hormones begin to flood their bodies and induce in them a form of insanity that has been called "girl craziness." . . . American popular culture-television, film, music, advertising, journalism, fiction-continues its portrayals of "girl crazy" teenage boys.

Dennis wants us to see that this was not always so.

The author's central argument is that in American popular culture from about 1900 to the end of World War II, a range of popular culture texts including teen fiction, film, serials, comic books, popular journalism, radio shows, and even high school yearbooks employed formulaic narratives and images for and about teenage boys engaged in "homoromantic," not "heteroromantic," relationships. Girl craziness in that period was seen as infantile or effeminate. Instead, boys "were encouraged to form intimate passionate bonds with other boys or with men, romantic friendships, or "homoromances" (p. ix). These relationships were more intense, intimate, and exclusive than "ordinary same-sex friendships," but the homoerotic gaze in these representations never crossed the line into homosexual acts. Dennis wants to know why these homoromance narratives flourished when they did and why they all but disappeared by the end of World War II. He understands that "hetero-mania" (p. 1) is an ideological construct, and he aims to show the ideological work of that construct.[13]

We'll have to question that "ideological" bit, but let's sum up

---

[13] Review by Jay Mechling in *Thymos*, vol. 2, no. 1. Speaking of summaries, Dennis provides a quashed-down version of the book here: "Love Laughs at Andy Hardy: The Rise of the Heterosexual Male Teenager" (GendersOnline, issue 41, 2005).

even more. Dennis shows that in pre-War American popular culture, the rules were:

1. All boys are straight.
2. At puberty, boys hang out with each other, or adult mentors.
3. Other than infants, only four-eyes, fatties, and fairies hang out with girls.[14]
4. At around 18, boys marry [a girl, we must add today], get a job, and raise a family, ending their period of fun and freedom

Get it?

Dennis divides his pop culture Boys into three types, inspired not by Caesar but by the usual academic Marxism—the first strike against the book, in our view. These are:

1. Boys Next Door
2. Lost Boys
3. Adventure Boys

Like a good pinko, Dennis distinguishes these along the lines of class and race.

Boys Next Door (e.g., Andy Hardy, Henry Aldrich, Jack Armstrong) are small-town WASPs who need an older male to toughen them up—although White Culture is the summit of evolution, it has an ironic feminizing effect; hence the need for Boy Scouts, "muscular Christianity," etc.

Lost Boys, by contrast, are immigrants or sons of immigrants, living in big city slums (e.g., The Dead End Kids, The Bowery Boys). Unlike BND's, these boys need some civilizing, and hence are the targets of kindly priests, kids from the neighborhood who made good, juvenile delinquency specialists, and the ubiquitous Boy Scouts.

Adventure Boys (e.g., Sabu, or Tarzan's son, simply called

---

[14] Four-eyed, fat, and girl-crazy; sounds like the average denizen of the Man-o-sphere!

"Boy"[15]) move these scenarios abroad to enact an imperialist narrative, policing and otherwise bringing the White Man's civilization to the exotic Others.

What he has in mind here, of course, is the kind of analysis put forward quite seriously at the time by writers familiar to our readers here, such as Madison Grant or Lothrop Stoddard, dealing with the enervating nature of modern civilization, mass immigration, or the "rising tide of color" abroad, which we Alt-Rightists can choose to give a more favorable interpretation.[16]

Moreover, I would suggest that the more interesting way to interpret these tropes is as instances of Indo-European male bonding, in either its pedagogic (Boy Next Door) or band of warriors[17] (Lost Boys) moments, with Adventure Boys simply taking it on the road.

3. Ideology vs. Ideology

And this kind of clichéd Leftist analysis is where Dennis disappoints more generally. Right in Chapter 1, he tells us that

> *Of course*, it [teenage homoromance] does not reflect real life. . . . *it is an ideological construct* . . . And as with all ideologies, we must ask who desires it or who profits from it. (p. 15)

---

[15] Or even Conan the Barbarian, at least in the one, early story set in his adolescence, "The Tower of the Elephant." In light of what we'll be discussing, it's interesting that the supposedly "complete" Kindle collection I had omits the story, and it took quite a while to locate a collection that did include it: *Conan the barbarian* [sic] *Twenty Stories* (Seng Book [sic]), which also includes Kipling's *The Jungle Book*, featuring his own Adventure Boy, Mowgli.

[16] See, for example, the recently republished *The Revolt Against Civilization* by Lothrop Stoddard, Introduction by Kevin MacDonald (Abergele, UK: Wermod & Wermod, 2011); and *The Passing of the Great Race* by Madison Grant, Introduction by Jared Taylor (Abergele, UK: The Palingenesis Project, 2012).

[17] Unlike the generational relations of the Boy Next Door, in gangs "only peers can experience homoromance" (p. 46). These are the peer-relations among warriors such as Achilles and Patroclus.

Dennis has half the story right; today's "girl-crazy" teen is indeed an ideological construct, and we'll soon look at his analysis of "who profits from it." But to say that teenage homoromance is equally ideological is just another Leftist knee-jerk, like "race is a social construct."[18]

Rather, as James Neill has shown, traditional (and, we would say, Traditional) societies have used the fact of human "ambisexuality" (as he calls it) to ingeniously craft various successful strategies for controlling male, and especially what we would call "teenage," sexuality.[19] In the main, they resemble the pre-War "homoromantic Arcadia" Dennis describes. Discussing traditional Muslim society, Neill points out that:

> Arguing that homosexuality among individuals in sexually segregated societies [such as prisons or sailors at sea] is due to the unnaturalness of these same-sex environments displays *a profound ignorance of the way sexual and reproductive patterns have manifested in nature*.
>
> The sexually segregated Muslim society in fact, seems *a nearly perfect example* of the sort of *natural sexual regulation* that appears among many animal species, where *heterosexual couplings are restricted primarily to mature individuals capable of providing the parenting necessary for the healthy growth of the offspring*. . . . The ambisexuality of Islamic societies, therefore . . . is not only *consistent with sexual patterns found among many other societies around the world*, but

---

[18] The idea that only ideologies manipulating us for Someone's profit can explain things is the sort of idea that could only explain, or occur to, modern man. Cut off from the Principles of Tradition, he is on the one hand literally formless of personality, subject to the whims of politicians or merchants, and on the other hand concerned solely with not merely his own benefit, but that only conceived in its lowest terms: money and copulation. See "Homo Modernus, Evolian-Gomezian Portrait of Modern Man" by Mark Rostkowski in *Aristokratia* II, 23–39.

[19] See James Neill's *The Origins and Role of Same-Sex Relations in Human Societies* (Jefferson, N.C.: McFarland, 2011) and my *A Review of James Neill's "The Origins and Role of Same-Sex Relations in Human Societies"* (Amazon.com Kindle Single, 2013).

seems *an inevitable product of human sexual nature.* (loc. 6217-23)

This traditional Muslim society still exists on what Western diplomats sneeringly call "the Arab street," and has been described by journalist John R. Bradley as one in which pubescent boys, rigidly kept apart from girls, are naturally expected to get up to some mischief amongst themselves, forming intense relationships with mentors and peers, that will structure their adult lives, but as long as they don't make a public spectacle of it, and obediently marry and settle down when old enough, there is no "problem."[20]

This is exactly the homoromance model Dennis illustrates in *We Boys Together*. The pre-War pop culture trope, in which, and thus by which, pubescent boys are safely steered away from women until old enough to marry and support a family, is both sanctioned by Tradition and rooted firmly in biological reality.[21] The notion of boys going "girl crazy" — and hey, whatcha gonna do about it? — is by contrast the real ideological construct.[22]

4. WHAT HAPPENED & HOW?

Well then, what happened, and why? How did girl-craziness "invade and ultimately conquer Arcadia"?[23] Amusingly, Dennis offers the exact date, if not time:

On March 12, 1937, the character of the Boy Next Door

---

[20] See *Behind the Veil of Vice: The Business and Culture of Sex in the Middle East* (New York: Palgrave, 2010).

[21] Michael Davidson was quite prescient to use the Persian term "purdah" to describe the fact (not, pace Dennis, the "ideological construct") that "most boys, during the two or three years after puberty, don't want to have girls." See his memoir *Some Boys* (London: Gay Men's Press, 1988).

[22] See our own discussion of homosexuality in Traditional societies, using the work of Alain Daniélou, John R. Bradley, and others, in "Tradition, 'Traditionalism,' and Really Existing Homosexuality" in *The Homo & the Negro*.

[23] See Evelyn Waugh, *Brideshead Revisited: The Sacred and Profane Memories of Captain Charles Ryder* (1945), ch. 1, "Et in Arcadia Ego."

changed forever. In a minor subplot in MGM's *A Family Affair*, small town Judge Hardy orders his sixteen-year-old son Andy to escort a girl to a party.... "Holy jumping Jerusalem, a party with girls!" Andy yelps. Suddenly the universe had changed ...

Andy's girl-craziness was problematic to the studio (see the Mayer quote above) but ultimately, it would prove to be "the first portent of the adolescent hetero-erotic mania that would invade and ultimately conquer Arcadia" (p. 94).

Dennis doesn't notice, though, that "A family affair" and especially "Holy jumping Jerusalem!" are the clues. What soon followed *A Family Affair* was WWII, which would usher in a wholesale reordering of American society along Judaic family-values lines. That's where we need to look for those profiteering from imposing an ideology, the shift to today's hetero-craziness. The clue is the time frame: just before, during and after WWII. *Cui bono?*

In the space of a decade, measured by the Andy Hardy series, "girl-craziness" went from being the mark of immature, infantile, effeminate sissies to being the *sine qua non* of red-blooded American youth. Why did it happen?

Dennis identifies two factors, though he doesn't see their ramifications or even their connection.

First, the rise of "scientific" psychology, in particular the "psychoanalysis" of Freud and the "sexology" of Magnus Hirschfeld. Building on the late 19th-century notion of the "homosexual" (and "heterosexual") as a fixed identity (rather than the more accurate "ambisexuality" Neill documents), Freud then asserted that children could "fail to mature" and wind up in this dreadful state of "inversion"; while Hirschfeld offered the contrary idea, that these were born as freaks of nature, a "third sex" possessing a feminine soul.

Either theory was bad news when the second factor came along: World War II. The last thing the Army needed was a bunch of what Colonel "Bat" Guano would deem "deviated preverts" or woman-souled men when there was a war to fight!

Thus, while beforehand the occasional homosexual characters were "tolerated as harmless eccentrics"[24] like Clifton Webb[25] or at worst "as jokes" like Franklin Pangborn (p. 89), now "The Homosexual" became a deadly threat to the war effort, not only incapable of fighting like a real man[26] but apt to spread the infection by deviating youth. He was a menace that needed to be faced up to and defeated.[27]

---

[24] "[A man who] used to be considered merely a little "odd" by his contemporaries, and avoided or tolerantly humored (unless, that is, he incurred the righteous wrath of the Church, in which case things could be made very hot for him) he is today declared by modern Freudianism to be mentally ill and unfit for the ancient protections of law; and this is surely indicative of the 'progress' we have made in a thousand years." —"Introduction" by Revilo Oliver to Yockey's *Imperium*.

[25] See my "The Babysitting Bachelor as Aryan Avatar: Clifton Webb in *Sitting Pretty*," http://www.counter-currents.com/2013/02/the-babysitting-bachelor-as-aryan-avatar-clifton-webb-in-sitting-pretty-part-1/

[26] The persistence of the myth that "fags can't/won't fight" shows the remarkable hold of ideology in the face of overwhelming evidence, from Alcibiades to Grand Duke Sergei Alexandrovich. Putin wishes he had Duke Sergei at his side today, and Americans, who haven't won a real war since 1945, might consider the career of English couturier, war hero, and dandy Bunny Roger, the inventor of Capri pants who, replying to a sergeant's question regarding approaching Germans, advised "When in doubt, powder heavily." See Trevelyan, Raleigh, "Obituary: Bunny Roger," *The Independent* (May 14, 1997); and for more of Bunny's wartime *bons mots*, see "Wild Boys vs. 'Hard men'" in *The Homo & the Negro*.

[27] As Dennis correctly points out, homophobia only exists once "The Homosexual" has been identified; as my own philosophy mentor would say, they are a "dialectic couplet," each requiring and implying the other—"The two terms of an opposition have no meaning apart from one another" (René Guénon, *The Crisis of the Modern World* [Ghent, NY: Sophia Perennis, 2001], p. 9). Thus, as Bradley observes, in the Arab world an occasional male might continue his youthful habits but, as long as he is discreet and married, this is seen as a harmless foible; homophobia only arises where the Western world has introduced its Freudian fallacies, so that the secular regard him as "sick" and the

The American answer was, as always, propaganda; we can adapt here Francis Parker Yockey's description of the war-propaganda machine that operated at the same time — and was, I argue, "girl-craziness" writ large:

> Europeans are [not] familiar with [America's] internal propaganda. This propaganda utterly dwarfs, in its scale as well as its effect, anything Europeans can readily imagine. . . . . [A notion like "Girl craziness"] is glorified on all public occasions, by all public officials, is taught in the schools and preached in the churches. . . . Newspapers, books, magazines, radio, television, films — all vomit for the same [idea, such as "girl craziness"] . . .[28]

So great was the need for propaganda that even the Hollywood movie machine was not adequate. Soon, minor companies, like Jam Handy (yes, Jam Handy) were to produce so-called "educational" films, to teach boys skills that, although supposedly "natural," were apparently beyond their ken, such as *What to Do on a Date* (1950).

These are easily available today on YouTube, but I would suggest also taking a look at the versions that have been produced by *Mystery Science Theater 3000*. Mike and the 'bots — over-educated Midwestern Whites — are always a good index of SWPL instincts; witness their constant quipping "Look how White everyone is" when viewing almost any pre-'60s film, and referencing Hitler whenever someone noticeably blond appears.

When these films are viewed today even the Counter-Currents reader will find them positively surreal, due precisely to their seeming to still have an odd, quasi-"homoerotic" atmosphere today, thus illustrating the historical change in the very

---

fundamentalists as "Western." This accounts for the shock, outrage and amusement directed by PC Liberals against Pres. Imadinnerjacket for his naively honest remark that "There are no homosexuals in Iran" and hence, no problem with "oppression." And yes, I know Iranians are Persians.

[28] *The Enemy of Europe* by Francis Parker Yockey, "Introductory Note."

process of happening. *What to do on a Date*, for example, still retains the *Männerbund* traces of the older best pal who provides guidance ("Are these two on a date?" asks the MST3k crew) and the advice to attend group activities and double date.

Another example of the *Männerbund* in transition to girl-craziness is *Mr. B Natural* (subtle, isn't it?) in which the problem is how to get the hollow-chested slacker "Buzz" accepted by the Group. The answer, of course, is: buy a genuine Conn brand trumpet and join the band! What's interesting here, and would provide fodder for a memorable MST3k episode, is that "Mr" B Natural is played, in the Peter Pan tradition,[29] by an androgynous female.

Here we see how the Traditional Aryan solution — find a gang of boys and obtain a mentor — is displaced by the empty "individualism" of consumerism and social conformity, but re-emerges in an almost surrealistically distorted form (literally, as the 'bots point out, "coming out of the closet"). It's an especially harrowing experience from our contemporary perspective — an androgynous figure in spangled jacket and tights visits the bedrooms of 12-year-old boys to dance about and instruct them in how to blow into instruments — the trauma of which Joel and the 'bots had to deal with by staging a mock debate over whether "Mr." B was a man or woman — with Tom as William F. Buckley, Mr. Post-War Conservative, taking the pro-female side:

JOEL: Mr. T. Robot, you have twenty minutes to rebut.
CROW: Mr. Servo, you've GOT to be kidding me! Let's assume for the moment that Mr. B Natural IS a man. My heavens! *What a confusing message to send to little kids*! Already, there's *the painful feeling of isolation*,[30] the horrible, scarring acne. And Mr. Servo here would have us place a cross-dressing man with a clarinet slap dab in their bedrooms! Why not men in Little Bo Peep costumes with stinky cigars explaining the facts of life to

---

[29] Another notable instance of the *Männerbund* in supposedly "popular" media, of course.

[30] As we've seen, it's all about ending the "isolation" of boys, and of the nation at large.

>   our unsuspecting daughters? I, for one—
> JOEL: Mr. Servo, your rebuttal!
> TOM: Yes! Yes! Mr. Crow! I don't think we should stop there! Let's break down ALL the barriers. Hairy men in Spartan costumes holding bake sales on shady boulevards! Naked jock-strap wrestling! Big—
> JOEL (interrupting): Gentlemen, I have Commercial Sign, I'm sorry.

Appropriately, many of these "educational" films were *au fond* thinly veiled commercials for one product or another (such as Mr. B's Conn Band Instruments), since the inculcation of "family values" was intimately tied up with consumerism. A remarkable example, not discussed by Dennis, is *A Young Man's Fancy*.

Perhaps because the Edison Institute was too focused on selling people on electrical appliances (again, inculcating post-War consumerism), or some personal predilection of the filmmakers, but although produced in 1952 the story, though superficially conforming to the *What to do on a Date* model, operates entirely on the pre-'40s Boy Next Door assumptions.

Judy's brother Bob enjoys a clean (the first thing they do on arrival is shower together), healthy relationship with Alex, who is praised by him to his family as both a scholar and "quite a girl hater." Otherwise, his "outside interests" are restricted to consumer appliances and . . . time management.[31]

Eventually, Judy wins his affection through her (electrically enhanced) cookery skills. This is not so much "look how enslaved women were" as an example of the old-paradigm idea of male bonds of friendship versus the inevitable reversal of interest and creation of a family unit. (That Judy's brother will still be around no doubt softens the blow).[32]

---

[31] The latter reminds me of that other epic girl-hater, Clifton Webb, who played the time-managing father in *Cheaper by the Dozen*; we analyzed his today-inexplicable box office appeal in "The Babysitting Bachelor as Aryan Avatar," *op. cit.*

[32] According to IMDb, the plot keywords are: "male in shower," "jealousy," "coming home," "brother," and "sister." What is this, Ten-

Good clean '50s entertainment!³³ The reaction of the MST3k group to the film (shown on the episode with Ed Woodian teen delinquent epic *The Violent Years* in 1994), borders on sheer dumbfoundedness. Surely, you can almost hear them say, surely everyone involved could *see* that Alexander Phipps is gay, gay, gay, and probably Judy's brother is too.

Another example, feature length this time, is their take on B movie *The Girl in Lover's Lane*, where the older hobo (they dub him "Big Stupid" due to the muddy audio) takes a young runaway, Danny, under his wing, sleeping together, getting into pointless alley brawls, and, above all, constantly "rescuing" him from any chance of getting laid. How this was filmed as late as 1960 can, again, only be explained by its status as a "B" film no one was paying attention to. "It's perfectly normal that Big Stupid would shy away from the pretty girl who works at the diner in order to go shack up with Danny and his parents. Perfectly normal. Nothing odd about it. What are you staring at??"

5. WHO BENEFITS?

Dennis suggests three reasons that girl-craziness replaced homoromance due to the war; whatever their contribution, I think the War itself is more important. Hearing that all this is a "post WWII phenomenon" really got my spidey-sense tingling. Was this not the *foetor judaicus*?³⁴

It was indeed no coincidence that the expulsion from the homoromantic Arcadia coincided with the campaign to stampede America into the war in Europe and, indeed, a situation of Permanent War. We can see the hand of the Jew in both.³⁵

---

nessee Williams?

³³ Oddly enough, the 1963 *Twilight Zone* episode of the same title, by Richard Matheson, reverses the process: a newlywed husband visits his late mother's house which he is reluctant to get rid of; she reappears and he becomes a child again, telling his wife to "Go away, lady — we don't need you anymore."

³⁴ "How does that coincide with your post-war Commie conspiracy, huh? It's incredibly obvious, isn't it?" says General Ripper, who seems to be having a bit of a bromance with Group Capt. Mandrake; see my "From Odd John to Strange Love," below.

³⁵ "But since the Second World War, the Jewish element of subver-

Yockey again:

> In Europe it has been impossible for the Jew to annihilate Tradition . . . but in America . . . because of its colonial origins . . . there were no barriers to the Jew. As a result, the success of the Jew has been greatest in America, and *in the year 1933*, [four years before Andy Hardy!] the entire continent of America passed into the control of the Jewish Culture-State-Nation-Race-People.
>
> The presence of a Culture-alien generates spiritual, political, economic, and *social phenomena of a kind which could never arise from domestic elements and happenings.* . . . [W]hen the Culture-alien intervenes in the public, and spiritual affairs of the host . . . he must of his own inner necessity *distort the life of the host, warping and frustrating its proper tendencies to make them serviceable to his alien needs.* The Jew is the only Culture-alien who at present exercises this Culture-distortion on the life of the Western Civilization.[36]

As Dennis summarizes elsewhere:

> Adolescents were singled out for special concern, since their heterosexual desire was still inchoate and developing. Freud and the Freudian pop-psychologists warned that boys could move from latency to "perversion" in any number of ways, through the deliberate or accidental *intervention* [sic!] of parents, teachers, peers, and strangers on the street. As Benshoff notes (1997: 139), the ongoing worry of adults during the period was "whether the boys would become successful, mature, adult males, and not turn gay along the way" (cf. Grant, 2001). *The mandate to promote heterosexual adulthood, plus the need to create a new national character at the end of the era of isolationism,* com-

---

sion has become hegemonic." Greg Johnson, *New Right vs. Old Right & Other Essays* (San Francisco: Counter-Currents, 2013), p. 43.

[36] *The Proclamation of London of the European Liberation Front*, 3rd ed. (Nordland Press, 1972), II.2.

> bined to produce a new "*all-American boy,*" resourceful, industrious, wisecracking yet serious when it counted, cautious yet brave when it counted, smart but not an egghead, sensitive but not a sissy, doting on his mother, obedient to his father, a big brother to the kids and a pal to his peers. . . . And, *for perhaps the first time in media history,* he was wild about girls. [37]

"When it counted" — when the American Golem needed to be sent abroad to destroy the rising of the European nation — "boys next door must be dragged, willingly or not, out of their homoromantic Arcadia" — just as America was dragged, unwillingly, into War.[38]

6. WHO CARES?

> **BERT COOPER:** "Even if this were true, who cares? This country was built and run by men with worse stories than whatever you've imagined here. . . . the Japanese

---

[37] Dennis, "Love Laughs at Andy Hardy," p. 7.

[38] Dennis notes but makes nothing of the way "inversion" is coded to the "bad" half of various polarities — White/dark, West/East, etc., including Allied/Axis. To this day the PC Left delights in imagining National Socialists as fags, while the notion reached its post-War peak in *The Pink Swastika,* a delirious work whose Evangelical authors imagine every German of note from the Teutonic Knights to Krautrock as a bunch of what Sgt. Bat Guano would call "deviated preverts." Perhaps it reached bottom when the creators of *Bottom,* Rik Mayall and Adrian Edmonson, guested on the "Private Plane" episode of *Blackadder Goes Forth,* which anachronistically projects the trope onto the Great War. Mayall portrays Squadron Commander the Lord Flashheart, whose name alone suggests boys' books like Biggles, but who is portrayed in proper WWII fashion as a maniacal skirt-chaser; Edmondson is his equally blond but rather epicene rival, Baron von Richthoven. When they meet in Richthoven's castle dungeon, and Richthoven begins bloviating about honor, combat, brotherhood of arms, etc., Flashheart blithely shoots him dead. with a disgusted "What a poof!" As Blackadder sums it up, "Dress it up in any amount of pompous verbal diarrhea, and the message is 'Squareheads down for the big Boche gangbang.'"

have a saying: a man is whatever room he is in, and right now Donald Draper is in this room. I assure you, there's more profit in forgetting this. I'd put your energy into bringing in accounts."[39]

Dennis, the PC academic, takes the same Judaic-influenced line as Bert, the Ayn Rand disciple. It's just two rival ideologies to him, and having documented the change, the book just peters out, seemingly more interested in detailed biographies of his favorite boy stars, like Jackie Cooper and Johnny Sheffield. So it's up to me to point out the malignant social effects of "girl-craziness."

First, what we might call the material effects on boys and society. As we said above, Dennis is aware that, as Neill points out, once The Homosexual is invented as a character type, he becomes a "problem" for society, calling into being his dialectic twin, The Homophobe. Boys are now expected, by society and by each other, to be "girl-crazy" as soon as puberty hits—and perhaps a little sooner, as child-raising fashions progress, just to "be sure." Play-dates, anyone?

Neill has aptly described the effects on teenagers:

> By diverting the sex drive away from inappropriate heterosexual involvement, [homoromance] among adolescents and young adults works to prevent pregnancies among these immature individuals, and helps to insure that the conception of children occurs within stable relationships between psychologically and emotionally mature adults.
>
> [M]odern Western culture places high expectations on teens to demonstrate heterosexual interest, bombarding them with heterosexual images and role models, whether in song lyrics of teen movies, which pound into them that to be normal is to be [having sex with girls]. . . . As a result, adolescents in Western societies and in westernized cultures of the Third World direct their sexual energies for the most part toward the opposite sex [with] a correspond-

---

[39] *Mad Men*, Season 1, "Nixon vs. Kennedy."

ing explosion of extramarital heterosexual permissiveness and its attendant problems [such as] teen pregnancy and single mothers [which are] virtually unknown among those aboriginal societies still unaffected by Western cultural and moral values [sic].⁴⁰

The evidence drives Neill to conclude that:

[T]he involvement with the opposite sex that is the norm among teenagers in Western culture represents a premature heterosexuality at variance with the ambisexual harmony observed among . . . many human societies.

And what is the response of the "conservative"? Repression (abstinence), ignorance (no sex ed.), and above all, a healthy dose of "good old fashioned family entertainment," the more girl-crazy the better! *Goyishe kopf.*

In a traditional society, these erotic energies would be recognized, valued, and safely diverted into "homoromances" (along the lines of Nietzschean "sublimation" vs. Judeo-Christian asceticism). This is possible because, contrary to Freud and Hirschfeld, humans are, as Neill documents, an "ambisexual" species, which allows society to shape and prune human sexuality in various ways and into various channels.⁴¹ In this way,

---

⁴⁰ Neill, *op. cit.*, loc. 1199–1208.

⁴¹ This was the insight of Hans Blüher, Hirschfeld's rival and, appropriately enough, the chief modern theoretician of the *Männerbund* and its contemporary appearances such as the Wandervogel movement and the Boy Scouts. Contrary to Freud, Blüher posited Eros as an undifferentiated prior energy, which when manifested is always already culturally differentiated. "Whenever sexuality makes itself noticed in man it has already been taken up into the workings of Eros and thereby acquired a meaning."

One sees here yet another way the War proved useful to Judaic interests, burying the work of Blüher and the other Stirnerite "Masculinists" and spreading the pseudo-sciences of such "exiles" as Freud and the Frankfurt School. See Alisdair Clarke: "Hans Blüher and the Wandervogel, talk from sixth New Right meeting in London, February 2006" (http://aryanfuturism. blogspot.com/2006/04/hans-

male/female relations are reserved for marriage at appropriate ages, and the whole problem of teenage pregnancy, STDs, knife-fights among pubescent Romeos, etc. is avoided.

This leads to our second, more general point. Traditional societies, especially Aryan ones, direct those teenage energies not only *away* from inappropriate heterosexual relations but also *into* two main forms of homoeroticism: inter-generational pedagogic relations, and bonds of loyalty and affection between peers; teachers and warriors, in short.[42]

These are the relations that create, and hand down (*traditio*) the unique cultural institutions of Aryan society—from the priesthood, to private/public schools, to the Boy Scouts. However, once The Homosexual arises as a "threat," all relations between males, especially between generations, become suspect. To revert to pop culture again, consider that pre-War American audiences reveled in the tales of Bing Crosby's Fr. O'Malley, and Clifton Webb's Mr. Scoutmaster, or Robert Donat's Mr. Chips; today, in movies or "real life," such men would be presumed child molesters.

Dennis notes at one point the similar effect on adult peer relations as well: "Men can be chummy 'pals', but they can never fully trust each other. Every masculine smile hides the potential for backstabbing and malice" (p. 232). This makes it almost impossible to create a true *Männerbund* in modern society.

Consider—as we so often do—the advertising world depicted

---

bluher-and-wandervogel.html); and generally, *Homosexuality and Male Bonding in Pre-Nazi Germany: The Youth Movement, the Gay Movement, and Male Bonding before Hitler's Rise*, ed. Hubert Kennedy (New York: Routledge, 1992).

As Clarke notes, one implication of Blüher's work is to render the whole issue of whether homosexuality is "natural" otiose; as I point out in my review of Neill, it is merely a Judaic misunderstanding of Stoic cosmology along the lines of monotheistic "laws."

[42] The failure to recognize this dichotomy, as if all sexual relations were between unequals, leads to such smugly ignorant attitudes as "proud, free, and virile Aryan men would never have sex with each other," rendering the widespread evidence of elite warrior cults and blood-brotherhood inexplicable.

in *Mad Men*.⁴³ *Mad Men*'s '60s setting is about halfway between us and Andy Hardy, and this triumphalist Judaic take on the last days of WASP hegemony can be usefully seen in the light of Dennis's analysis. Don, whatever his title, is clearly the creative leader of a shifting collection of *Männerbünde*, sometimes a small staff working on a project, sometimes reconfiguring the whole set of partners on the spur of the moment—leading a Christmas Eve mutiny to start a new firm, then sabotaging their IPO by merging with a hated rival. His selfishness renders these "bad" or "fake *Männerbünde*" like those of Capt. Ahab or Al Capone, which I have analyzed elsewhere.⁴⁴

Moving from the Gang Leader mode to the Pedagogic, Pete and Peggy (note the similar names, as well as Peggy/PEdaGoGY) both seek Don as a mentor, but Don, his womanizing establishing his hetero cred from the start, takes on the rather mannish Peggy and treats Pete as a rival to be stymied at every turn. That the "chauvinist" Don mentors Peggy is treated as surprising—another legacy of the previous paradigm—but it only makes sense; anything else would be "crypto-homo."⁴⁵

In Peggy's rise in the industry we see how this "premature heterosexuality" as Nell calls it, inculcated by popular culture, as Dennis shows, has led not only to the decay of the *Männerbund* but also to the parallel, only superficially paradoxical, result of a feminized culture. As Yockey observed:

> The true American People is a unit based upon matriarchy. . . . The soul of this People is too oriented to the femi-

---

⁴³ See my *End of an Era: Mad Men & the Ordeal of Civility* (San Francisco: Counter-Currents, 2015).

⁴⁴ See my essay on De Palma's *The Untouchables* in *The Homo & the Negro*.

⁴⁵ Dennis illustrates the point by looking at the peculiar relationship of Superman and Jimmy Olsen, who is less an object of romance or sidekick than a sad sack and fall guy in one of the Man of Steel's plans, often near death while Superman chuckles nearby, waiting to "save the day" at the last minute. I immediately thought of *Superdickery*, the website devoted entirely to illustrating, with vintage DC covers, the thesis that Superman is, in fact, a smug dick.

> nine pole of existence, and it therefore cherishes peace, comfort, security, in short, the values of individual life. War, conquest, adventure, the creation of form and order in the world—these do not interest the American People. Empire-building demands sacrifice; yet, for sacrifices to be made . . . there must be an Idea. [46]

War, conquest, adventure, the creation of form and order in the world through sacrifice for an idea—these are the values created by the *Männerbund*.

> The Masculine Principle is to realize higher ideas through art, warfare, Politics. Nothing could be further from the American ideal than that.[47]

We can see here a phenomenon similar to what Andy Nowicki has noted in his critique of the "Game" culture of the man-o-sphere:

> There is, I think, something essentially degraded about a mindset which takes it as self-evident that *sex in itself is a thing to be prized and sought after and salivated over, simply because cultural forces scream to us that indulging our appetite is some kind of biological imperative*. It is, of course, no revelation to admit that the male libido is a potent, often growlingly insistent force, but *this does not mean that it must be placated, or that it defines who we are as men*. In fact, is there not something appalling in the prospect of being led by the nose to do the bidding of our loins? Think of how easy it is for this drive to be harnessed and manipulated by those who, for one reason or another, seek control over us! I am in fact astounded that fewer manosphere-scribes and readers haven't wised up . . .[48]

---

[46] *The Enemy of Europe*.
[47] *Op. cit*.
[48] See Andy Nowicki's "Manning Down" (http://alternative-right.blogspot.com/p/manning-down.html) as well as his Counter-Currents article "In Defense of 'Squares'" (http://www.counter-

How could they "wise up" as long as everything from "orthodox" Christianity to Hollywood Nihilists have drummed the same message for three score and ten years?[49]

One could, perhaps, see in this another turn of the cycle of the regression of the castes,[50] from the aristocratic priestly and military, arising from and structured as *Männerbünde*,[51] to the purely bourgeois or even plebian merchant, organized purely as selfish individuals pursuing material advantage for their private families — the ideal of the modern "conservative," epitomized by Margaret Thatcher (beloved by conservatives as "The Iron Lady") snapping "There is no such thing as society."[52]

The post-war, crypto-Judaic transformation of bromance into

---

currents.com/2012/03/in-defense-of-squaresa-response-to-jack-donovan/%20/%20_blank) which prompted a reply from Ferdinand Bardamu, "Can You See the Real Me?" (http://www.inmalafide.com/blog/2012/04/02/can-you-see-the-real-me-a-response-to-andy-nowicki/%20/%20_blank) as well as Greg Johnson's "Be Yourself?" (http://www.counter-currents.com/2012/04/be-yourself/).

[49] Neill notes with some wry amusement that William Davenport, who studied the sexual practices of the Santa Cruz Islanders in the 1960s, discovered 20 years later that *"both government and church* had worked hard" to replace traditional sanctions against heterosexual permissiveness, resulting in an explosion of same (*op. cit.*, Loc. 1038).

[50] See Evola, *Men Among the Ruins*, p. 164.

[51] It is within the *Männerbund* that spiritual initiation is conducted; this is what creates the true aristocracy, not mere blood, race, or ethnicity. In Evola's political theory, the aristocrat is the differentiated man, that is, the man who has *differentiated himself* from the mass, whatever his supposed race or genetics. See Gwendolyn von Taunton, "The Once and Future King: The Political Philosophy of Julius Evola" in *Aristokratia* II, esp. pp. 82–85. The idea of a nation or ruling class defined by mere biology is a Judaic notion, despite its popularity in European racist circles from Gobineau to Hitler to today.

[52] By contrast, in aristocratic Rome, the patrician family was more than a group of related genes: "the rite . . . enjoyed primacy over all other elements . . . that were related to nature . . . 'The cult shaped the family into a united body . . . the ancient family was more a religious than a natural association' [de Coulanges]" (Evola, *Revolt Against the Modern World*, p. 39).

family values could not be better shown than in Dennis's analysis of Isaac Asimov's 1948 *Second Foundation* (pp. 192–94). Unlike the earlier, wartime Foundation stories, bromance is nonexistent, "pals" turn on, betray and torture each other at the drop of a hat, and the asexual Mule is replaced by the leaders of the newly discovered Second Foundation—Pappa and Mamma. It's hard to type it without cringing, but the new, Judaic or Judaic-friendly writers like Asimov could churn it out endlessly. Sci-Fi, once home to Aryan bromance, was now occupied territory; it's no surprise that the State of Israel was *founded* in the same year.

The results of "girl-craziness" have been out-of-control teen sex and the decline of all culture-forming institutions, now tainted with "gayness."[53] As Yockey was analyzing the American character in the early '50s, the deleterious results for White America were already plain.

> The tragic fact is that the attenuation of the national instinct has proceeded so far that one cannot envisage how a Nationalist Revolution would be even possible in America. For practical political purposes, *the "White America" which still existed in its strength in the 1920s has today ceased to exist*. Whether that submerged spirit will rise again in some remote future is unforeseeable . . .[54]

---

[53] Evola, as usual, seems to be unique on "the Right" for understanding that the modern "population crisis" is both quantitative—too many *Untermenschen*—as well as qualitative—too few of the elite. The answer to the first is abortion and birth control, to the second, homoromantic *Männerbund* (Evola calls them "celibate"). (See Paul Furlong, *Social and Political Thought of Julius Evola* [New York: Routledge, 2011], p. 84, and Gwendolyn von Taunton, *op. cit.*, p. 112). Needless to say, both are anathema to the "conservative" who counsels instead: more girl-craziness!

[54] *The Enemy of Europe* by Francis Parker Yockey, "Introductory Note." "White" America is the key here. Just as America has been feminized, it has also been Negrofied. The Negro manifests hysterical hyper-heterosexuality in both his out-of-control sexuality and his inability to form true *Männerbünde* and hence create and sustain culture. As a commenter at *Stuff Black People Don't Like* observes: "I have often heard

Welcome to the Club 41

By the time of the ironically named, Judaically led "Summer of Love," the transformation was complete.

> Every teenage boy in mass culture, whether he was drawn for children, teenagers or adults, whether he was a star, sidekick or villain, would be portrayed as aggressively and unequivocally girl-crazy. The homoromantic Arcadia had vanished. (p. 242)

The results were a disaster for white culture, from the uprising of Charlie Manson's appropriately named Family to the epidemics of teenage pregnancy and STDs that are now simply taken for granted.

Today, any boy expressing the kind of emotional intensity expected of pre-1940 boys would be labeled a fag, to be curb stomped by some skinhead as "conservatives" cheer on the negroidally bald, reggae-loving champion of white values; while any adult male showing an interest in boys—priest, teacher, scoutmaster, etc.—is presumed a pervert until proven otherwise; Bing Crosby's Fr. O'Malley and Clifton Webb's Mr. Scoutmaster would soon find themselves in the crowbar hotel, where "conservatives" would cheerfully look forward to their rape and murder by those other well-known champions of white values, negro convicts who have proven their real-manliness by raping white girls and fathering dozens of offspring with innumerable

---

that negroes gestate faster, mature faster and die faster, but this is really an eye-opener. PDK often opines on the fast reproductive strategy but here it is out in the open. *While Whites and their minds are still growing (and will continue to grow till 25) negroes seem to be completely "done" by 18.* After that, they get coarser and uglier till 35 and then they begin to die off. The average life span of a negroid is 69 years. Probably the natural life span of a groid is 35, but *their lives are extended by White man's medicine, White man's laws and White man's technology*, like Water Purification and food tech. Astonishingly, negroes lives are extended by prison (!) due to their *large amount of leisure time*, [the basis of culture, as Josef Pieper observed] while you stupid Whites are out there slaving away to pay your taxes [like good family-valuers]," http://stuffblackpeopledontlike.blogspot.com/2014/03/two-of-marshall-coulters-black-14-year.html

"baby mamas."

In response, the "conservative" has his usual panoply of useless and irrelevant fixes—no sex ed., chastity rings, etc.—and above all "censor that Hollywood dreck"—little realizing that the "traditional family values" entertainment he proposes instead is just another brand of Hollywood dreck, and is itself the root of the problem!

And so we see how "conservatives" have concentrated their ire on the relatively piddling "gay agenda" (the Leftist notion that "we're all the same and probably better parents anyway") while ignoring, or rather, helping promote, the wide-spread illusion of teenage boys as "just naturally girl-crazy." Like their unwitting models, the Pharisees, they strain at the gay marriage gnat and swallow the girl-crazy propaganda at a gulp.

Just as Neill's book, as I show in my Kindle essay, establishes that male-bonding is both rooted in evolutionary biology and culturally productive—as opposed to the unnatural and culture-distorting "family values" of the Semites—so Dennis's book demonstrates that popular culture, at its origins, reflected these same healthy values, before they were distorted, calumniated, and buried beneath a filthy flood of Judaic pseudo-psychology and war propaganda.

"Conservatives" are right to complain about "Hollywood shoving the gay agenda down our throats" but wrong (again!) to imagine that the answer is "bring back Andy Hardy." As Dennis shows, Andy Hardy and the rest were culturally foreign ideologies already forced down our throats long ago, first to prepare us for "The Good War" (good for you-know-who), and ultimately for "the anti-national impetus of the [post-War] American System, which wars on the forces of history, culture, and nature."[55]

The good news is, if we labor under the delusions of a foreign ideological system, then we can change that, if we set our minds to it. As Christian Larson, a spokesman of the New Thought movement—America's native-born Neo-Platonism and two-fisted Traditionalism, itself the decades-long target of the knife-

---

[55] Michael O'Meara, "2009: Crisis or Opportunity?" in *Towards the White Republic* (San Francisco: Counter-Currents, 2010).

happy Judaics of the American Medical Association—put it a century ago:

> [E]very undesirable inheritance can be removed. Every impression formed in the mind is a seed that will produce some tendency; therefore we should not only remove those impressions that we do not wish to cultivate, but should also prevent inferior and undesired impressions from forming in the mind in the first place.
>
> We are therefore not in bondage to what we have inherited, because we can change everything and bring everything in ourselves into harmony with natural law.[56]

As Greg Johnson has said:

> [T]his regime was not imposed on our people by a violent revolution. They accepted it because of the transformation of their consciousness. They can be saved the same way.[57]

With Chuck Hagel proposing that the military be cut back to its 1940 level (and being denounced by the Judeo-cons as an "isolationist," of course), perhaps there is a chance to take our culture back—back to the days of Aryan boyhood.[58]

Stop pontificating about "Faustian Man" and bring back Adventure Boy!

Counter-Currents/*North American New Right*
March 13, 2014

---

[56] *How to Stay Well* (Los Angeles: The New Literature Publishing Co., 1912), pp. 85–86.

[57] Greg Johnson, *New Right vs. Old Right*, p. 29.

[58] As this goes to press, looks like Hagel, for one, is out.

THE LEAVEN OF THE PHARISEES:
THE JUDEO AS CUCKOO

"'How is it you do not understand that I did not speak to you concerning bread? — but to beware of the leaven of the Pharisees and Sadducees." Then they understood that He did not tell them to beware of the leaven of bread, but of the doctrine of the Pharisees and Sadducees. (Matthew 16:11–12).

Having, for a number of years now, used the archetypes of the Homo and the Negro in performing what some have been kind enough to dub "cultural criticism," it is perhaps time to remember that behind the Negro, hidden away, as always, is the darker, more sinister figure of the Judeo. The Negro is the shock troop; the Judeo is the ultimate beneficiary.

Sometimes, the Judeo hides in plain sight: you can hear him when the Christian speaks, and not only the really nutty ones that claim to be the "real Israelites" or want to enact Deuteronomy into positive law in their new kingdom.

Speaking of creating new kingdoms (while making sure that Judeos feel comfortable) you can hardly peruse the Comments sections of White Nationalist websites without eventually coming across something like:

> Once our homeland has been set up, without any homos, then we can . . .

I confess I find the mentality hard to understand. Now, I'll admit that in the context, "no Jews" and "no negroes" go without saying, so, yes, literally, they aren't said. But homos? Really, that's your biggest concern as you look over your imaginary Whitopia?[1]

---

[1] Jack Donovan figures that "the percentage of exclusive male homosexuals within the mainstream male population [is probably less than 3-5 . . . So everyone is talking about "expanding" the institution

This sort of thing always reminds me of Alan Watts' great insight that the Christian church had become first moralistic to the exclusion of any concern with spirituality (hence, the well-known "spiritual hunger" among the young); then obsessed specifically with sex:[2]

> What can you get kicked out of the church for? Any church—Presbyterian, Roman Catholic, Episcopalian, Baptist, and the synagogue I think too. What's the real thing for which people get kicked out, excommunicated?
> For "envy, hatred, malice, and all un-charitableness"? "Pride, vainglory, and hardness of heart"? Owning shares in munitions factories? Profiting off slums? No *sir*. You can

---

of marriage to benefit 50% of 5% of the male population. With some insanely generous rounding, that's what—maybe 200,000 dudes, including male children and senior citizens"; hardly the biggest "problem" facing White America, especially since "Every day American culture is a little more like a Black Mass against nature and manhood and anything decent or beautiful or noble or worth saving. Western Civilization has become a Black Mass for Western Civilization. Everything our better fathers believed in has been spit on and placed like a tainted Host between the yeasty thighs of a giggling whore." See "Gay Marriage: 'What-The-Fuck-Ever'" by Jack Donovan, April 9, 2013, http://www.jack-donovan.com/axis/2013/04/gay-marriage-what-the-fuck-ever/

[2] Here, if nowhere else, Watts agrees with Evola: "Some people have sought to favor a watered-down idea of Tradition, marked by moralizing and religious [i.e., exoteric dogmas and ritualism] concerns" (*The Path of Cinnabar* [London: Arktos, 2013], p. 234); "As for the character of official Catholicism today—a parochial, moralistic, socialistic, politicizing, and frankly paternalistic Catholicism which abhors all 'medieval-isms' in its attempt to prove itself up-to-date—there is little to be said" (*op. cit.*, p. 133). And of course, there was nothing to be said about Protestantism. See, for example, Guénon's "The Origins of Mormonism" in *Miscellanea* (Ghent, NY: Sophia Perennis, 2004), and then try and take Mitt Romney or Glenn Beck seriously. While Guénon, for example, spent decades trying—rather like Breton with psychoanalysis, Marxism, occultism, etc.—to create a rapprochement with Catholicism, Evola simply dismissed Christianity as having been a pseudo-tradition from the get-go.

be a bishop and live in all those sins openly. [Or live in a White Nationalist homeland] But if you go to bed with the wrong person, you're out.

So one has to conclude that, for all practical purposes, the church is a sexual regulation society; and it really isn't interested in anything else. Christianity is more preoccupied with sex than even Priapism or Tantric Yoga [are]. Because that's the *thing* that counts, that's the sin, the really important sin.[3]

The parallel here is between elevating sexual etiquette into the *sine qua non* of being a good Christian as well as being a good White citizen. Just as the all-too eager decline of Christianity into Protestantism and then into moralism is a tribute, or backhanded compliment, to Judaic subversion—Judaism itself being hardly a religion itself, being empty of all spiritual content; nor even a moralism, being, as Gilad Atzmon has pointed out,[4] dedicated to the anti-universalism of "Jews *über alles*,"[5] but simply a form of obsessive compulsive disorder inculcated in the Jewish masses to facilitate the domination of the rabbis[6]—so is the decline of

---

[3] Audio lecture, "Beyond Theology."

[4] While Atzmon is no more than a pseudo-ally, Greg Johnson notes that "Atzmon's first argument, of course, is correct: Jews are guilty of deception when they preach universalism to us and practice partiality among themselves." See Greg Johnson's review "The Self-Exterminating Jew: Gilad Atzmon's *The Wandering Who?*," http://www.counter-currents.com/2011/10/the-self-exterminating-jew-gilad-atzmons-the-wandering-who/

[5] Atzmon writes: "Israel has always been the Jewish State, it has never been a liberal place nor has it been committed to justice or equality. The deepest truth is that universal humanism and ethical culture is [sic] foreign to Judaic thinking that is tribal and legalistic." —"I Support Israel's National Bill," November 25, 2014, http://www.gilad.co.uk/writings/2014/11/25/i-support-israels-national-bill0

[6] "Rabbis quite literally rule the life of their congregants (this is particularly true in the case of Orthodox and ultra-Orthodox Judaism) as *halakhah* literally has thousands of rules based off of the 613 *Mitzvot* ('Commandments') derived from the (Written) Torah. Thus it

what we might call "cultural building" among White Nationalists, having, like the political Right and the Neo-cons, swallowed a whole lot of Judaic ideas—such as "No Homo!"—under the illusion that they represent "tough talk" and "serious thinking."[7]

Since Jews and culture, in the context of delineating how to compose the ideal society, have come up, we might profitably look who T. S. Eliot, no mean traditionalist himself,[8] thought should be excluded. As the *Forward* describes it:

> During a 1933 lecture in Virginia, published in 1934 as "After Strange Gods," (which he later refused to reprint[9]) Eliot, following Maurras, stressed the importance of social "unity of religious background.... Reasons of race and religion combine to make any large number of free-thinking Jews undesirable," Eliot declared.[10]

---

is necessary for the rabbi's congregation to materially support him so that he can provide *'expert guidance'* at a moment's notice for his flock in all matters of religious law (*halakhah*) and custom (*minhag*)." See "Blogging the Jerusalem Talmud: Tractate Bikkurim" http://semiticcontroversies.blogspot.com/2014/11/blogging-jerusalem-talmud-tractate.html

[7] As well as "our proud Viking heritage"—MST3k Episode 810: *The Giant Spider Invasion*.

[8] It should be remembered that Eliot, Anglo-Catholic that he was, played a not inconsiderable role in the presentation of Traditionalism to the Anglosphere. His publishing house, Faber & Faber, produced both the first English translation of Schuon's *The Transcendent Unity of Religion*, trans. Peter Townsend (London: Faber & Faber, 1953), with a cover blurb from Eliot, and Watts' *The Supreme Identity: An Essay on Oriental Metaphysic and the Christian Religion* (London: Faber & Faber, 1950); as well as Josef Pieper's *Leisure, the Basis of Culture*, trans. Alexander Dru, with an introduction by T. S. Eliot (London: Faber & Faber, 1952), which just happened to be the text of my Intro Philosophy class at Assumption.

[9] Though of course it's on the internet, such as at archive.org.

[10] Benjamin Ivry, "T.S. Eliot's On-Again, Off-Again Anti-Semitism: Letters to Friends and Colleagues Repeatedly Denigrate Jews," *Forward*, September 23, 2011, http://forward.com/articles/142722/ts-eliots-on-again-off-again-anti-semitism/#ixzz3Kf6Jzua7

Now the phrase in question is certainly more than enough to brand Eliot an "anti-Semite" by today's hair-trigger standards (as the *Forward* article attests[11]), which amount to nothing more than what Steve Sailer calls "noticing things."

But looked at closely, as Eliot would advise us to read any poet's work, the phrase is rather restrictive: "any *large* number" and "*free-thinking* Jews." Eliot seems to be insinuating that a small number of Orthodox Jews would not be a problem,[12] perhaps would lend a little color to drab London.[13]

The idea seems to be the old saw about the role of the Jew as cultural "outsider," providing a needed, indeed a necessary, "objective" and "critical" perspective.[14] Needless to say, it's a popular idea . . . among Jews.[15]

---

[11] As Joe Sobran said, "anti-Semite" no longer means "someone who hates all Jews" but "someone some Jew dislikes."

[12] After writing this, I discovered (through idly searching new Kindle releases on Amazon) a similar reading: "The notorious passage in *After Strange Gods* is capable of the interpretation that a community of *orthodox* Jews would be socially desirable because of the strong social bonds established by Jewish solidarity." Roger Kojecky, *T. S. Eliot's Social Criticism* (London: Faber, 1971; Amazon Kindle Direct Publishing, 2014), "Introduction." Of course, it all depends on what the aims of that "solidarity" (i.e., "ethnic networking") are. Michael A. Hoffman, II — whose otherwise invaluable researches into Judaic subversion are vitiated by a typically Protestant insistence on stubbornly distinguishing evil Talmud Jews from God's Chosen Ones of the Old Testament — would insist that Eliot "naively" accepts the claims of Rabbinic Judaism to be kosher.

[13] Similarly, editor Leslie Klinger seems puzzled by H. P. Lovecraft's virulent antipathy to "the Jews" and other swarthy foreigners, while nevertheless enjoying trips to Chinatown and the Lower East Side and admiring the colorful native dress. See my "Notes on *The New Edited Lovecraft*," http://www.counter-currents.com/2014/10/notes-on-the-new-annotated-h-p-lovecraft/

[14] I discussed this before in "The Eternal Outsider: Veblen on the Gentleman and the Jew," reprinted in *The Eldritch Evola*.

[15] I've frequently described this "culture of critique" (Kevin MacDonald) as producing "cockroach literature" due to the iconic role Kafka plays in it; however, recent a biography has led me to think the icon of Kafka himself, ironically, has been faked; see my review "Kaf-

To suggest what might have been in the back of Eliot's mind, preventing him from just calling for the summary expulsion of "the Jews," consider one of his greatest epigones, Marshall McLuhan. McLuhan, though born on the Canadian prairie,[16] developed, after attending Oxford, a loathing for the Puritan provinciality he saw all around him, even—or especially—in Canada's grand metropolis, Toronto—then a bastion of Presbyterian righteousness known semi-ironically as "Toronto the Good."[17]

---

ka, Our Folk-Comrade," below.

[16] "The graying professor from Canada's western hinterlands . . ." — From "The *Playboy* Interview: Marshall McLuhan," *Playboy Magazine*, March 1969, http://www.nextnature.net/2009/12/the-playboy-interview-marshall-mcluhan/

[17] While avoiding the excesses of Prohibition—though Quebecois Jews like Joseph Seagram were happy to sell whisky to Irish gangsters like Joe Kennedy—Canada, like England, enjoyed the restriction of drinking through a network of arcane rules and regulations (government-run stores, separate rooms for men without women, curtains on all windows to prevent ladies fainting after catching a sight of the debauchery, etc.). To see, in cultural terms, what McLuhan was up against, see Wyndham Lewis' fictionalized memoir of the same period in the same cities, Toronto and Windsor, *Self Condemned* (Methuen, 1954; Voyageur Classics, Toronto: Dundurn, 2010). A generation later, Joyce Carol Oates wrote a series of inter-connected stories satirizing the desperate lives of her colleagues at the fictionalized "Hilberry College" where "everyone felt superior to the college, even to the country, Canada itself!" See *Crossing the Border* (New York: Vanguard Press, 1976) and *The Hungry Ghosts: Seven Allusive Comedies* (San Francisco: Black Sparrow, 1974). Significantly, two stories were published in *Playboy Magazine* and never collected by Oates, despite award-winning acclaim: "Saul Bird Says: Relate! Communicate! Liberate!" (Oct., 1971; *Playboy* Editorial Award, 1971; O Henry Award, 197; reprinted in *Playboy Stories: The Best of Forty Years of Short Fiction 2*, New York: Dutton, 1991), which portrays the destructive influence of what Kevin MacDonald would call a typical Jewish guru-type; and "Gay" (*Playboy*, Dec. 1976, reprinted only in *The Best American Short Stories* 1977), which details the self-destructive career arc of an English professor who seems to be the only person who "doesn't realize he's gay": "Harvard, Oxford . . . somewhere in Canada? Impossible!" Both stories are relevant to our concerns here, of course.

To deal with this cultural atrophy, McLuhan proposed a simple, sweeping remedy: the immediate importation of a couple million Jews.

In an unpublished article titled "Canada Needs More Jews," he put forth a notion he had picked up from Wyndham Lewis that the importation of two million Jews might liven the place up.[18]

Now, in this, I think Eliot and McLuhan were quite wrong. One might only call their attention to the Elizabethan Golden Age, when writers not merely equal to Shakespeare but the man himself, flourished with not one Jewish foot trodding upon England's green and pleasant land. And one also needs to add, if one is adding up the cultural accounts, the deficit produced by the deliberate *subversion* of Aryan culture by the Judaic elites; to say nothing of their other impudent and vicious distortions of politics, religion, etc.

But there is another, broader, sense in which they were quite right. To put it in terms the Right understands, all societies have elites; moreover, all societies need elites, to set standards of culture and even decorum. This is what McLuhan sensed was lacking in Canadian society of the 1950s, as did de Tocqueville when observing America a century before;[19] as did Henry James, and Eliot, who pulled up stakes to rejoin the British homeland, and H. P. Lovecraft, who lived in the 18th-century England of his dreams.

But why the Jews, of all people?[20] A glance at the complete

---

[18] Philip Marchand, *Marshall McLuhan: The Medium and the Messenger: A Biography* (Cambridge, Mass.: The MIT Press, 1998), p. 82.

[19] De Tocqueville already noted that behind the much vaunted "individualism" the lack of social stratification actually produced socially sanctioned conformity. In Kafka's novel (usually known as) *America*, "What seems like popular democracy merely disguises the authoritarian rule of the political and economic elite." Ritchie Robertson, "Introduction" to *The Man Who Disappeared (America)* (New York: Oxford University Press, 2012).

[20] "How odd of God/To choose the Jews" wrote William Norman

lack of any development, to say nothing of dominance, in the arts, sciences, or technology, from Biblical times to their post-Napoleonic civil emancipation,[21] would make them an odd choice to be our elite. But was it a "choice"?

In fact, evidence that our "elite" is basically devoted to the doctrine of "Kill Whitey" should give us a clue as to the problem—and the cause.

Watts, I think, was onto more than he seems to be; not just a diagnosis of Western religion but of Western, particularly American, society itself.

The lack of a natural elite, requiring the import of Jews, is itself a product of the same "family values" regime imposed—via Christianity—by the Jew.

Ewer; interestingly, though he began as a Chestertonian sort of "guild socialist" he eventually became a Communist and a Soviet spy, according to Wikipedia, http://www.nextnature.net/2009/12/the-playboy-interview-marshall-mcluhan/

[21] Documented by Israel Shahak, in his *Jewish History, Jewish Religion: The Weight Of Three Thousand Years* (London: Pluto Press, 1994). Shahak notes that Jews have simply recently colonized arts and sciences established by non-Jews: "Except for a purely religious learning, which was itself in a debased and degenerate state, the Jews of Europe (and to a somewhat lesser extent also of the Arab countries) were dominated, before about 1780, by a supreme contempt and hate for all learning (excluding the Talmud and Jewish mysticism). . . . Study of all languages was strictly forbidden, as was the study of mathematics and science. Geography, history—even Jewish history—were completely unknown. The critical sense, which is supposedly so characteristic of Jews, was totally absent, and nothing was so forbidden, feared and therefore persecuted as the most modest innovation or the most innocent criticism." Even the much vaunted "Jewish sense of humor" is an even more recent construct; there are no jokes anywhere in classical Jewish writings: "Not only is humor very rare in Hebrew literature before the 19th century . . . but humor and jokes are strictly forbidden by the Jewish religion—except, significantly, jokes against other religions. Satire against rabbis and leaders of the community was never internalized by Judaism, not even to a small extent, as it was in Latin Christianity. There were no Jewish comedies, just as there were no comedies in Sparta, and for a similar reason." *Op. cit.*, Chapter Two: "Prejudice and Prevarication."

We see, in all this, the hand of the Jew. First, replace the authentic initiatic Traditions of paganism with the pseudo-Tradition of Christianity, with its fake, phony initiatic substitute, the so-called "Eucharist" — thus robbing the West of its culture-creating abilities.[22] Then, having knocked out the esoteric props, reduce the exoteric shell to moralism, and ultimately, to the Judaic obsession, sex. And a large part of that obsession, coincidentally or not, is what's come to be known as homophobia.[23] As a result, the natural elite of the Aryan peoples is rendered into un-persons, and waiting to fill the vacuum is . . . the Jew.[24]

---

[22] On the role of entheogens in culture, see the extensive research of Michael Hoffman (not Michael A. Hoffman, II, though the fact that two Hoffmans, one of which is "II," are involved in these areas is rather amusing) collected at his website, egodeath.com; for the role of drugs and drug-inspired Mysteries in creating classical culture, see D. C. A. Hillman, *The Chemical Muse: Drug Use and the Roots of Western Civilization* (New York: Thomas Dunne, 2008); for the Germanic tradition, see Christian Rätsch on "The Sacred Plants of our Ancestors," *TYR* 2.

[23] Yes, I know, the Right complains about "all our disagreements with the Left get pathologized and tagged with a diagnostic term" but here at least the virulence and single-mindedness does suggest something of a syndrome rather than an opinion.

[24] A similar process of cultural decapitation occurred under the name of "Denazification," to say nothing of the atrocities and deprivations visited upon Germany in the postwar years: see Thomas Goodrich: *Hellstorm: The Death of Nazi Germany, 1944–1947* (Sheridan, Colorado: Aberdeen Books, 2010) as well as in the wake of the Iraq War II. The latter purge was explicitly called, half-jokingly, "De-Ba'athification," and it's interesting to note that cultural destruction was an explicit element of it. When asked about the destruction of not just Iraq's cultural heritage but that of the "cradle of Western civilization," Defense Secretary Rumsfeld shrugged and mused that "'Freedom's untidy, and free people are free to make mistakes and commit crimes and do bad things['] . . . Looting, he added, was not uncommon for countries that experience significant social upheaval. 'Stuff happens,' Rumsfeld said." "Rumsfeld on looting in Iraq: 'Stuff happens'; Administration asking countries for help with security" by Sean Loughlin, CNN Washington Bureau, April 12, 2003, http://www.cnn.com/2003/US/04/11/sprj.irq.pentagon/

Now, before everyone starts hootin' and hollerin', let me just make it, as William Burroughs would say, country-simple for ya'll. The origin and the handing down (*traditio*) of culture, at least in the Aryan world, lies not in the family (the subject of the "family values" so dear to the Jews and their Neocon contingent?, including the Christian Right), essential though it may be in itself, but in those who have broken from it and established their own groups for those purposes: the various *Männerbünde* of warriors, priests, scholars, vigilantes, etc.[25]

As Wulf Grimmson outlines it:

> The *Männerbund* is a system of social ties found in traditional Indo European societies which is very difficult for men living in a modernist (and/or monotheistic) society to understand . . .[26]
>
> Among our Germanic ancestors these groups were composed of sexually mature male youths who under guidance of an elder formed a closed cult or society. They were dedicated to Odin, had special rites of pedagogical training, initiation and esoteric practice and combined the functions of a sorcerer or shaman and a warrior. . . .
>
> [T]he role of the blood brother and the *Männerbund* was seen as the foundation of Germanic society with the family unit of far less significance. This changes the whole structure of how we see archaic society when we realize that these societies held a virile warrior ethic based in male-male affection superior to family life.
>
> The *Männerbund* was a unique social and initiatory institution; it stood at the centre of the hierarchy of archaic

---

[25] See generally the work of Wulf Grimmson, and my discussion of it in "A Band Apart: Wulf Grimsson's *Loki's Way*" and my use of it in "'God, I'm with a heathen.' The Rebirth of the *Männerbund* in Brian De Palma's *The Untouchables*"; both are reprinted in *The Homo & the Negro*.

[26] And by "monotheist" read "Judeo-Christian"; however "anti-modernist" the White Nationalist may be, he tends, as we have seen, to remain a Judeo-Christian at heart; his conversion is only partial and inadequate.

society offering a path to initiation into the esoteric Mysteries and providing stability to the tribe below it. In comparison to the Third Function of the tribe and family *the Männerbund was certainly an outsider institution yet it was this outsidernesss that allowed it to take such a significant role within the traditional hierarchy.* It was not swayed by nepotism or by tribal or familial pressures; it was a separate, distinct and unique structure. It had a warrior ethic yet also trained scribes, shamans, rune masters and many others; it combined the First and Second Functions in a very special and profound way.[27]

As Evola says,

> It was this *Männerbund*, in which the qualification of "man" *had simultaneously an initiatory (i.e. sacred) and a warrior meaning*, that wielded the power in the social group or clan. This *Männerbund* was characterized by special tasks and responsibilities; *it was different from all other societies to which members of the tribe belonged*. In this primordial scheme we find the fundamental 'categories' *differentiating the political order from the 'social' order*. First among these is a special chrism—namely, that proper to 'man' in the highest sense of the word (*vir* was the term employed in Roman times) and not merely a generic *homo*: this condition is marked by *a spiritual breakthrough and by detachment from the naturalistic and vegetative plane*. Its integration is power, the principle of command belonging to the *Männerbund*. We could rightfully see in this one of the 'constants' (i.e. basic ideas) that in very different applications, formulations and derivations are uniformly found in theory or, better, in the metaphysics of the State that was professed even by the greatest civilizations of the past.[28]

Elsewhere, Evola is a little more explicit on the role of sexuali-

---

[27] See Wulf Grimsson, *Loki's Way: The Path of the Sorcerer in Age of Iron*, 2nd. ed. (Lulu.com, 2011), p. 7 and p. 89.

[28] See Julius Evola, *Men Among the Ruins, op. cit.*

ty, like drugs, in the rites, rituals and mysteries designed to produce the desired "breakthrough":

> The defining trait of all sexuality is a kind of hyper-physical excitement not dissimilar from all the conditions that the ancient world regarded as *potential paths leading to the direct experience of the super-sensible* (as Plato himself clearly acknowledged).

However,

> *Physical procreation weakens the impulse to pursue the highest aim of sexuality*: the insignificant physical community of the species through the succession of perishable individuals [the essentially Judaic idea of "family values," immortality through the survival of the race, etc.] here replaces the conception of a being capable of transcending the cycle of confined existence, and mere moral life.[29]

In sum, we see that in Aryan societies the family is superseded by (though not denigrated, in fact supported by) male groups formed by sexual and esoteric rites (the "mysteries" which undoubtedly involved entheogenic substances) that, living as outsiders, nevertheless created and sustained the cultural superstructure of each society.

And here we see the evil genius of the Judaic subversion; is it any surprise to see all this—basically, drugs and sex, both employed to escape the ties of family[30]— is on the Judeo-Christian hit list?

---

[29] *Op. cit*, p. 208. This is the usual displacement of verticality (transcendence) with horizontality (dispersion among the physical states of the world) that is the essential feature of modernity, "progress," *Lebensraum*, etc., and is even lauded by propagandists of science or the Renaissance.

[30] See Erik Davis's discussion of teenage drug use as a means of escape in his *Nomad Codes: Adventures in Modern Esoterica* (Portland, Or.: Yeti Publishing, 2010), which I reviewed on Counter-Currents, http://www.counter-currents.com/tag/nomad-codes/

Having ensured that Aryans would only be able to form basic social groupings based on families (mere "societies" as Evola calls them) but not true, hierarchical States,[31] who then stands to benefit by stepping forward into the vacuum?

It's important to realize that Jews make themselves all warm and snuggly within Western culture by a strategy of not only distortion but also deception or disguise. For example, take "open borders." This policy both distorts the public life of the United States (over 90% native born White before the 1965 Immigration "Reform" Act) and disguises the Jew (just another one of dozens of loyal, patriotic immigrant groups).

In the same way, the Judaic acts to not only short-circuit the natural elite of Aryan society by imposing religiously based "family values,"[32] but also positions himself (one is tempted to say, "pushes himself forward") as the "real" or at least "new" elite, while actually being a foreign, hostile elite.[33]

Thus is Athens transformed into Jerusalem, via Salt Lake City; we might call it the "Cuckoo Strategy."

During the Cold War, man-in-the-street conservatives of the Archie Bunker variety were wont to sneer at their com-symp opponents that if Russia was so great, "why don't you go live there?" Later, this would be extended to Cuba, Viet Nam, or whatever the latest Leftist Utopia was located.

---

[31] Thus the Judaic fury directed against the SS Order State that was to be the ultimate goal of Himmler; this was the only element of National Socialism that maintained Evola's interest; see his *Notes on the Third Reich*, trans. E. Christian Kopff (London: Arktos, 2013). Needless to say, the whole National Socialist project was vitiated from the start by a crypto-Judaic (and downright creepy) obsession with Master Races and "births" — "prole" notions whose "vulgarity" Evola appropriately scorned (see Evola, *op. cit.*, ch. 3); paralleling in miniature the cultural distortion of Western society that we've been discussing here.

[32] Using the patented one-two, heads I win tail you lose Judaic strategy of rigging the debate to include only the false alternative of homophobia vs. gold lamé hot pants.

[33] See these articles tagged "Jews as a hostile elite" at *Occidental Observer*: http://www.theoccidentalobserver.net/category/jews-as-a-hostile-elite/

In the same spirit, we might suggest to those who make "no homos" the knee jerking, word-association answering, Pavlovian responding *sine qua non* of their Whitopia, that it already exists; why don't you move to Salt Lake City? Or perhaps a nice ultra-Orthodox settlement in *Eretz Israel*?[34]

So our problem is not that we have no elite, but that we have *the wrong one*. Rather than a natural elite we have an alien elite that means us harm.

Natural? Formed from the non-procreative—an evolutionary tactic essential to the evolutionary survival of *homo sapiens*[35]— Homos indeed form a natural elite, being of the same race as the rest of (White) society, and even can show up in any family— spouse, child, cousin. etc.—thus giving every clan a tie to the elite, or at least a better chance than winning the lottery.[36]

Thus, when the people ask for the true bread of the entheogenic Mysteries, the Judeo gives them the stone of the Eucharist; when they ask for an elite, the Judeo gives them . . . himself.[37]

---

[34] And, by contrast, an actual Whitopia, if based on historical knowledge rather than Judaic-approved fantasies, would more closely resemble the camps of the eponymous warriors of Burroughs' *The Wild Boys: A Book of the Dead*. (New York: Grove, 1971); and before anyone mentions it, let me point out that Burroughs' Boys make full use of "modern technology" when useful and appropriate (including cloning and time machines).

[35] Contrary to man-in-the-street biology favored by bloggers of the Right, see James Neill's *The Origins and Role of Same-Sex Relations in Human Societies* (Jefferson, N.C.: McFarland, 2009) and my review/essay thereon (Amazon Kindle Single, 2013).

[36] After all, a race is, as Steve Sailer puts it, a partially inbred extended family. "A race is a family, and families tend to behave alike. In Ferguson, we're seeing one kind of behavior—the same kind Darren Wilson faced when he met Michael Brown walking down the middle of the street."—"Ferguson Fallout—Red Is Not The New Black" by James Fulford, November 27, 2014 (http://www.vdare.com/articles/the-fulford-file-ferguson-fallout-red-is-not-the-new-black).

[37] "There is every reason to believe that 'stone' is the code-word [in Biblical literature] for beast-man, ape."—Dr. Jorg Lanz von Liebenfels, *Theozoology, or the Science of the Sodomite Apelings and the Divine Electron* (originally published 1905; Europa-House, 2004), and

The point here is not to idolize or "liberate" the poor, downtrodden homosexual, but rather, that having made non-reproductive sexuality the Ultimate Sin, a process (not unlike what the rabbis call "building a fence around the Torah") ensues in which all "taint" of it must be avoided by manly men. Thus, the male societies that comprise the culture-creating institutions of White society—from the Boy Scouts to the priesthood, from athletics to the arts to the military—are enveloped in a cloud of cultural sniggering, and any self-respecting White male looks to the promiscuous Negro for his self-validation. One thing you can say about Detroit: it may not have any culture, but there's no homos! Of course, it's perfectly understandable that anyone would want to exclude and dissociate from the kind of people put forward by the Left and the Liberal Media as representatives of this minority.[38] But this, as I've argued elsewhere, is precisely because of the fake "gay" identity, manufactured by the Left in order to corral the homosexual into their Rainbow Coalition of culture-wreckers.[39] The real interests of both homosexuals and White society in general are elsewhere:

> The fact that homosexuals have become pillars of the cultural left is deplorable—*and quite unnecessary. Homosexuals have ethnic interests just like everyone else, and they can promote those interests even if they don't themselves have children . . . This would be the rational thing to do.*[40]

---

available for free online (http://www.american-buddha.com/cult.theozoology.htm).

[38] Jack Donovan, I believe, has observed that if most homosexuals weren't annoying twerps, "'fag' wouldn't be an insult in the first place."

[39] See, of course, the title essay of my collection *The Homo & the Negro* as well as the late Alisdair Clarke's seminal essay "Paris Shockwaves": "the blandishments of the Gay-Liberationist-hucksters led us away from our Western civilization, our antecedents; Plato, Hadrian, Michelangelo and Tchaikovsky, turned our folk community into strangers, and deposited us in the heart of the enemy camp," http://aryanfuturism.blogspot.com/2006/08/paris-shockwaves.html

[40] "Psychopathology and Racial Self-Hate Among Whites" by Kevin MacDonald, *Occidental Observer*, October 7, 2014, http://www.

I would suggest that here is another case where the alt-Right would learn from the New Left, rather than from the Old Left or the Old Right.[41] To paraphrase Eliot, no White society could thrive without a small number of — tradition-minded — Homos.

The Occidental Observer
June 24, 2015

---

theoccidentalobserver.net/2014/10/psychopathology-and-racial-self-hate-among-Whites/.
[41] Just as, self-styled "radical" Leftists, who have learned how to recognize what Chomsky, Parenti, or Petras have called "institutional analysis," are more useful to our cause than "official" Rightists or "conservatives" who have been taught (by Whom?) that they must eschew what they call "conspiracy theories."

KAFKA:
OUR FOLK COMRADE

James Hawes
Excavating Kafka
London: Cuercus, 2008
US edition: *Why You Should Read Kafka Before You Waste Your Life*
New York: St. Martin's Press, 2008

> "Turns out, Kafka was a wealthy, porn-loving, loyal German citizen. Who knew?"
>
> —Amazon reviewer

That face. You've seen it. You're sick of seeing it. The Prophet of the Holocaust, the Gulag, and worst of all, the Orwellian aspects of the Bush/Obama Administration. The corporate logo of Judaic Cultural Supremacy, the ikon of Holocaustianity. The emblem of all that you hate.

You want to smash it so hard, then put it together again to smash it again, and again.

James Hawes has good news for you: it's a fake. A big, phony fake:

> ... the international trademark of Prague ... was actually taken in a department store in Berlin ... about eight months before his death, when he knew logically he was doomed. ... This state of mind is ... liable to make anyone look profound.
>
> But still not profound enough. [I]n the early fifties ... S. Fisher Co. artists retouched this picture to give Kafka's eyes the desired gleam. *Prophetic Kafka* is now as famous and vague an icon as *Saintly Che Guevara*—and with about as much historical accuracy.

Hawes hates the photo too, but for other reasons. For him, it's the all-too-appropriate ikon of what he calls "The K-Myth" (using "myth" as a good-thinking liberal does, to mean "phony fake").

The K-Myth is:

> [T]he idea of a mysterious genius, a lonely Middle European Nostradamus, who, almost ignored by his contemporaries, somehow plumbed the depths of his mysterious, quasi-saintly psyche to predict the Holocaust and the Gulags.

In reality,

> Kafka was not only a literary insider but a social one too, a millionaire's son, a well-paid senior functionary of the Habsburg empire, a member of Prague's German elite who consciously—and subconsciously—wanted Germany and Austria to win the First World War. A German-speaking, German-thinking Jew who foresaw the horrors of the Holocaust no more than anyone else did. A writer who, when he first read out *The Trial*, reduced his friends to "helpless laughter."[1]

Yes, They have been lying to you from the beginning; from before the beginning, for as we will see, Kafka himself was an eager participant in the early parts of the stage-managing of his literary career, like any young writer, though he would have collapsed in "helpless laughter" himself to see how monstrous the K-Myth has grown.

Hawes devotes most of his book to deconstructing the K-Myth piece by piece. First off, that guff about poor Kafka, working long hours at his stifling office job, living with his parents, snatching a few hours for writing his masterpieces in the late nights—the original Millennial Slacker. "Actually, Kafka was . . . an '80s Yuppie; more Gordon Gekko than Quentin Tarantino. Far from being alone and poor, he lived with his family in up-

---

[1] James Hawes "Tumbling the author myth: Why such anger about my revelations of Kafka's interest in pornography? His legacy could stand a little debunking," *The Guardian*, Friday, August 29, 2008, http://www.theguardian.com/commentisfree/2008/aug/29/franzkafka.civilliberties

per-middle-class comfort..."²

Actually, even that understates the case; Kafka's father (who, as we'll see, takes a lot of heat from the myth-makers) was a millionaire, owning not merely an apartment to share with Franz but an apartment building (more Proust than Gregor Samsa) as well as an admittedly not well-performing asbestos factory.

The rent-free accommodations are especially lucrative, since Kafka, holding a doctorate in Law, has scored a plum job at the Workers' Accident Insurance Institute, taking home the modern equivalent of *$90,000 a year* for a six-hour day, most of it spent discussing Heine with his boss.³

Kafka writes only a few hours a day, mostly in the late nights, only because, as he admits gleefully, he spends all his free time and money in cafes and brothels, and is just lazy to boot. In short, a fairly typical rich young man with literary ambitions but little ambition; hardly a Genet scribbling on paper bags in prison.

Now, about that writing. All that time out socializing on the town sure comes in handy. Before publishing a single word, his pal, Max Brod—"a classic literary networker with fingers in many literary pies"—inserts, into a review of an established author he's publishing in an important Berlin literary journal, the observation that this Kafka chap seems to be a great stylist. The author under review, one Franz Blei, then reviews Kafka's first, tiny little pieces, favorably, of course; later, Kafka's publisher will arrange the hasty publication of one story as a stand-alone chapbook, so as to qualify for—and win—the prestigious Fontane Prize (rather like the National Book Award)—judged, that year, by Franz Blei.

Which is not to say that the work itself is unworthy of such judgment; only that, such assiduous log-rolling, as certain tribe well versed in it would say, "couldn't hoit."

But back to that day job again; it's going to furnish Hawes with

---

² Louis Bayard, "How Kafka-esque is Kafka? The Czech writer has become the prophet of our absurd era, but a new book intends to strip the author of his saintly reputation," *Salon*, Friday, August 1, 2008, http://www.salon.com/2008/08/01/kafka/

³ Apparently a typical German occupation, shared by Dietrich Eckhart; see my review of *Hitler's Mentor*, http://www.countercurrents.com/2014/05/hitlers-mentor/

some of his most powerful, or at least controversial (and, like Kafka, he knows the value of controversy to word of mouth sales) evidence for the K-Myth.

First, although I've been calling K a "yuppie" for shock value, he did not at least share the same kind of single-minded individualism characteristic of the Reagan-era model. No, this chap closely identified himself with his ethnic comrades. Unfortunately for the K-Myth, those comrades were not the poor, downtrodden, persecuted Jews, but the German-speaking elite of the Hapsburg Empire. Kafka, in short, was a German patriot.

For example, Kafka invested a considerable portion of his savings — remember, even with all the *Kaffee mit Schlag* and Czech waitress-whores (the Prague equivalent of today's "actress-models"), he's got $90,000 a year, and living rent-free — in Austrian War Bonds. That's right, Kafka helped pay for the bayonets those Huns were skewering Belgian babies on. They paid 5% or so interest, backed up by the Hapsburg Empire, making them the no-brainer investment of the century. Ironically, it turned out to be the most "Kafkaesque" thing he ever did, the equivalent of selling the family jewels for Confederate currency, but, as the Tribe would say, who knew? And this is the schlemiel who supposedly could foresee the Holocaust?

Even more "damning," though, was his wartime write-up of an appeal for a hospital for German-speaking — and *only* German-speaking, no Czech or Yiddish riff-raff need apply was made clear — wounded war veterans. I'll let Hawes tell the tale:

> There've been countless attempts to present Kafka as a closet socialist, a friend of Czech aspirations, and so on. The fact is that in a public proclamation of late 1916 (to raise funds for a hospital exclusively for German-speaking mentally-damaged soldiers of Kaiser Franz Josef's multinational army), Kafka speaks explicitly as a "German-Bohemian Folk-Comrade." His thinking vis-à-vis the Habsburg Empire seems to have been "non-political." Not in an oppositional sense at all, simply as conformism to the state of affairs. As Reiner Stach (whom I was very sad and surprised to see rubbishing my book even while admitting he hadn't read it)

says of Kafka's apparent views on Habsburg Foreign Policy, "the ease with which Kafka parroted the official jargon is disconcerting."[4]

Notice how Hawes tries to insinuate that even Franz Josef (with his anachronistically "multinational" army) was more "diverse" than white-bread Franz Kafka? "Disconcerting" to the Tribe, perhaps, or to those who "parrot" in their turn British War Office propaganda as history.[5]

Now, if you've been peeking at my footnotes, you noticed the references to "pornography" and even "Kafka's porn cache." Yes, it all comes together in one big ball of scandal; as George Costanza once said, in a rather Kafkaesque moment, "This thing is like an onion: The more layers you peel, the more it stinks!"[6]

For it turns out that Kafka liked to spend some of that salary on subscribing to an expensive, "arty" porn journal. And, as Hawes says, while puffing his book elsewhere,

> [T]he publisher of this porn in 1906 was the same man who, in 1908, was to become Kafka's own first publisher—and the same man who would, in 1915, arrange for Kafka to very publicly receive the prize-monies from the most prestigious German literary award of the year.[7]

Even for Prague at the *fin de siècle*, it seems a small world, after all!

As for the porn itself, Hawes tries to make a big meal out of it, as it were; but while he's correct that despite the literally millions of books, theses, and articles on Kafka, no one else has ever commented on it, it's hardly as earth-shatteringly lewd as he keeps

---

[4] Scott Horton, "In Pursuit of Kafka's Porn Cache: Six questions for James Hawes," *Harper's*, August 19, 2008, http://harpers.org/blog/2008/08/in-pursuit-of-kafkas-porn-cache-six-questions-for-james-hawes/

[5] See again my review of Eckhart in note 3 above.

[6] *Seinfeld*, Episode no. 136 "The Soul Mate" (Original air date 26 Sept 1996), http://www.seinfeldscripts.com/TheSoulMate.html

[7] "The Kafka Myth," http://www.readysteadybook.com/Article.aspx?page=kafkamyth

insisting; more like the censored parts of Beardsley's drawings.[8] Of course, your mileage may vary.[9]

Yes, one by one, Hawes knocks the props out from under the K-Myth, until, like one of those giant *papier-mâché* puppet heads the anarchists wave around at their demos, it comes crashing to the ground.

Or rather, to use a more literary metaphor, it's like a palimpsest, and after stripping the later monkish nonsense off, a lost classic stands revealed. Kafka, as I've been insinuating all along, the greatest writer, certainly the greatest European writer, of the 20th century — is One of Us! A White Guy!

But you shouldn't let yourself think Hawes is One of Us. He hates the "real" Kafka, the rich, sexually-active, free-spending Yuppie, and above all, the German patriot.[10]

He's arguing against the K-Myth because he thinks it distorts our understanding of the writings, distracts us from the texts themselves. It does so by creating a sickly secular saint of the typically Judaic sort.

> We all love the myth of the great dead romantic *outsider genius* (for what dubious reasons I leave you, dear reader, to wonder yourself). But knowing who Kafka really was — and

---

[8] Speaking of which, Mark Anderson's *Kafka's Clothes: Ornament and Aestheticism in the Habsburg Fin de Siècle* (Oxford: Clarendon, 1995) has a similar agenda, but limited to revealing Kafka the Dandy, almost a metrosexual.

[9] Having already pooh-poohed the "sexual explicitness" of Houellebecq ("Michel Houellebecq's Sexual Anti-Utopia," below), I may not be the right person to make the call.

[10] One senses, over and above the log-rolling, that Hawes wishes Kafka had not written in German at all, and, like the supposedly resigned prisoners at Auchwitz, had willingly entered the ghetto of Czech literature. Or perhaps, Yiddish — he did cultivate a taste for the Yiddish theatre — or even, dare one hope, Hebrew — thus assuaging beforehand that annoying fact, that the super-talented Jewish State has produced not one writer — or any other artist — of any distinction. Perhaps Veblen was right, and the Jew thrives only on adversity? See my "The Eternal Outsider: Veblen on The Gentleman and the Jew" in *The Eldritch Evola*.

therefore who he wasn't—is the only way we'll ever be able to read his wonderful writings in all their true, black-comic glory.[11] If it takes a bit of shock therapy to dispel the myth, so be it.

"We"? And what "dubious reasons" are behind it?

To combat it, he constructs his supposedly historically accurate counter-figure, not as a new idol, but to disgust us with Kafka altogether as a real, individual man, leaving us with the works alone—the things themselves, as Kafka's contemporary tribesman Husserl would say. In fact, it would be safe to say that Hawes despises the "real" Kafka and wants to dissociate him from the Holocaust precisely because he is unworthy of being its patron saint.[12]

Having supposedly liberated us from the K-Myth which distorts our reading of Kafka's works in—as he would not say—a typically Judaic fashion as the works of a tortured, prophetic outsider, Hawes, under the pretense of giving us a reading of "the works themselves," merely substitutes a new, equally Judaic though more secular reading, as works of "black comedy."

While the original British title, *Excavating Kafka*, reflects the first part of the agenda, the subsequent American title, *Read Kafka Before You Ruin Your Life* (clearly meant to capitalize on the success of such DIY culture texts as Alain de Botton's *How Proust Can Change Your Life*), reflects the second, more insidious part of the agenda: Kafka as the prophet, not of the Holocaust, but of postmodernism. As he puts it clearly elsewhere:

> What Kafka is obsessed with is our suicidal readiness to buy into grand narratives of redemption and absolute certainty,

---

[11] "No other writer's work suffers from this kind of prejudgment" Oh? I can think of dozens: Hitler, Goebbels, Rosenberg . . .

[12] Hawes is such a believer in the Church of Holocaustianity that he actually absolves the Red Army of "whatever else they may be guilty of" in recognition of their "liberation" of the "death camps." Millions of dead and living though brutalized German and "liberated" Slavic civilians might beg to differ, although I suppose it's a sign of progress that he even acknowledges the "whatever else."

> however ramshackle and visibly corrupt they may be. The vital element in his works that the K-Myth obscures is that his heroes are utterly complicit in their own "entrapment." These are *not* tales of innocent people suddenly swallowed up by miscarriages of cosmic justice. Of all the philosophical roots of Kafka's thought, *I believe that the single most important is Nietzsche's famous and terrifying insight regarding the "nihilism" of modern, post-religious man* (my translation is necessarily a free one): "mankind would rather long for nothingness than have nothing to long for." This Nietzschean analysis of why modern people do what they do may well be very apposite to both the killers of 9/11 and the blank-eyed porn-stares of the Abu-Ghraib abusers.[13]

Note the clever use of the porn trope to rope in "us" with Kafka and the Moslem extremists—moral equivalence, as the Neo-Cons would say. We're all—except Hawes and his vaguely Marxist academic cohorts—zombies in the grip of "grand narratives," etc.

> And why read Kafka today? Because his analysis of the way we're so fatally, suicidally *tempted by visions of a gold-lit past, complete with all its alleged certainties and securities,* is more needed today than ever. His works are one great warning against swallowing the grand illusions, one great demand that if we want to really live, we have to grow up and look life in the eye.[14]

Of course, one might suggest that it is the purveyors of this somehow simultaneously smug and stale po-mo cliché that needs to "grow up" or at least leave the '60s behind, man. Still, as the reference to Nietzsche shows, there's something to this kind of thing. But if we are to assimilate Kafka to Nietzsche as a "Good European," we need to take our Nietzsche as Baron Evola did; useful as a solvent of bourgeois liberalism, but useless—indeed, poisonous—when taken as a guide to the way forward.[15]

---

[13] "In pursuit of Kafka's Porn Cache," note 4 above.
[14] *Ibid.*
[15] See most notably *Ride the Tiger: A Survival Manual for the Aristo-*

And speaking of academic po-moists, the reaction of the "orthodox" Kafka specialists was swift and predictable; yes, Max Brod was a mythmaker, but we've known this for years, blah blah blah. Hawes, himself something of a Kafka specialist, may have his own reasons for tweaking the experts. He may have simply chosen the wrong target; it may be that "Walter Benjamin exploded the Kafka myth is the '30s" in some unreadable bit of Eurosludge (after all, if Kafka wasn't the biggest Judaic Genius, then Benjamin was, right?), but so what? Kafka, like Dickens and Orwell, is one of the few writers to have his own adjective, and we all know what "kafkaesque" means; that's Hawes' real target.

Perhaps the silliest, but most symptomatic, response is from tribesman Sander Gilman, no doubt put out that Hawes fails to mention his own biography, modestly titled *Kafka*.[16] Gilman (related to Lovecraft?) fouls the waters with some typical Judaic claptrap, smuggled in through Stanley Fish, that "all biographers lie," and so he modestly, cringingly politely, can't really complain that Hawes sees Kafka as a regular guy, rather than being "special" (i.e., a Jewish genius jewishly obsessed with his Jewish jewitude). But it sure would be good for the Jews if Hawes would just go away:

> Hawes misrepresents—but then again, as Fish believes, so do all biographers. It *could be argued*, for example, that I needed my Kafka to be ill and anxious and creative in order to shore up my reading of the situation of European Jews at the turn of the century. [No! Who could doubt you, *boychik*?] *But* the major difference between *this writer* and James

---

crats *of the Soul*, trans. Joscelyn Godwin and Constance Fontana (Rochester, Vt.: Inner Traditions, 2001), especially "Part 2: In the World Where God Is Dead." Interestingly, Evola admits in his autobiography that two of his adolescent guides were Nietzsche and Oscar Wilde, with the latter suggesting a connection to Kafka through his Beardsley porn cache; see *The Path of Cinnabar* (London: Arktos, 2009), p. 8. Evola also names Otto Weininger, who also greatly influenced Kafka as well.

[16] Sander L. Gilman, "Everyman's Kafka," *Azure: Ideas for the Jewish Nation*, no. 35, Winter 5769/2009, http://azure.org.il/include/print.php?id=487

Hawes is that while we all have stories we tell about the lives we write, *some of us* are more concerned with *the nuances of the research we do and of the world that we try to describe*. [I.e., is it good for the Jews?] In the end, however, it is the believability of those lies by the widest community that defines the successful biographer. Let us see whether time is kind to Hawes's Welsh-comic [Gilman, true tribesman, found it funny that Hawes teaches in Wales], literary intellectual Franz Kafka.

Oh, boo-boo. If all biographers lie, then why should I believe your lies? I say phooey-kerflooey! Away with all this Judaic *quatsch*! Gilman is right; the "nuances" of Hawes's portrait of Kafka are worrisome — they encourage the *goyim*, though surely that would be the "widest community" of all, one would think. Let us have a real Kafka, Kafka as he was, Kafka as he saw himself, Kafka as he wanted to be seen, however you want to put it: a proud member of the German literary and cultural tradition.

Kafka: our folk-comrade!

Counter-Currents/*North American New Right*
July 3, 2014

MICHEL HOUELLEBECQ'S SEXUAL ANTI-UTOPIA

Michel Houellebecq
The Elementary Particles
Translated from the French by Frank Wynne
New York: Knopf, 2000

> "I get my kicks above the waistline, Sunshine."[1]

> "The universe is nothing but a furtive arrangement of elementary particles. . . . And human actions are as free and as stripped of meaning as the unfettered movements of the elementary particles."
> —Michel Houellebecq, *H. P. Lovecraft: Against the World, Against Life*

> "Frolicking has never been so depressing."
> —MST3k Episode 609: Coleman Francis' *Skydivers*

It really does seem odd that I have until now managed to avoid reading the novels of Michel Houellebecq. It's especially odd I didn't plunge right in after reading his excellent essay on Lovecraft,[2] and even quoting it my very own first essay on Lovecraft, published right here on Counter-Currents.[3] Why, we even share the same year of birth![4]

The appeal of Houellebecq to elements of the Right should be obvious; his enemies seem to be our enemies, from American consumer culture to modernity itself, as well as not just the French

---

[1] "One Night in Bangkok," from *Chess* by Tim Rice and Benny Andersson.

[2] Michel Houellebecq, *H. P. Lovecraft: Against the World, Against Life* (San Francisco: Believer Books, 2005).

[3] Now republished in *The Eldritch Evola … & Others*.

[4] Although not, like Thomas Ligotti, the same city of birth, college, and first job.

versions of PC but French culture itself, at least in its postwar state.⁵

His basic notion is that, contrary to the foolish dreams of the '68ers, and dogmatically enforced today by both academic and consumer establishments, "The 'decentred self' remains a selfish unit; *the death of hierarchy merely nurtures the cult of the individual and an incoherent, deviant society.*"⁶

These fiercely individualized entities are the elementary particles left to spin aimlessly by the smashing of the bonds of traditional society.

> It is interesting to note that the "sexual revolution" was sometimes portrayed as a communal utopia, whereas in fact it was simply another stage in the historical rise of individualism. As the lovely word "household" suggests, the couple and the family would be the last bastion of primitive communism in liberal society. The sexual revolution was to destroy these intermediary communities, the last to separate the individual from the market. The destruction continues to this day.⁷

This is pretty consistent with the model explored by Baron Evola in, for example, *Ride the Tiger: A Survival Manual for the Aristocrats of the Soul*.⁸ Liberalism has atomized⁹ society by a Nietzschean smashing of all our idols. All members are now "free" to "realize themselves" and "become what they are." The problem being, Nietzsche intended this to apply to an elite, the potential Supermen—what Evola calls "differentiated [from the

---

⁵ His narrator from the future laconically notes that "Foucault, Lacan, Derrida, and Deleuze" have fallen into "global ridicule" and "suddenly foundered, after decades of inane reverence."

⁶ "Confused extremes: *Platform*, Michel Houellebecq's follow-up to *Atomised* [a.k.a. *The Elementary Particles*]" by Anna Lynskey, http://www.oxonianreview.org/issues/1-2/1-2-5.htm

⁷ "Death Dreams" by Rob Horning, http://thenewinquiry.com/essays/death-dreams/

⁸ 1961; see especially "Part Two: In the World Where God is Dead."

⁹ The title of the UK edition of the book.

social herd] men" — not society at large. Left to his own devices, the Underman resorts to what he knows best: sensation, and thus to shopping and sex.

Houellebecq's characters are notable for how completely they embrace the consumerist ethos: believing that youth is society's primary index of value, *that sex is the only pleasure and is eminently commodifiable*, that disposability is natural, that *quality is ultimately reducible to quantity* [cf. Guénon], that the quest for novelty is our only genuine tradition, that secular materialism has triumphed once and for all over atavistic spirituality.

So far, he seems to be on our team. Of course, someone who hates as much as Houellebecq is apt to be an uncomfortable ally.

I know that Islam — by far the most stupid, false and obfuscating of all religions — currently seems to be gaining ground, but it's a transitory and superficial phenomenon . . . [All but Guénon & Co. shout Yah!]
. . . in the long term, Islam is even more doomed than Christianity. [Crickets][10]

And just to be clear on that: "I was talking about the stupidity of all monotheistic religions."[11]

Alrighty then, moving along . . . Besides being a fountain of opinions either bold and scintillating or mean and stupid, de-

---

[10] Of course, some on the Right would be fine with that: "Ben Jeffery makes a comment on this, saying: 'It is not that Houellebecq is a reactionary writer exactly. For example, it is never suggested that religious faith is the solution to his character's dilemmas; the books are all resolutely atheist.' But I guess Jeffery has never heard of the likes of Mencius Moldbug, neoreactionary atheist . . ." Craig Hickman, "Ben Jeffery's *Anti-Matter: Michel Houellebeq and Depressive Realism*," May 19, 2013, http://darkecologies.com/2013/05/19/ben-jefferys-anti-matter-michel-houellebeq-and-depressive-realism/

[11] Suzie Mackenzie, Interview with Michel Houellebecq, *The Guardian*, August 31, 2002.

pending on whose ox is being gored,[12] Houellebecq is a damned good, clear—lucid, the French would say, I suppose—writer; here, if anywhere, worthy of the comparisons made to Camus.

But unlike Camus, he's a funny guy[13] (though perhaps rather like Joe Pesci is "funny" in *Goodfellas*):

> As a teenager, Michel believed that suffering conferred dignity on a person. Now he had to admit that he had been wrong. What conferred dignity on people was television.
>
> Rumor had it that he was homosexual; in reality, in recent years, he was simply a garden-variety alcoholic
>
> The beach at Meschers was crawling with wankers in shorts and bimbos in thongs. It was reassuring.
>
> Whatever, in the showers at the gym I realized I had a really small dick. I measured it when I got home—it was twelve centimeters, maybe thirteen or fourteen if you measured right to the base. I'd found something new to worry about, something I couldn't do anything about; it was a basic and permanent handicap. It was around then that I started hating blacks.

Not that Old Grumpypuss will let you just have your fun:

> Irony won't save you from anything; humour doesn't do anything at all. You can look at life ironically for years, maybe decades; there are people who seem to go through most of their lives seeing the funny side, but in the end, life

---

[12] "I don't begin by wanting to be provocative exactly, no. But when I realize that what I say is provoking, I don't change it because of obstinacy. It's up to me. Nobody asked me to say it again." —*The Guardian,* August 31, 2002.

[13] "Yet Houellebecq possesses one quality in which the Left Bank existentialists of the '40s and '50s were notably lacking, namely, humor. Houellebecq's fiction is horribly funny. Often the joke is achieved by a po-faced conjunction of the grandiloquent and the thumpingly mundane." —"Futile Attraction: Michel Houellebecq's Lovecraft" by John Banville, *Bookforum,* April/May 2005, http://www.bookforum.com/archive/apr_05/banville.html

always breaks your heart. Doesn't matter how brave you are, or how reserved, or how much you've developed a sense of humour, you still end up with your heart broken. That's when you stop laughing. In the end there's just the cold, the silence and the loneliness. In the end, there's only death.

And, as in liberal society, until then, when all else fails, there's also the sex.[14] Perhaps I've consumed more than my share of pornography, but this did not seem as overwhelming or perverse as reviewers would have us believe. I suppose it serves the purpose of shocking the shockable, but if you find it off-putting, or just boring, go ahead and skip it, it really adds nothing to the message of the book.

Now, at this point, fifteen years later, there's little to be gained in adding yet another review; so with the book taken as read, I'd like to take a look at that message and try to place it in relation to some other, rather grander works.

First off, the book has an odd structure that only becomes apparent with the Epilogue. "Despite the essentially elaborate scope of the plot revealed in the novel's conclusion (i.e. the eventual emergence of cloning as a replacement for the sexual reproduction of the human race) . . ."[15] It's not entirely mind-shattering, but if you've been told that, like Joyce's *Ulysses*, it's just a book about sex, you might wonder what the point is. Even the *New Yorker* reviewer found himself frustrated by what he called "editorials" cropping up throughout the text, which he felt were Houellebecq putting in his two cents.[16]

Actually, they are another feature of, and clue to, the structure and intent of the book. Certainly other odd features, such as the long poem that opens the book, become clearer at this point. What you have here is another one of those "future histories" that I've

---

[14] "Now the wife and I are going to have the sex." — MST3k, Experiment #0612 — *The Starfighters*.

[15] http://en.wikipedia.org/wiki/Atomised#Plot_summary

[16] "Paris Journal: Noel Contendere: A political impasse gives way to a literary scandal" by Adam Gopnick, *New Yorker*, Dec. 28, 1998 & Jan. 4, 1999, p. 61.

been reviewing recently;[17] a biography, from the near future (apparently around 2030) of the main protagonist, the geneticist Michel, and the effects of his work in our near future (actually, now right about today).

In particular, though, it reminded me of a far older, and much more substantial one than those. Then it finally hit me: Hermann Hesse's *The Glass Bead Game*.[18]

Hesse's novel takes place around 2500 and presents itself as a biography of a recently deceased and rather controversial Game Master, one Joseph Knecht. To orient the reader (both fictional and real) to both the Game and the history out of which it emerged (which is our own, of course) it opens with a long section presenting "A General Introduction" to the Game's history "For the Layman."[19] It ends with a supposed selection of poems from Knecht's student days documenting his struggle to assimilate the game, and to allow himself to be assimilated by it.

The Game, we learn, arose out of the ruins of The Century of Wars, which was, not coincidentally, the "Age of the *Feuilleton*," symbol of journalistic and scholarly frivolity.[20] At the last moment, Europe pulled back from the brink, and initiated a movement dedicated to Truth rather than Interest, to Platonically purify and uplift society by purifying the arts and sciences of fraud, triviality, and irrelevance; above all, by demonstrating their unity and interconnection.

Fortunately, the same *Zeitgeist* was expressing itself by the slow development of The Game; conveniently indescribable, it seems to be a system, akin to music or mathematics,[21] by which

---

[17] Such as Jeff Frankas's *De-World*, http://www.counter-currents.com/2014/05/jeff-frankas-de-world/ and Ann Sterzinger's *The Talkative Corpse*, http://www.counter-currents.com/2014/04/the-talkative-corpse-a-love-letter/

[18] *Das Glasperlenspiel*, 1943; English as *Magister Ludi* (1949) and *The Glass Bead Game* (1969).

[19] If you have a kindle, you can download the whole Introduction as a "sample" from Amazon.

[20] Imagine *American Idol*, although Hesse couldn't think of anything more degrading than crossword puzzles and popularizing literary biographies.

[21] Music, of course, properly understood, *is* mathematics. For this,

the content of any science can be stated, developed, and, most importantly, interwoven with any other, in a kind of scientific or cultural or spiritual counterpoint. The result is a spiritual exercise, akin to meditation but often performed publicly and ceremonially, "an act of mental synthesis through which the spiritual values of all ages are seen as simultaneously present and vitally alive." The celibate scholars of the province of Castalia are the secular monks of this new quasi-religious order that orders society as Catholicism did mediaeval Europe.

While there is a certain intellectual thrill in contemplating this picture (perhaps a clue as to whether the reader would be a suitable candidate for the Order) the dramatic heart of the work is the *Bildungsroman* in the center, in which Joseph Knecht is initiated into the game and the Order, rises to the very highest position, only to abdicate and return to the world when he begins to sense that the Game itself has become arrogant, sterile, and alien to human society, which may someday decide they no longer need to support it; and as Marx would say, the same shit would start all over again.

What does this have to do with *The Elementary Particles*? Houellebecq has essentially inverted Hesse's novel, both structurally and thematically.

Structurally, he has placed at the beginning an unattributed poem that strikes the same themes as Hesse's work, resembling one of Knecht's final poems of contentment with the Game, "Stages."

> We live today under *a new world order*
> The *web which weaves together all things* envelops our bodies
> Bathes our limbs,
> In a halo of joy.
> A state to which *men of old sometimes acceded through music*
> Greets us each morning as a commonplace.
> What men considered a dream, perfect but remote,

---

and the Traditional doctrine by which musical systems are methods of creation rather than arbitrary systems of pleasant noise, see the material presented in my essay "Our Wagner, Only Better: Harry Partch, The Wild Boy of American Music" in *The Eldritch Evola . . . & Others*.

We take for granted as the simplest of things.
But we are not contemptuous of these men,
We know how much we owe to their dreaming,
We know that *without the web of suffering and joy which was their history, we would be nothing.*

Now, rather than Hesse's long, clear, conveniently labeled Introduction to the Game and our history we have the unexpected and puzzling epilogue, which details Michel's self-exile to Ireland (land of monks where "most of them around here are Catholics") and his breakthrough in genetics that results in the replacement of sexual reproduction with perfect, immortal clones. The bulk of the novel shows us the modern, secular society that Michel comes to doubt and reject.

Genetics, of course, easily lends itself to metaphors of weaving, but Michel's breakthrough, which somehow bases itself on quantum mechanics, seems especially Game-like: "Any genetic code, however complex, could be *noted in a standard, structurally stable form*, isolated form disturbances and mutation . . . every animal species could be *transformed into a similar species . . .*"

Moreover, the descriptions of his thought processes and inspirations constantly recur to similar tropes; he takes inspiration from the *Book of Kells* and writes works like "Meditations on Interweaving" — "Separation is another word for evil; it is also another word for deceit. All that exists is a magnificent interweaving, vast and reciprocal" — while his protégé's article "Michel Djerzinki and the Copenhagen Interpretation" is in fact a "long meditation on a quotation from Parmenides" while another attempts "a curious synthesis of the Vienna Circle and the religious positivism of Comte."

Meanwhile, the popularizing of Michel's ideas adds to the popular ferment. We live in "the age of materialism (defined as the centuries between the decline of medieval Christianity and the publication of Djerzinki's work)" whose "confused and arbitrary" ideas have led to a 20th century "characterized by progressive decline and disintegration." But now, "There had been an acceptance of the idea that a fundamental shift was indispensable if society was to survive — a shift which would credibly restore a sense of community, of permanence and of the sacred."

The key to this is "the global ridicule in which the works of Foucault, Lacan, Derrida and Deleuze had suddenly foundered, after decades of inane reverence," which "heaped contempt on all those intellectuals active in the 'human sciences.'" Now "they believed only in science; science was to them the arbiter of unique, irrefutable truth."

What we have, then, is in effect a re-write of Hesse's novel, but now centered on the (in Hesse's work, anonymous by choice[22]) inventor of the Game, rather than his later descendant; the celibate monks of Castalia, selected in childhood and separated forever from their mundane families, have now been generalized to the entire population of the Earth: "Having broken the filial chain that linked us to humanity, we live on. We have succeeded in overcoming the forces of egotism, cruelty and anger which they [us!] could not."[23]

While it's pretty cool and all, one can't help but think, especially if one has already read Hesse's novel, that Houellebecq has simply passed the buck. Remember that whole middle section about Joseph Knecht? Hesse had played around with the idea of a utopian society devoted to intellectual contemplation for years; who hasn't, from Leibniz all the way back to Plato? And he, like Plato, had seen, living through the Century of Wars himself, that it was the only hope for mankind, or at least for culture.

The problem was, however, less one of how to do it—Step One, invent cloning—than Step Two, how would it work; or rather, how would it be maintained? Houellebecq's narrator speaks with the same placid self-satisfaction as the narrator of Hesse's introduction: "Science and art are still a part of our society; but without the stimulus of personal vanity, the pursuit of Truth and Beauty has taken on a less urgent aspect." Indeed. What Joseph Knecht realizes is that dealing with the "less urgent aspect" (his scholars can, if they choose, while away whole careers freely pur-

---

[22] See Guénon's *The Reign of Quantity*, Chapter 9, "The Twofold Significance of Anonymity."

[23] "Our people have forgotten, they have been made to forget. For centuries. But I have learned how it once was. Families. Brothers and sisters. There was happiness . . . there was love." — *Teenagers from Outer Space* (1959).

suing research so inane that even our Federally-funded researchers would be embarrassed) may be the key to avoiding sterility (admitted, not a problem perhaps with cloning) and self-defeating social irrelevance.

Simultaneously and synchronistically, while Hesse was writing away in Switzerland Thomas Mann was comfortably ensconced in LA, writing his own very similar book, *Doctor Faustus: The Life of the German Composer Adrian Leverkühn As Told by a Friend*.[24] Given its resemblances to Hesse's novel, it's not surprising to find similarities to Houellebecq's. Mann's narrator is contemporary with us, not a few decades in advance, but also writing about our own (then) recent times—Germany from Bismarck to Hitler. His subject, Adrian Leverkühn, is, like Houellebecq's Bruno, an artist, though also, like Michel, a whiz at mathematics, at least of the cabalistic kind (thus relating him to Hesse's Castalians). Like Bruno, he is sexually twisted, though in a Wilhelmine German way—like Nietzsche, he has sexual contact once, with a prostitute, in order to deliberately infect himself, like Nietzsche, with syphilis. Like both Bruno and Michel, his one, last object of love, his nephew, is torn away from him through an agonizing, grotesque death.

But most significantly, after that last catastrophe, he conceived his ultimate work, before sinking, again like Nietzsche and Bruno, into madness—*The Lamentations of Dr. Faustus*, a blasphemous atonal work by which he intends "to take back the *Ninth*." I think Houellebecq's novel can be seen as performing a similar function—taking back *The Glass Bead Game*, or at least its dramatic sections, where the personal and historical conflicts are lived through and at least somewhat resolved; instead settling comfortably in with the rather pompous narrator of the Introduction, refusing to face the task of working out the problems of the interactions of the human particles and simply saying, "Oh, sure, the modern world sure sucks so let's just let Science clone us and be done with it!"

Counter-Currents/*North American New Right*
June 11, 2014

---

[24] Theodore Ziolkowski explores the remarkable parallels in his "Foreword" to the 1969 translation.

THE FRAUD OF
MISS JEAN BRODIE

Muriel Spark
The Prime of Miss Jean Brodie: A Novel
London: Penguin Books, 1965 (1st ed. 1961)

> "Brodie, of course, is a follower of Hitler, Franco and Mussolini. . . . In that context it doesn't take a great leap of the imagination to see the elite *'crème de la crème'* as an SS in miniature with Miss Brodie as its Duce or Führer."
>
> — Alan Taylor, "Little Miss Imperfect"[1]

This is a book whose title has been rattling around in my head for decades, mainly due to the popular movie, for which Maggie Smith won the Oscar for 1969 (and which I haven't seen). So I was happy to find an old but solid Delta paperback (the old upscale line from Dell) from 1962 for a buck, and read it over two afternoons (it's a short novel, really one of James' dear *nouvelles*).

For those of you not up on the book, here's a recap of the film (whose ending is slightly different, though not in any way relevant to us here):

> One thing I recalled from references to the movie over the years is that Miss Brodie is supposed to be an Evil Person, as shown by her so inspiring a student to live dangerously that she gets killed in the Spanish Civil War. Since "fighting the fascists" is supposed to be a Good Thing by our Elite, I had always supposed it was the girl's youth that was the problem. On reading the book, however, it is revealed that Miss Brodie is a Bad because she is herself a Fascist (that is, her 'elitism' leads her to approve of Fas-

---

[1] Alan Taylor, "Little Miss Imperfect," *Sunday Herald*, January 12, 2003.

cism) and persuaded the girl to switch sides to the Bad Guys; the girl's death (not even in combat) is only the last straw, leading another of Her Girls to "betray" her to the administration.

Constant Readers will know that I continue to be amazed at how not only are mass murderers of the Left still presented as heroes (Mao) or sexy icons (Che) or at least sadly mistaken (Stalin), but even such a minor figure of the Right as Franco is still regarded with the same dread and loathing one might be expected to feel for Cthulhu. As I said here:

> You would think that on points, Franco would come out pretty good; Spain liberated from a murderous terrorist government, Europe avoids eventual encirclement by Stalinist puppets, thousands of Jews not rounded up and sent East, Spain kept out of the war and avoids the fate of Eastern Europe; eventually, prosperous and free, joins the EU. Of course, as soon as the "social democrats" got their hands on it, the country was run straight into the gutter, as we can see today.[2]

But as we know, the Left will tolerate not one minute deviation from its doctrines or its whims, and so Franco must be a monster of horror.

So I expected to have my usual counter-culture experience of reading about some "horrible" person and actually admiring them. And indeed, I found it hard to not admire Miss Brodie, an experience apparently quite common among readers, as well as filmgoers, who not only adored Maggie Smith's character but even have the double-exposure effect of her role in the Harry Potter films, which she has described as "Miss Jean Brodie in a wizard's hat."

There is indeed something odd and contradictory about Miss Brodie, and it's not the "fascist" sympathies or her being, as one of the girls realizes, "an unconscious Lesbian" (p. 120). She

---

[2] http://jamesjomeara.blogspot.com/2010/05/sunic-on-sunday-tom-sunic-has-great.html

doesn't resemble any "fascist" character I've run into, or even much of a stereotype of one.

Miss Brodie preaches free thought and individualism, and scorns "team spirit": "Phrases like 'the team spirit' are always employed to cut across individualism, love and personal loyalties" (p. 79).

Yet is not "fascism" supposed to privilege the mass over the individual? Of course, while praising "free thought," Miss Brodie is quite prepared to ram her own ideas down their willing throats:

"Who is the greatest Italian painter?"

"Leonardo da Vinci, Miss Brodie."

"That is incorrect. The answer is Giotto, he is my favourite." (p. 11)

In line with this "free thought" and "individualism," and her Calvinist upbringing, she is a fervent anti-Catholic: "Her [Brodie's] disapproval of the Church of Rome was based on her assertions that it was a church of superstition, and that only people who did not want to think for themselves were Roman Catholic" (p. 85).

And yet, were not the classic '30s Fascists, Hitler, Mussolini, and Franco, all Catholics of one kind or another?

Far from being easily imagined as a miniature SS elite, the "Brodie Girls" are a rag-tag assortment of misfits and fuck-ups. One will later die while panicking in a hotel fire, another will be blown up on a train before reaching the battlefield in Spain.

Rather than merit, or blood, her selection process emphasized different qualities:

> Miss Brodie had already selected her favourites, or rather *those whom she could trust;* or rather *those whose parents she could trust not to lodge complaints about the more advanced and seditious aspects of her educational policy, these parents being either too enlightened to complain or too unenlightened, [...] or too trusting to question the value of what their daughters were learning at this school of sound reputation.* (p. 26)

We're getting warmer. We'll have reason to come back to those parents, drawn from either the *Lumpenproletariat* or the "enlightened" elite.

As for her "educational policy" which might be "questioned," Miss Brodie refuses to move to a more progressive school, preferring a "school of sound reputation" to a "crank school." Her questionable methods and results include these:

> At that time they [the girls] had been immediately recognizable as Miss Brodie's pupils, being *vastly informed on a lot of subjects irrelevant to the authorized curriculum, as the headmistress said, and useless to the school as a school.* . . . These girls were discovered to have heard of . . . the love lives of Charlotte Brontë and of Miss Brodie herself. . . . They knew the rudiments of astrology but not the date of the Battle of Flodden or the capital of Finland. All of the Brodie set, save one, counted on its fingers, as had Miss Brodie, with accurate results more or less. (pp. 5-6)

> She turned to the blackboard and rubbed out with her duster the long division sum she always kept on the blackboard in case of intrusions from the outside during any arithmetic periods when Miss Brodie should happen not to be teaching arithmetic. (p. 45)

Are not "fascists," or at least their near-cousins, "conservatives," constantly denouncing "progressive" education and demanding that students learn "the 3 Rs"?

Most bizarrely of all, Miss Brodie, a spinster and anti-Catholic, falls in love with the married Catholic art teacher (male), and then schemes to have one of her "suitable" girls have the affair for her, while she arranges equally secret "booty calls" with another unmarried, non-Catholic male instructor.

I'm not sure what disorder this falls under, but again, isn't the classic "fascist" either sexually rigid or else sadistically debauched (the W. Reich-Visconti pendulum)?

After a little meditation, I think I've figured it out, and I submit my hypothesis for general discussion.

Spark, like most Good Thinkers, doesn't know anything

about any real "fascism" or know any of those dirty fascists herself (so *infra-dig*, after all; when Sandy, she of the "unconscious Lesbian" insight, becomes a Catholic "she found quite a number of fascists less agreeable than Miss Brodie"). How then, to construct her "fascist" character?

Obviously, Miss Brodie must be based on herself, or some other Good Thinkers, and her doctrines and methods accordingly are merely some kind of extreme Good Thinking; hence the notion of "that's why they're so damned attractive at first" central to the paranoid "anti-fascist" genre.

The double exposure arises from the fact that Miss Brodie's "fascism" is actually an extreme form of Liberalism, which today we now know as PC or, as Keith Preston has analyzed it, "Totalitarian Humanitarianism."

For Spark and her kind, "fascism" is a strawman of ignorance, a mere "boo-word" for anything they dislike. In this case, it's been applied to what we now can see is the most recent and logical development of Liberalism itself.

Perhaps, to inject some element of rigor, we might line up Miss Brodie to the schema of "Modernity," the enemy of the Right, provided at the outset of "The French New Right in The Year 2000" by Alain de Benoist and Charles Champetier (reprinted as "Manifesto for a European Renaissance" in Appendix III of new edition of Tomislav Sunić's *Against Democracy and Equality*: "Modernity . . . is characterized primarily by five converging processes."[3]

1. "[I]ndividualization, through the destruction of old forms of communal life": Miss Brodie scorns "team spirit" and preaches her own form of individualism: agreeing with her.

2. "[M]assification, through the adoption of standardized behavior and lifestyles": "You are all Brodie girls!" "Miss Brodie would prefer it."

3. "[D]esacralization, through the displacement of the great religious narratives by a scientific interpretation of the world." Miss Brodie is fervently anti-Catholic, rejecting the great religious narrative of European Man for a narrow, presumptuous

---

[3] Tomislav Sunić, *Against Democracy and Equality: The European New Right*, third edition (London: Arktos, 2011).

Calvinism that has been secularized to the extent of her assuming the determining role of the Calvinist God herself, as Sandy correctly intuits: "'She thinks she is Providence', thought Sandy, 'she thinks she is the God of Calvin, she sees the beginning and the end'" (p. 120) just as secularism has replaced God with Man himself.

4. "[R]ationalization, through the domination of instrumental reason, the free market, and technical efficiency." Not so much; Miss Brodie scorns science, economics, and efficiency, and has her girls rely on their fingers to count, as does she; however, this is really in the service of ensuring that science will not intrude on her dogmas, *à la* PC taboos on racial science or questioning the dogmas of natural selection and global warming.

5. "[U]niversalization, through a planetary extension of a model of society postulated implicitly as the only rational possibility and thus as superior."

The implicit assumption of Miss Brodie's whole program, creating little models of herself and sending them forth; she may say she "educates" in accordance with the etymology of "drawing out what is within" but actually assumes that "inner" content to be identical with herself, or else to be discarded; "all people are equal, except when they disagree with me, in which case they are merely stupid or sick, and may be taken out of consideration." Indeed, her very discussion of the issue itself illustrates this: hers is "the only correct understanding of the word."

In short, Miss Brodie is no Fascist (although technically she may be a quote-fascist-unquote) but rather the adumbration of a then-new type, very familiar to us today: the withered old Methodist-Presbyterian-raised but now secularly righteous Public Scolds. Like Hilary Clinton, for example.

Or consider Nancy Pelosi, La Passionara de San Francisco, who tells us that: "[I]t doesn't matter so much who wins the election, because we have shared values about the education of our children . . . elections shouldn't matter as much as they do."[4]

These are the women, not the "fascist" skinheads, who are sending our girls and boys to their deaths to "fight injustice" in

---

[4] http://gatewaypundit.rightnetwork.com/2011/04/radical-pelosi-elections-shouldnt-matter-as-much-as-they-do-video/

every shithole on the planet.

It's pretty *counter-stereotypical*. Women's suffrage was originally justified in part on the grounds that women were less likely to vote for war. But Clinton, Power, and Rice all come out of the Clinton-era ideological tradition of hawkish humanitarian interventionism.

It's also interesting to recall that *Power had to resign from the Obama campaign* after calling Clinton a "monster" in what she thought was an off-the-record interview. Now they're teaming up. The "stereotype" is woman=liberal=good, which lies behind the idea that a Miss Brodie *must* be a nasty "fascist"; and, as a spinster and even an "unconscious Lesbian," she's *not even a real woman*, so there! Of course, that part's a bit behind the times now. And for "humanitarian interventionism" read: Totalitarian Humanism. As for a "monster," is that not exactly how we are supposed to regard Miss Brodie?

Although Benoist doesn't mention sexual "liberation," viewing Brodie as PC *avant la lettre* even makes sense of her batty molestation/adultery/voyeurism scheme; isn't that just exactly the sort of "enlightened" brainstorm some Bloomsbury type would dream up, to the cynical guffaws of a Lytton Strachey? Keynes' (another Bloomsberry, let us not forget) infamous "In the long run we are all dead" might be taken as the male version of Miss Brodie's dictum "I am in my prime!"

One is also reminded of a similar triple play idea dreamed up by the supposedly "sensible wife" in *The Big Chill*; another group of mis-educated PC losers, one dead, all bemoaning their bad but sophisticated life choices and pontificating wildly.[5] Here's a very Brodie exchange:

Don't you have any music from this century?

There's no other music here.

Now we see exactly why Miss Brodie insinuates herself into an established school, not a "crank school." And why she selects

---

[5] See my "Of Costner, Corpses, and Conception: Mother's Day Meditations on *The Untouchables* and *The Big Chill*," in *The Homo & the Negro*.

only pupils whose parents are either too disinterested to care about what she teaches their girls, *or enlightened enough* to agree with her. Either way, the perfect subjects of PC indoctrination, with none of those pesky "Right-wing" buttinskis to get in the way.

It's interesting, is it not, that our own "highly educated elites" are constantly bemoaning the paltry results of our educational institutions, and rightly so; yet it is also clear that they link, more or less explicitly, "education" with adherence to their ideology, and "lack of education" with any residual traces of "bad old" ideas. This despite the easily attested fact that the "well-educated man" (in Evola's phrase) of the bad old days held precisely these opinions.

Evola, I suppose, is a lost cause, but read some "patron saint of free speech" like Mencken or even as far back as Voltaire, and see how they freely spoke about "noble savages" or Jews or "the feminine" or any other hobbyhorse of the PC Left.

The standard reply of the half-mis-educated (Shaw) Negro on the Internet, "You ray-cists beez ig-nor-ant" not only serves as a summation of this "education=liberal cant" meme, but we could also imagine it to have been spoken, in both content and grammar, by one of Miss Brodie's Girls.

And yes, despite their "we're so smart" blather, even turning out students who count on their fingers is quite compatible with the Liberal Project. Is not Liberalism the doctrine of the Public Sector? And is not the Public Sector, as James Jackson reminds us, "[T]the chief vehicle by which the witless, the retarded, and the pathologically lazy can find employment. They produce nothing, they do nothing, they mean nothing. *It is why the political left embraces them and why they in turn cling to the political left*—all at the poor bloody taxpayer's expense."[6]

Yes, girls, enter the warm embrace of Miss Brodie! She has selected you, so you must be Special! And your parents will silently foot the bill!

Counter-Currents/*North American New Right*
January 23, 2011

---

[6] http://takimag.com/article/fuck_the_public_sector

TO CUT-UP A MOCKINGBIRD:
HARPER LEE'S *GO SET A WATCHMAN*

Harper Lee
Go Set a Watchman
Nashville: Thomas Nelson, 2015

"I almost don't care what the critics say as long as I can write another one."[1]

"*Mockingbird* is a classic, but you've probably read it before, and it's no more relevant to your future legal career than *12 Angry Men* is to picking a jury. They're both realist presentations written through idealist, dramatic glasses."[2]

On Friday night, a comedian died in New York. Somebody knows why. Down there, somebody knows . . .
No, wait, sorry — wrong *Watchman*, wrong pop culture meme.[3]
Constant Readers who recall my inability to join the teenage cult of Tolkien will not be surprised to hear that I have never read (Nelle) Harper Lee's *To Kill a Mockingbird*, nor seen the film. It seems to be the sort of pious claptrap that "everyone" reads, and I just can't stomach.[4]

---

[1] Nelle Harper Lee (Sandra Bullock) interviewed in *Infamous* (2006).

[2] *Outside the Law School Scam*, "Alternative Summer Reading for Pre-Law Students," http://outsidethelawschoolscam.blogspot.com/2015/07/alternative-summer-reading-for-pre-law.html

[3] "Which century?" replies John Caradine's engineer to a reporter's question about "the desperadoes who came through here back in '62," the year of the *Mockingbird* film, in the MST3k version of *Night Train to Mundo Fine* (Coleman Francis, 1965).

[4] Gregory Peck is not enough. It took the prospect of seeing an unbeatable array of now-classic character actors in their youth (Jack Klugman as an angry ex-juvie!) to get me to watch *Twelve Angry Men*. Speaking of "young adult books," I did read *Catcher* on my own, and came away with a loathing not for the hapless residents of Pency Prep but for the real "phonies," Upper West Side Jews like the pretentious

In any event, I never read "the original." For all I know, it may have been "assigned," but in that case I didn't read it either — a not infrequent occurrence in my slapdash schooldays.[5]

Nor can I be bothered to figure out the conflicting, *Rashomon*-like accounts of just what relation this book bears to the sainted classic.[6]

Relying on the redoubtable Margot Metroland's account of the hidden genesis of *Mockingbird*,[7] I think we can say that what we have here is close to the original MS Lee submitted, before the editors told her to junk the narrative of present-day, 26-year-old Jean Louise, write more about the recollections of 6-year-old Jean ("Scout") into the main narrative,[8] expand the rape trial into the moral and narrative centerpiece, and for God's sake cut all the talk about racism, pro and con.

And I don't propose to read it now, so here's your special treat: a review by someone with no preconceived ideas about the story, or vested interest in preserving blessed childhood illusions. And the death of childhood illusions is what the book is about.

Well, it's an enjoyable if forgettable read, written with an intelligent though not flashy style. The editors who read this and or-

---

author and his protagonist.

[5] I'm pretty sure I was assigned *Lord of the Flies*, and I know I didn't read that, as the cover of the Capricorn paperback I found repulsive. *Mockingbird* has a nice cover, at least in hardcover, and the new book shares the same look; is the illustrator still alive, toiling away for Harpers?

[6] Serge F. Kovalesti and Alexandra Alter, "Harper Lee's 'Go Set a Watchman' May Have Been Found Earlier Than Thought," *New York Times*, July 2, 2015, http://www.nytimes.com/2015/07/03/books/harper-lee-go-set-a-watchman-may-have-been-found-earlier-than-thought.html

[7] Margot Metroland, "Y'all Can Kill That Mockingbird Now," http://www.counter-currents.com/2014/09/yall-can-kill-that-mockingbird-now/. See also "Atticus in Bizarro World: Harper Lee's *Go Set a Watchman*," http://www.counter-currents.com/2015/07/atticus-in-bizarro-world/

[8] Perhaps this increase in the role of her playmate Dill, based on Truman Capote, is the origin, and perhaps the truth, behind the rumors of Capote getting involved in the writing or at least the recollections.

dered a complete re-write were, I think, wrong, although with two years on the best seller list, a Pulitzer Prize, and a hit movie, it's hard to argue with them; perhaps they "sensed" they could make something more out of it. The experience, however, did seem to sour Ms. Lee on the whole writing thing.

Oh, but then there's also the horrible "racism" of the first draft. That issue is perhaps best handled while looking at the style itself, the unity of style and message being itself a sign of the talent behind the writing.

On her first Sunday back in her childhood home, Jean Louise of course attends church with her family. The church organist essays the doxology at a faster, High Church tempo, and the congregation sticks to their lugubrious Southern Baptist rendition. This leads to a stern rebuke from Uncle Jack after services, where we learn that the music director has just got back from choir camp, where the leader—from New Jersey, no less—has given him a whole list of supposed "improvements" for the church's music.[9] He's dubious, and the stubborn resistance of even worldly, bachelor aesthete Jack—who drops the Catholic phrase "D. V." which he glosses for Jean as "God willin'" and seems tailor-made for this kind of "smells and bells"—convinces him he's right to drop the whole matter.

It may seem like a delaying tactic—come on, make with the inbred racism already!—but it neatly encapsulates the whole position the South finds itself in—stubbornly resisting "improvement" suggested—or demanded—by the North, in the name of preserv-

---

[9] Bad people, like this New Jersey mook, or later the school principal from up in the Hill Country of Alabama, always like things written down: the latter "doesn't believe anything unless it's written down" and then "when it's written down he believes every word of it." Tradition, by contrast, is non-literate. This goes back to the curious Genesis 9:22, where Ham (father of the negro race) is cursed for "seeing the nakedness" of his drunken father, Noah. Alexander Jacob suggests may refer to "the public dissemination of the ancestral wisdom among the highly literate Hamitic civilizations of Sumer and Egypt, whereas the other Indo-Europeans preserved it in purely oral form." "The Indo-European Origins of the Grail" in Leopold von Schrodeder and Alexander Jacob, *The Grail: Two Studies* (Numen Books, 2015), p. 169, n402.

ing local traditions.[10]

As we move on, apart from a few flashback sequences that are

---

[10] The New Jersey snob, we hear, is not a family man. Catholicism, or High Church tendencies within Anglicanism, has long been a comfy place for curmudgeons, bachelors, homosexuals and other oddballs to hide in plain sight. In *Brideshead Revisited*, Charles' cousin sternly remonstrates him when going up to Oxford to "Avoid Anglo Catholics; they are all sodomites with atrocious accents." On the *fin de siècle* in general, see Ellis Hanson, *Decadence and Catholicism* (Cambridge: Harvard University Press, 1997), which discusses Oscar Wilde, Charles Baudelaire, J.-K. Huysmans, Walter Pater, Paul Verlaine, and even Frederick Rolfe (who went so far as to style himself "Fr. Rolfe" when he wasn't playing as the Sicilian Baron Corvo). For the American, or at least Northern, angle, see Douglass Shand-Tucci's *Ralph Adams Cram: Boston Bohemia, 1881–1900* (Amherst: University of Massachusetts Press, 1995). On the Catholic side, there's always one in every parish that want more incense, High Masses, and sermons on Meister Eckhart; see J. F. Powers' *Morte d'Urban* (New York: Doubleday, 1962), itself winner of the 1963 National Book Award for Fiction. To understand Powers, you must understand that he was that rare bird, a sort of proto-Leftist, pre-Vatican II Irish Catholic who thought America was a nation of knuckle-dragging, war-mongering, racist Protestants, to whom his kind were superior in politics and culture, as well as ethics and religion. He fights both incense and homos, which he associates with the Right: McCarthy and Cohen, Whittaker Chambers, Cardinal Spellman. Also in the early '60s, even J. D. Salinger gets in the act; his narrator in the *New Yorker* story "Zooey" disparaging a boy his mother, Irish Catholic Bessie, recommends to sister Franny as being a weepy mother's boy "who probably sleeps with a rosary under his pillow."

Alan Watts describes his own struggle as a "spike" during his brief Episcopal priesthood in his autobiography, *In My Own Way*; later, in *Beyond Theology*, he will try to appreciate the other side: "The insides of most Protestant churches resemble courthouses or town halls, and the focal point of their services is a serious exhortation from a man in a black gown. . . . If I try *to set aside the innate prejudices which I feel against this religion*, I begin to marvel at the depth of its commitment to earnestness and ugliness. . . . I begin to realize that those incredibly plain people, with their almost unique lack of color, may after all be one of the most astonishing reaches of the divine Maya-the-Dancer of the world as far out from himself as he can get, dancing not-dancing" (*Beyond Theology*, ch. 2).

apparently the origin of the more assertively 1930s content of *Mockingbird*, we meet various characters in what is to today's readers now their twenty years later form,[11] and Jean Louise, fresh from another year's stay in New York,[12] is horrified each time by some new — to her, at least — manifestation of "racism."

Aunt Alexandra is a splendid creation, all corsets and scented face powder, the very embodiment of the Southern Way of Life

---

[11] I thank Ms. Metroland, *op. cit.*, for identifying the speaker from the North as perhaps Robert Welch of the John Birch Society himself. When we first meet Atticus, he's reading with disapproval a book titled *The Strange Case of Alger Hiss*. Thanks to Google, we can instantly date this to 1953, when this book (New York: Doubleday & Company, 1953. $3.95.), by one Earl Jowitt, that is, "The" Earl Jowitt, a parlor pinko no doubt, appeared. This "Earl" business explains why Atticus thinks he "shows a childlike faith in the integrity of civil servants," imagines the Congress to "correspond to their aristocracy," and in general has "no understanding of American politics a-tall." The Earl's book is anti-Chambers and apparently one of the first exercises in what the Clintons have dubbed "the politics of personal destruction." It has always puzzled me as to why the Hissites claim that Chambers was in love with Hiss, since it is clearly they themselves who have a big ol' crush on dashing young diplomats improving the world from their positions in the One World Government.

Later, Louise will find a pamphlet back at the house entitled "The Black Plague," essaying forth a eugenic perspective about "brain pans, whatever they are." It's an obvious enough title to be her own creation, but I do find there is a pamphlet by that title by that old conspiracy-monger, Eustace Mullins. The version I can find online is obviously from the late '60s (there's a Black Panther on the cover and Malcolm X is referenced on the first page; there's even talk of the Zebra killer) and the emphasis is culture, not physiology.

[12] New York newspapers are a note that ties the book together. "You've been reading those New York papers," Atticus points out during their final confrontation. When she first arrives, he asks her "how much of what's going on down here gets into the newspapers" and she responds "Well, to hear the *Post* tell it, we lynch 'em for breakfast down here." Later, when she bristles as a former schoolmate makes a crude negro joke, she says "I'm getting like the *New York Post*." Younger readers need to know that at the time, the *New York Post* was a Liberal newspaper.

("They endured" as Faulkner would say).¹³ Appropriately, then, she gets to deliver some of Lee's toughest "racist" lines, as do Scout's former gal pals: "Keeping a nigger happy these days is like catering to a king . . ."

The men are a different story, weak and temporizing. Uncle Dr. Jack is a bachelor eccentric, living in a literary 19th century of the mind, and delivers a rambling, evasive, analogy-ridden defense that Steve Sailer could put in one sentence: a race is a large extended family that occasionally practices incest. He evidences the "we acknowledge some problems but we're still proud of our land and its traditions" attitude currently under attack by those banning the Confederate battle flag and digging up the bones of Nathan Bedford Forrest.

Hank, Jean Louis' intended, is revealed a monster of social conformity that compares well with Lane, Franny's obtuse boyfriend in *Franny and Zooey*. He sullies Jack's views by adding a strong dollop of Babbitty "get along to go along" but then, like Clarice Starling, he's only a generation away from trash.¹⁴

Finally, she confronts the Big Guy himself, Atticus, her father and, as a result of the subsequent book and film, apparently most of (White) America's father. And now the book's big shock: Atticus is a racist!

At first they reach common ground on rejecting the Court's judicial overreaching, effectively repealing the 10th Amendment. This, of course, is already enough to sicken today's Liberal. But what follows will scare the pants off them.

"Jean Louise," he said. "Have you ever considered that you

---

¹³ Like most such, it "escaped her notice" that "the son had developed all the latent characteristics of a three-dollar bill."

¹⁴ "You know what you look like to me, with your good bag and your cheap shoes? You look like a rube. A well-scrubbed, hustling rube with a little taste. Good nutrition's given you some length of bone, but you're not more than one generation from poor white trash, are you, Agent Starling?" Dr. Hannibal Lecter, *The Silence of the Lambs* (Demme, 1991). Jean Louise may not know what a brain pan is, and be horrified by those who do, but she's eager to join with the rest of the town to denigrate the poorer members of her own race.

can't have a set of backward people living among people advanced in one kind of civilization and have a social Arcadia?"

"Let's look at it this way . . . You realize that our Negro population is backward, don't you? You will concede that? You realize the full implications of the word 'backward,' don't you? . . . You realize that the vast majority of them here in the South are unable to share fully in the responsibilities of citizenship, and why?"

"Now think about this. What would happen if all the Negroes in the South were suddenly given full civil rights? I'll tell you. There'd be another Reconstruction. Would you want your state governments run by people who won't know how to run 'em? Do you want this town run by — now wait a minute — Willoughby's a crook, we know that, but do you know of any Negro who knows as much as Willoughby? Zeebo'd probably be Mayor of Maycomb. Would you want someone of Zeebo's capability to handle the town's money? We're outnumbered, you know . . . They vote in blocs.
"[T]he Negroes down here are still in their childhood as a people . . . The NAACP doesn't care whether a Negro . . . tries to learn a trade and stand on his own two feet — oh no, all the NAACP cares about is that man's vote."

And so on. *The Guardian*, bringing the *frisson* of distaste one might bring to, say, scraping a squashed raccoon off the driveway, finds the offense of Lee in her recourse to "biological determinism," not just to account for racism but even for her own superiority, explaining that she was just "born color blind."[15]

My readers, however, may find all this rather tepid. Atticus is

---

[15] As always, it's impossible to fathom the Liberal mind, or to follow its never-ending, shall we say, revolutions. Wasn't it just last year that Liberals were pumping their fists — or other body parts — to Lady Gaga's insistence that she and her Little Monsters were "born this way"? (Vigilant Citizen)

simply what we would today call a "race realist,"[16] with a dash of paternalism thrown in. But as *The Guardian* sternly advises us, both paternalism and "color-blindness" are badthinking today. To the modern Liberal, the more or less fierce confrontations between the Northernized Scout and her Southern role models are like arguments between the inmates of some racial insane asylum — a rather Southern Gothic notion at that.

Neither Atticus nor Scout convinces the other, of course, and Uncle Jack is brought back to cobble together a kind of "higher" moral position: take no man as your infallible moral guide, and recognize and honor the human fallibility in all of us.

The moral, if you will, is not one that will sit well with the Liberal either. Smash your idols? Kill the Buddha on the road? Sounds good, since the Liberal, like the proverbial college sophomore, only imagines smashing his own parents at the Thanksgiving table, not himself; that is, smashing idols by attacking and silencing them, not questioning his own views.

> What does a bigot do when he meets someone who challenges his opinions? He doesn't give. He stays rigid. Doesn't even try to listen, just lashes out.

In short, the Liberal is as bigoted as any Klansman. What Uncle Jack means by tolerance is something rather different:

> "Good grief, baby, people don't agree with the Klan, but they certainly don't try to prevent them from puttin' on sheets and making fools of themselves in public."

Well, these days "they" certainly *do*, most certainly, and that applies to a lot of things Uncle Jack couldn't imagine anyone being crazy enough to believe could happen, such as flying the state

---

[16] "Race realism is one of the intellectual foundations of White Nationalism. Race realism is the thesis that racial differences are *objective facts of nature*, which pre-exist human consciousness, human society, and even the human race itself." Greg Johnson: "Why Race is Not a 'Social Construct,'" http://www.counter-currents.com/2015/07/why-race-is-not-a-social-construct/

flag, too. After all, some things are Just Wrong and someone — preferably the Government — should Do Something About It; otherwise, you're As Bad as They Are.

You could call what Jack and Atticus espouse, and bring Scout back to a grudging acceptance of, Olde Tyme Liberalism, I suppose, just as Atticus calls himself a "Jeffersonian Democrat" although, as Jean Louise points out, he voted for Eisenhower.[17]

You could also call his views on race "olde tyme Liberalism," too. Atticus believes that the negro is a childlike race, but he also believes in Progress: the negro can grow into his role in a modern society; the NAACP and the other Liberal busybodies are trying to force not only Southern society but the negro himself into too fast a rate of change. The stir-up negroes are more dissatisfied with their lot than ever, sullen and by turns demanding and ungrateful; a condition easily observed today. The ancient family retainer, Calpurnia, Scout's surrogate mother, now barely recognizes her, seeing only just another White oppressor.

If this is indeed what Lee wrote some 50 or 60 years ago, or close to it, and looking at today's Birmingham, a disaster,[18] or Selma, where a movie celebrating the "victory" of MLK there fifty years ago can't be shown, since all the movie theaters, along with most every other business, are closed, one can only applaud her prescience.[19]

But let's stick with this theme, as the intertwining of theme and style illustrates the perhaps unconsciously subtle style that Lee brings to the novel.

Those who have made the transition away from the modern

---

[17] The foolishness of electoral politics: Eisenhower was the one sending troops in to enforce desegregation, out of Cold War necessity. And right on time for the book's appearance, calls to remove Jefferson and Jackson from the Democrat pantheon (and the currency); racists, don't you know?

[18] As chronicled by Paul Kersey on his invaluable blog, *Stuff Black People Don't Like*, and compiled in his collection *The Tragic City: Birmingham 1963–2013* (CreateSpace, 2013).

[19] All this has been chronicled, not, of course, in those "New York newspapers," but on Paul Kersey's invaluable blog, *Stuff Black People Don't Like*, stuffblackpeopledontlike.blogspot.com

dogmas of Liberal goodthinking often use the metaphor, derived from *They Live!*, of *being able to see*.[20] And so during their final confrontation, Atticus frequently asks Scout to see, to look around, and to open her eyes. "Let's look at it this way . . ."

Scout, as we've *seen,* diagnoses herself as "born color-blind," which she of course thinks is a good thing, while Atticus tries to convince her that it its, in fact, a handicap.[21]

"You must see things as they are, as well as they should be."[22]

"See" occurs, with varying tenses, dozens of times in the course of the novel,[23] along with synonyms like "look" or "watch."[24] Indeed, the latter is the chief symbol of the book, occur-

---

[20] Such as, obviously, the blog Those Who Can See, thosewhocansee.blogspot.com For my own discuss of Carpenter's film—a prior, and implicitly White, version of *The Matrix*, see my "He Writes! You Read! *They Live!*" in *The Homo & the Negro*.

[21] It would appear that in the occluded world of *They Live!*, the color-blind would indeed be immune to the alien's brainwashing.

[22] Is that English? He means "as well as what they should be" I guess. From a man arguing the inferiority of the negro? This is the only place where the book feels like a first draft.

[23] Graham: "Because everything with you is seeing, isn't it? Your primary sensory intake that makes your dream live is seeing. Reflections. Mirrors. Images. . . ." *See* my "Phil and Will: Awakening Through Repetition in *Groundhog Day, Point of Terror*, and *Manhunter*, Part 2," http://www.counter-currents.com/2013/12/awakening-through-repetition-part-2/. "I asked my mother what I had seen, and she told me that he was not just a white man turned brown, but a different kind of man called a 'Negro.' But I already *saw* the differences before I was *told* the name and explanation. Indeed, I asked for an explanation *because* I saw the differences. My mother and I certainly did not construct the differences that were apparent to all." Greg Johnson, *op. cit.*, emphases his.

[24] Scout sneaks into the courthouse and *sees* Atticus and Hank at the Citizens' Council meeting, and wonders if anyone *sees* her there (they do). Calpurnia, the old family retainer who's been radicalized by the civil rights interlopers, can no longer see Scout. Even the long reminiscence about Scout and Dill—the character based on Truman Capote and a favorite of readers, involved Dill and a supposed machine to see

ring in the title and inserted way back at that early chapter at church, where in the sermon text JHVH "sets a watchman" and Scout later muses, "Mr. Stone set a watchman in church yesterday. He should have provided me with one. I need a watchman to lead me around and declare what he seeth every hour on the hour."[25]

As Uncle Jack says, in his convoluted "literary" way, and in what would appear to be the book's moral: "Every man's island, Jean Louise, every man's watchman, is his conscience. There is no such thing as a collective conscience."[26]

This, of course, is why the modern Liberal has abandoned the "Watchman" metaphor, with its "biological determinism," for one which emphasizes the passive, docile role of the masses: *The Guardian*. You must not *see*, you must be *taught*.[27]

Speaking of conscience, that reminiscence about Scout's falsies flap that Ms. Metroland singled out for enjoyment also contains an interesting lead related to sight: the insight that Atticus "wouldn't be above throwing a little dust in a juryman's eyes." As she noted in her discussion of *Mockingbird*, in the famous rape trial

> [W]ise paterfamilias Atticus Finch emerges as one very sleazy lawyer. He does not merely provide competent defense for Tom Robinson, he gratuitously defames the poor girl Mayella Ewell. With no real evidence at hand, he weaves a tale in which she lusted after a crippled black man, and seduced him into fornication. It's a hair-raising, lurid tale, but it is completely unnecessary.... Atticus knows they're not going to acquit his client, so he makes

---

through walls.

[25] Scout goes on to say she needs the watchman to "proclaim to them all that twenty-six years is too long to play a joke on anybody," which could indeed be said of those Whites who have bought into the whole "color-blind" idea. Negroes, as Atticus points out, "vote in blocs."

[26] Again, the text seems wrong here; surely this should be "conscience," or is Jack meant to be confused, misled by Jung's "collective consciousness," or is there some other symbolism here I'm missing?

[27] "The foundation of race realism is sense experience, not scientific theorizing." —Greg Johnson, *op. cit.*

up an unpleasant tale about Mayella, all the while feigning pity for the pathetic lass. But it's all invention and false sentiment, just like the fantasies that the *Daily Worker* conjured up about Willette Hawkins and Willie McGee.

Of course, sacrificing the White trash so that one can preen over one's moral righteousness is a trait Scout has, unknowingly, inherited from her father—childhood pal and sometime suitor Hank can be dismissed as White trash as soon as he starts with the racism, even though he's working alongside her father.[28] But then that's White privilege for ya.

This is the kind of moralistic shystering that modern lawyering has become: drunk on *Mockingbird* and other pop legal memes, today's law schools are full of so-called "idealists" who don't intend to practice law so much as "overturn the system, man," using any kind of legal trickery—theories far more sophisticated that Atticus' courtroom shenanigans—to establish Liberal dogma as the law of the land, whatever the masses may think about it.[29]

It amuses me that two generations of lawyers apparently claim to have been "inspired" by Atticus Finch. Two generations of sanctimonious scumbags, who, from "freedom rides" to "marriage equality" to "sanctuary cities" have, as Jack and Atticus would predict, ripped the legal system, and the country, apart, all in the name of some unseeable—because always receding into the perfect, abstract future—notion of "fairness." And now they, along with their hero, stand revealed as the shysters they are; at least, the handful who get jobs "a-tall."[30]

---

[28] And speaking of the Finch family, we also wonder about how Uncle Jack made so much money off his poor Alabama patients during the Depression so as to retire wealthy in his forties.

[29] Ironically, the uber-shysters running the "schools" are fleecing the little lambs blind, pocketing their federally guaranteed loans and sending them out as debt slaves, most of whom will either have no jobs, or find themselves forced into lucrative corporate slavery rather than indulging in "pro bono defense." In a further irony, only the rich can afford such society-wrecking concern for "the poor," while the poor themselves are suckered into . . . law school ("diversity") and debt slavery.

[30] Similarly, *TKAM* has bred two generations of lambs that, faced

It's hard to tell what upsets the Lib-elite more: having the truth about race exposed, or having Atticus Finch show up with his pants down.

I suspect they fall back on the Mark Twain strategy and ban it from the schools for use of the N word.

Let's return now to the issue of style, and look at some touches that seem purely aesthetic, rather than carrying any message.

---

with the overwhelming fact that law school is a disastrously bad bet (unless your parents foot the bill, or it's a "tier 1" school) respond as Special Snowflakes: "When I got into law school a few months ago a law school professor (who is also a family friend) sent me a glut of articles . . . and said to read them, then read *To Kill a Mockingbird* again. Realize that you are not part of that statistic if you remember why you really want to practice law. So, dear Gawker, I am going to just say that I am rubber and you are glue and all the law school bashing rolls off me and sticks to you." Really, if I *were* a liberal constituency, I'd be very afraid of being represented by delusional idiots like this. Generally, see "Do Not Go to a Second-Tier Law School Under Any Circumstances" by Hamilton Nolan, *Gawker*, 3/05/12, http://gawker.com/5890655/do-not-go-to-a-second-tier-law-school-under-any-circumstances: "In case you've forgotten, let us take this opportunity to remind you: do not go to law school. Law school is worthless. Even more worthless than you think. Law school will not make you happy. The smart kids are not going to law school. You should not go to law school." Although himself a law professor, Paul Campos has been at the forefront of exposing the "law school scam": "The odds of a graduate getting a job that justifies incurring the schools' typical debt are essentially 100 to 1. . . . The result is a system that has produced an entire generation of over-credentialed, underemployed, and deeply indebted young people." (*The Atlantic*, September, 2014, http://www.theatlantic.com/features/archive/2014/08/the-law-school-scam/375069/). Ironically, or appropriately, the worst hit have been the "solo practitioners" who wanted to be just like Atticus: "Solo practitioners, the largest single group of American lawyers and the heart and soul of the profession, have struggled for a quarter of a century. . . . In 1988, solo practitioners earned an inflation-adjusted $70,747. By 2012, earnings had fallen to $49,130, a 30% decrease in real income. And note, $49,130 is not the starting salary for these lawyers. It is the average earnings of all 354,000 lawyers who filed as solo practitioners that year." Benjamin Barton, "The fall and rise of lawyers," CNN, May 22, 2015.

In a nod to Modernism, or the avant-garde, Lee renders several passages which Scout can't bear to listen to—a "racist" rant, the inane chatter of grown and married childhood friends—as a sequence of broken sentence fragments. It's an interesting effect, which, if it represented the narrator's own exasperated consciousness, would suggest Céline. It also suggests William Burroughs at his most refractory, the period of the so-called "cut-ups."[31]

Moreover, at least one passage of ordinary prose suggests a parallel to no less than *Naked Lunch* itself:

> At the end of the table, sitting like a great dropsical gray slug, was William Willougby. . . . William Willoughby was indeed the last of his kind. . . . There were mutations, like Willoughby [who] chose to run the county not in its most comfortable office, but in what was best described as a hutch—a small, dark, evil-smelling room with his name on the door, containing nothing more than a telephone, a kitchen table, and unpainted captain's chairs of rich patina.

It seems, to me at least, very reminiscent of the "County Clerk" section, although I can't really find any verbal parallels, just a kind of tone:

> Lee listened in horror. The county clerk often spent weeks in the privy living on scorpions and Montgomery Ward catalogues. On several occasions his assistants had forced the door and carried him out in a state of advanced malnutrition.

Could Burroughs have had an influence on this beloved middle-school classic? I'm sure it would delight him.[32] Alas, further re-

---

[31] See my review of *The Magical Universe of William Burroughs*, "Curses, Cut-Ups, and Contraptions: The 'Disastrous Success' of William Burroughs' Magick," http://www.counter-currents.com/2015/01/curses-cut-ups-and-contraptions/

[32] Burroughs, perhaps hopefully, described *Nova Express* as "an action novel that can be read by any twelve year old." See Oliver Harris' "Introduction" to *Nova Express: The Restored Text* (New York: Penguin,

search shows that *Mockingbird* was in the stores before the County Clerk sections were generally available.[33]

Ironically, some have speculated that Capote wrote some part of *Mockingbird*.[34] If Lee—which was also Burroughs' pen name, e.g., for the pseudonymous *Junky*, as well as the characters "Lee" in *Naked Lunch* and "Inspector Lee" of the *Nova Trilogy*—was influenced, at least unconsciously, by Burroughs,[35] it's clear not only why her publishers would have deleted such "far-out" writing, but also why Lee never mentioned it: Burroughs and Capote hated each other. Burroughs, in fact, put a curse on Capote—in a letter of 1970, after the success of *In Cold Blood*—which reads like it could just as well suit Harper Lee:

> *The early work was in some respects promising*—I refer particularly to the short stories. You were granted an area for psychic development. It seemed for a while as if you would make good use of this grant. *You choose instead to sell out a*

2013), p. xliv.

[33] "In 1962, Grove Press issued a promotional booklet to accompany the November 20, 1962 American publication of *Naked Lunch*. . . . The promotional pamphlet includes an eight-page selection of *Naked Lunch*. Not surprisingly, Rosset chose sections that support the critical readings of the novel. The "Meeting of International Conference of Technological Society" and "The County Clerk" section highlight the satirical nature of *Naked Lunch* to the fullest. Rosset also featured these pieces (along with a section entitled "Interzone") in *Evergreen Review* No. 16 of January / February 1961. They present Burroughs' humor, language and voice at their most obvious." "Burroughs Ephemera 2: *Naked Lunch* Prospectus," (http://realitystudio.org/bibliographic-bunker/ephemera/naked-lunch-prospectus/). Note that "The County Clerk" is preceded by "Meeting of International Conference of Technological Society" which involves horrifying insect/human mutations, like the slug-like Willoughby and "his kind."

[34] "Harper Lee: the 'great lie' she didn't write *Mockingbird* rears its head again," Glynnis MacCool, *The Guardian*, July 15, 2015, http://www.theguardian.com/books/2015/jul/20/harper-lee-to-kill-a-mockingbird-authorship-women-writers

[35] And perhaps we should note the similarity of *William* Will*ough*by to William Burroughs?

talent that is not yours to sell. You have written a dull unreadable book which could have been written by any staff writer on the New Yorker — (an undercover reactionary periodical dedicated to the interests of vested American wealth).

You have placed your services at the disposal of interests who are turning America into a police state by the simple device of deliberately fostering the conditions that give rise to criminality and then demanding increased police powers and the retention of capital punishment to deal with the situation they have created. You have betrayed and sold out the talent that was granted you by this department. That talent is now officially withdrawn.

Enjoy your dirty money. You will never have anything else. *You will never write another sentence above the level of In Cold Blood. As a writer you are finished.* Over and out. Are you tracking me? Know who I am? You know me, Truman. You have known me for a long time. This is my last visit.[36]

Indeed, Capote never regained the level of talent or success shown by *In Cold Blood*, and Lee never wrote another book at all.[37] And the line about

You have placed your services at the disposal of interests who are *turning America into a police state by the simple device of deliberately fostering the conditions that give rise to criminality and then demanding increased police powers* . . . to deal with the situation they have created.

---

[36] "William S. Burroughs Trashes Truman Capote In Open Letter" by Jen Carlson, *Gothamist,* August 2, 2012, http://gothamist.com/2012/08/02/william_s_burroughs_trashes_truman.php. The "stunning opening" to *Nova Express* was originally titled "Open Letter" and is signed by "J. Lee"; see Harris, *op. cit.*, pp. 193, 199.

[37] "Of course, much like Lee was never able to publish anything after *To Kill a Mockingbird*, Capote's writing fizzled after *In Cold Blood*, so perhaps their literary relationship was more symbiotic than one-sided." Steve Sailer, "Harper Lee's 'To Kill a Mockingbird' Pre-sequel," Unz Review, July 2, 2015, http://www.unz.com/isteve/harper-lees-to-kill-a-mockingbird-pre-sequel/.

Sounds today like exactly the strategy one might attribute to the Civil Righters and disciples of Saul Alinsky — force desegregation and then expand the Police State to deal with the inevitable chaos resultant — although that would have been not at all Burroughs' meaning. But then, that's the thing about curses and magick: it works, but often not the way you intended.[38]

Is this a "rejected first draft"? Whatever the answer, *Go Set a Watchman* is an interestingly written first novel that addresses race in a realistic manner. The "classic" *Mockingbird* is New York's response: dumbed down for kids and retconned into a "saintly blacks" narrative as part of Operation Destroy the South.

Forget about setting a watchman. Atticus Finch was a freakin' prophet.

Counter-Currents/*North American New Right*
July 27, 2015

---

[38] See my review of *The Magical World of William Burroughs*, op. cit.

SOUR CREAM:
MICHAEL NELSON'S *A ROOM IN CHELSEA SQUARE*

Anonymous (Michael Nelson)
A Room in Chelsea Square
Richmond: Valancourt Books, 2014

> "Well," said John, "*I'm* thought queer because I have more brains than most children. Some say I have more brains than I *ought* to have. *You're* queer because you have more *money* than most people; and (some say) more than you ought to have."
>
> —Olaf Stapledon, *Odd John*

I've long enjoyed reading almost exclusively Old Books; not "the classics" as such, but books from a recognizably modern period, but prior to the cultural upheaval of the '60s—say, from 1920 to 1965. Although it's a personal predilection, I think I can recommend it as an interesting and instructive exercise. Such books reveal, innocently and therefore reliably, a whole world in which PC attitudes were unknown—and everyone was perfectly OK with it. It's a world alt-Rightists would do well to contemplate, if only for encouragement.

It's a world where it was perfectly natural for James Gould Cozzens—a Gentile!—to write *Guard of Honor*, a novel not so much "pro-military"—since its dialectic opposite, the "anti-military," was unthinkable prior to the "black comedy" of *Catch-22* or *Dr. Strangelove*—but simply realistic; a novel in which honest men—and women—try to do what's necessary at a homeland base during wartime, with greater or lesser levels of competence, rather than cartoonish psychopathy; where running a minor military base in a segregated county is a problem for men of good will to work out more or less satisfactory arrangements, rather than a moral imperative to be shoved down the throats of inbred cracker colonels. And not only win the National Book

Award, but get his picture on the cover of *Time*![1]

By the time you get deeper into the '50s, even the Young Lions become problematic. These are the books that keep troubling the PC gatekeepers in the media and especially the academy; still "relevant"—i.e., anti-White—but loaded with land mines that keep springing up anew as the cultural goalposts keep changing—progressing ever onward to ever greater liberation! As the PC crowd grinds on relentlessly, one "radical" after another becomes a "cretinous reactionary" the embarrassed teacher needs to justify to the outraged student, and ripe for reclamation by the alt-Right.

We all know about Mark Twain and "the N-word"—as if Twain were a whip-cracking straw boss—but consider the way the Beats, like Kerouac or Burroughs, presented "Negro," Mexican, or Arab cultures with a fetishistic relish that was intended to "stick it to the Man" but now appear to the cultural overseers as "racist," "essentialist," and "Orientalist." Reading Burroughs' letters makes him seem less Wise Old Junkie and more the embarrassing old fart at Thanksgiving who rants about the darkies stealing from him at the home. And yet this was the Avant Garde that scared all the old fogies!

Another aspect of this process: as a condition of their joining the Rainbow Coalition of the Left's culture destroyers, homosexuals have accepted—clung to—their own version of the Judaic's "lachrymose history," in which a tiny, wholly innocent, constantly harassed but courageous little minority struggles against The Man. As I've pointed out for some time, the reality was quite different; asking only a little discretion, the Establishment was happy to welcome the talents of such men as Sir Noël Coward, J. Edgar Hoover, Whittaker Chambers, Roy Cohn, and Francis "Franny" Cardinal Spellman, who, in turn, became pil-

---

[1] This was indeed too much for the rising Judaic literary cabal, who commissioned their *shabbos goy* Dwight MacDonald to pen the most famous and effective literary smear in history, "By Cozzens Possessed" in *Commentary*. 25 years later, *Commentary* was now "neo-conservative" so they commissioned Joseph Epstein to do a half-assed reassessment. And last year, D. G. Meyers tried his hand there as well: "James Gould Cozzens at 109." What is he, a Nazi "war criminal"? Never forget!

lars of the Establishment.² Conversely, it's the in-your-face outrageousness of "camp" and other aspects of "liberation" that creates, now, violent homophobia that liberationists then anachronistically—and opportunistically (donate money to us or else the bad old days will return!)—read back into the past.³

Apart from the Beats and a tiny selection of acceptably "modern" works, most of these naively non-PC books are almost entirely forgotten, certainly not to be recommended for reading or reprinting by the PC academics. The internet, however, has made them easier to find; and some offbeat publishers are still to be found, operating under the radar of the New York cabal. One such, Valancourt Books, a plucky little outfit—a "specialty micropress," if you will—gives us a rare chance to glimpse the normal life of the 1950s British homosexual world; it's not a pretty picture, but not for the reasons you probably think. It's a world in which not repression, but social dominance, has curdled the cream of Wilde's wit into the sourness of "camp."

In recent years Valancourt has put us all in their debt with lovely little editions, some quite scholarly, of the most obscure sort of Gothic novels of the 18th and 19th centuries ("Many of the titles in the series existed in fewer than five copies worldwide before our new editions; scholars and readers interested in reading these wonderful texts were forced to travel thousands of miles to a university rare book room or pay thousands of dollars to obtain a copy from an antiquarian bookseller") and "decadent" or "weird" British and European literature from the turn

---

² See, for example, my review of *The Noel Coward Reader* or the discussion of Bogart's interaction with Truman Capote; both reprinted in *The Homo & the Negro* (San Francisco: Counter-Currents, 2012).

³ I realize it's hard to believe such a Copernican idea. But take a look how this occurred in an entirely different context—the Arab world. As documented by John R. Bradley (see *Behind the Veil of Vice: The Business and Culture of Sex in the Middle East* [New York: Palgrave MacMillan, 2010]), it was pushy Western "liberationists" that disrupted the discrete playground of Burroughs, Capote, and others, creating the Puritan backlash wrongly attributed to "Medievalist Islam." Even James Neill, though he accepts most of the lachrymose theory, agrees here, as I point out in my review of his *The Origins and Role of Same-Sex Relations in Human Societies* (Amazon Kindle, 2013).

of the last century, concentrating on either obscure authors or obscure works by the well-known, such as Ann Radcliffe's posthumous *Gaston de Blondeville* (1826), Arthur Conan Doyle's *Round the Red Lamp* (1894), and Forrest Reid's *The Garden God* (1905).

For example,

> [T]he first-ever scholarly edition of Le Fanu's novella [*Carmilla*] follows the rare original text as it appeared serially in *The Dark Blue* in 1871-72 (including the original illustrations) and includes a new introduction and footnotes by Jamieson Ridenhour. Also featured in this edition is a wealth of contextual material, including texts by Yeats, Coleridge, Stoker, Padraig Pearse, and others, and the complete texts of Le Fanu's "The Child that Went with the Fairies" and F. G. Loring's "The Tomb of Sarah."

More recently, they've been moving into the area of our topic by delving into British fiction from the 1950s, including "angry young men" that are more familiar to us stateside from films, authors such as Keith Waterhouse (*Billy Liar*), John Braine (*Room at the Top*), John Wain (*Hurry on Down*, a somewhat more interesting book than Braine's that takes on the reverse theme of deliberate downward mobility), and the late Colin Wilson (the Gerald Sorme trilogy as well as the Lovecraftian pastiches).[4] It was the Wilson books that got my notice, but I confess I stayed to explore the others not only because of the vague sense of seeing the film or recalling Colin Wilson's discussion in one of his many memoirs.[5]

One book which they advertise as "coming soon" is one I already have: *A Room in Chelsea Square*, first recommended to me years ago by Jeremy Reed.[6] I must confess I never found it en-

---

[4] Perhaps they might be encouraged to reprint Wilson pal Bill Hopkin's fascist/Lawrencian *The Leap*.

[5] Such as Wilson's *The Angry Years: A Literary Chronicle* (London: Robson, 2007).

[6] Whose own story of a young man from the provinces in search of London accommodations can be found in his first novel, *The Lipstick*

gaging enough to finish years ago, but having kept it around—due to its vintage Edward Gorey dust jacket, of which more anon—I was inspired by Valancourt's notice to give it another try. I found it to be rather dull and surprisingly unpleasant.

Valancourt tells us:

> Patrick, the book's opening line tells us, is 'very, very rich'. He's also single, and he has his sights set on Nicholas Milestone, a handsome young provincial journalist. Having lured Nicholas to London with the promise of a job on a tabloid magazine, Patrick moves the young man into his suite at a posh hotel, where he lavishes money and expensive gifts on him. Nicholas enjoys his luxurious new lifestyle and meeting Patrick's amusing and fashionable friends, but he soon understands what Patrick's really after. Knowing he won't be able to resist the older man's advances forever, the greedy Nicholas will have to choose between his conscience and his newly acquired love of money.

It's the virtuous provincial girl plot, familiar since at least Richardson's *Pamela*, continuing through the wolfish *Mad Men* salivating over a new secretary, given a twist by setting it amidst the metropolitan London branch of what Auden described as the Homintern. And therein lies the problem.

Valancourt adds that Nelson's book, "was published anonymously both because of its frank gay content at a time when homosexuality was still illegal and because its characters were thinly veiled portrayals of prominent London literary figures."

I rather suspect the latter was more important than the former. As for the "gay content," it's not really all that "frank." I mean, it's obvious what's going on, but no one really does anything. That the traditional roles are all played by men is no more shocking than a school pantomime or "authentic" period production of *Romeo and Juliet*. The closest we get is Patrick telling a tired out Nicholas that, "An hour on your back with your legs up will do you the world of good."

Boys (London: Enitharmon Press, 1984)

Otherwise, it's about as offensive as *Auntie Mame*.⁷

Moreover, the reviewers at the time were quite enthused, treating it more like, well, *Auntie Mame* than *Last Exit to Brooklyn*:

> Consistently diverting, this may be the novel about homosexuality to end all novels on the subject . . . [W]ill make many a reader's day.
> —Julian MacLaren-Ross, *Punch*

> Talented, amusing . . . the story is told with sustained suspense: the various men in it are not merely types, but flesh and blood, even if one wishes that Patrick had never been born.
> —John Betjeman, *Daily Telegraph*

> Odiously funny and delightfully unwholesome . . . a distinct relief after the ponderous treatment homosexuality has tended to get in some recent novels.
> —*Sunday Times*

Nor did it have any trouble finding a major American publisher, Doubleday, who assigned the dust jacket to its now-famous in-house illustrator, Edward Gorey.⁸

The problem must have been in that "not merely types, but flesh and blood" bit, given England's famously generous libel laws. An Amazon reviewer clarifies matters for us:

---

⁷ A contemporary work (1955) although set earlier, where the ingénue is "Patrick" and the urban corrupter the nevertheless safely female Mame. Of course, "Auntie" Mame has no doubt been played by innumerable gay men, perhaps especially in the provinces. I actually only became acquainted with the book and movie quite recently, and while loving the '50s Technicolor, was actually shocked at utterly how subversive both are: Jews are to be catered to as our betters, Southerners are racist rednecks, children should attend nudist schools in Greenwich Village and sing the "Internationale," suburban couples are materialistic boobs; the whole New Left agenda.

⁸ See "Gorey Goes Gay" here: http://ukjarry.blogspot.com/2009/09/286-gorey-goes-gay-1.html

"Patrick" is a thinly veiled portrait of Peter Watson: associated for a long while with Cecil Beaton, co-founder of the ICA and wealthy homosexual sponsor of Bacon, Colquhoun, MacBryde, Vaughan, Minton and other homosexual painters. Michael Nelson (the "Nicholas" of the book) was in reality pursued by Watson, who bought him Picassos and Sutherlands as part of his seduction technique. Nicholas—like the real life Nelson—is prevented from starting at his Tabloid newspaper by the dangling of a greater carrot, a job on a new arts magazine "Eleven" (which was "Horizon" in real life) together with his friend Michael, Christopher Pyre (Stephen Spender in reality) and a former protégé of Patrick's: the bon-viveur Ronnie Gras (Cyril Connolly). It is Nicholas' constant prevarication as to whether to succumb to Patrick's gentle but lavish onslaught that eventually causes his downfall.

I suppose a modern equivalent would be one of those post-campaign *romans a clef*, like *Primary Colors*, since we no longer have public intellectuals (to use that ghastly neo-con term) or an intellectual public, to experience the frisson of scandal behind ... founding a cultural magazine.

However, the problem is not just that everyone is long dead and forgotten and in another country anyway; it's that the people are, frankly, bloody stupid.

William Burroughs, around the same time, wrote about meeting up with the Homintern a decade earlier at Harvard ("a fake English university for graduates of fake English public schools" as he called it):

> By accident I met some *rich homosexuals, of the international queer set* who cruise around the world, bumping into each other in queer joints from New York to Cairo. I saw a way of life, vocabulary, references, a whole symbol set as the sociologists say. *But these people were jerks for the most part* and, after an initial period of fascination, I cooled off on the setup.[9]

---

[9] *Word Virus: The William S. Burroughs Reader*, ed. James Grauerholz

So today's reviewers, unless they're personally interested in promoting "gay fiction," are a little harsher. Here's an online bookseller on his own wares:

> Unwholesome book deals with the complex contrivances by which Patrick, a very rich and inordinately nasty queer, seeks to break the will of a silly and rather greedy young man.

It's not clear if he thinks these are selling points, or he just can't control his rage and bile.

And on Amazon:

> I do have a capacity to endure novels even if they bore me early on. I gave up on this one. It's just too dated—a bit like trying to read *Upstairs Downstairs* without the drama. Quite grating on the nerves just reading about the wealthy and their day to day worries—which gold cigarette case they should purchase for a new beau.

The problem is not simply it being "dated." Patrick is the central character, and it's impossible to want to spend time with him since he's so bloody awful and boring—unless, as in the book, you're being paid for your services, which isn't an option for the reader.

And it isn't that he's a predatory homosexual—unless you're so dotty with homophobia that you can't stand the very idea of one, even as a plumber—since, as I've said, we've seen his hetero version time and again. After all, Hannibal Lecter is a serial killer *and* a cannibal, yet the whole world seems to want to spend as much time with him as they can.[10]

---

and Ira Silverberg (New York: Grove, 1998), p. 48. The quote is from his 1953 *Junky*, another disguised autobiography full of libel, this time among the world of drug addicts; for its complex legal and publishing history, see Oliver Harris's "Introduction" to *Junky: The Definitive Text of "Junk"* (New York: Grove, 2003).

[10] That's "Lecter" as in Anthony Hopkins' *Phantom of the Opera* version, not Brian Cox's much more interesting "Lecktor" who conse-

Lecter, unlike Patrick, is interesting, and that's because, as our parents used to tell us, he is himself interested (not interested in himself); he's interested in ideas.[11] I don't mean the way Patrick uses the set-up of an new cultural journal as a mechanism to reward his friends and discomfort his enemies—who wouldn't, that's the whole point of having a journal, isn't it?—but that he seems to have no notion of anything else to do with it.

Patrick exemplifies a certain type of urban homosexual—based on F. R. Leavis's notion of the "metropolitan cultural clique" one might call him a "metrosexual" if that word hadn't already been taken—in whom the genuine love of ideas, playfully expressed as "wit," found in an Oscar Wilde[12] has soured and

---

quently makes *Manhunter* a vastly more interesting film. Cox's outwardly schlubby Lecktor, who seems to have just gotten off a crosstown bus, seem to prefigure his role as an oddly sympathetic child molester in Michael Cuesta's 2002 film *L.I.E.*

[11] Unlike the Pet Shop Boys, Patrick is always being boring. This was the root of Colin Wilson's disgust with English culture, and love of America; the British were uninterested in ideas—or at least, his ideas. For example: "When I saw Amis's review of *The Outsider* in the *Spectator*, I was not surprised that it was entitled 'The Legion of the Lost', and began: 'Here they come—tramp, tramp, tramp—all those characters you thought were discredited, or had never read, or (if you were like me) had never heard of: Barbusse, Sartre, Camus . . .' I took this for a tongue-in-cheek pose, Amis pretending to be the intellectual barbarian. . . . It was not until after his death, when I read his vitriolic comments on me to Larkin in his collected letters, that I realised that, where I was concerned, there was a genuine dislike tinged with alarm. It was then that I understood that the attitude he had expressed in the review was more than a flippant affectation." — http://www.colinwilsonworld.co.uk/Pages/TheRiseandFallofAngryYoungMen.aspx

[12] Readers who find it hard to take Wilde seriously, or who are surprised to learn that Wilde was the earliest intellectual influence Baron Evola deigns to acknowledge in his autobiography, *The Path of Cinnabar* (London: Arktos, 2009) might examine *The Soul of Man Under Socialism* (1891), an admittedly witty presentation of the viewpoint more ponderously expressed by Spengler's "Prussian Socialism" or Yockey's "Ethical Socialism," and far more influential than either (ranging from Godwin to Žižek).

curdled into the brittle bitchiness known as "camp."[13]

This shows itself on the micro level, in his conversations, which are meant, I suppose, as "camp" but actually, unlike the Wilde they ape, betray an utter philistinism; hence, they are profoundly wearying.

The conventional explanation for this conversational tic—a more politely British version of the poisonously brittle repartee immortalized in now-reviled *The Boys in the Band*—is to blame it on the conditions of "the closet," but the openly though not explicitly sexual content, and the rapturous reviews quoted above, make that unlikely.

Patrick's problem is not that he is somehow "discriminated against" as one of today's far from predatory, marriage yearning gays would loudly whine—but quite the opposite; he's simply too rich to have developed a real personality.[14]

The answer, as usual, lies with one of those healthier-minded authors from the turn of the last century, one of the leading lights of our native-born, manly Neoplatonism, our own two-fisted Traditionalism, the "New Thought" movement; in this case, William Walker Atkinson:

> You must want a thing hard enough before you can get it. You must want it more than you do the things around you, and you must be prepared to pay the price for it. The price is the throwing overboard of certain lesser desires that stand in the way of the accomplishment of the greater one. *Comfort, ease, leisure, amusements, and many other things may have to go* (not always though). It depends on what you want. As a rule, the greater the thing desired, the greater the price to be paid for it. Nature believes in adequate compensation. But if you really Desire a thing in earnest, you will pay the price without question; for the

---

[13] It is appropriate that the "Gay Men's Classic" edition comes with an Introduction by one Philip Core, a British painter of the Bacony school whose literary efforts amounted to a rather silly book called *Camp: The Lie That Tells the Truth* (London: Plexus, 1984). Oh, but that's the point, isn't it? Silly me!

[14] Unlike Wilde, an arriviste and an Irishman to boot.

Desire will dwarf the importance of other things.[15]

Making things worse, Patrick's money is inherited, putting him in the British equivalent of what Paul Fussell has identified, in America, as the real elite, the Top Out of Sight.

> The way they have their money is largely what matters. . . . The main thing distinguishing the top three classes from each other is the amount of money inherited in relation to the amount currently earned. The top-out-of-sight class (Rockefellers, Pres, DuPonts, Mellons, Fords, Vanderbilts) lives on inherited capital entirely.
>
> No one whose money, no matter how copious, comes from his own work — film stars are an example — can be a member of the top-out-of-sight class, even if the size of his income and the extravagance of his expenditure permit him to simulate identity with it. Inheritance—"old money" in the vulgar phrase—is the indispensable principle defining the top three classes, and it's best if the money's been in the family for three or four generations.
>
> "When I think of a really rich man," says a Boston blue-collar, "I think of one of those estates where you can't see the house from the road." Hence the name of the top class, which could just as well be called "the class in hiding." Their houses are never seen from the street or road. They like to hide away deep in the hills or way off on Greek or Caribbean islands (which they tend to own), safe, for the moment, from envy and its ultimate attendants, confiscatory taxation and finally expropriation. It was the Great Depression, Vance Packard speculates, that badly frightened the very rich, teaching them to be "discrete, almost reticent, in exhibiting their wealth." From the 1930s dates the flight of money from such exhibitionistic venues as the mansions of upper Fifth Avenue to hideaways in Virginia, upper New York State, Connecti-

---

[15] "The Transmutation of Negative Thought" in *Thought Vibration: Or, The Law of Attraction in the Thought World* by William Walker Atkinson (1906), p. 53.

cut, Long Island, and New Jersey.[16]

Now, the point of this detour becomes apparent when Fussell asks the reader which class would he like to belong to, and it gets a little tricky. You see, he says, it might seem obvious that one would want to belong to the top out of sight—where you'd never have to worry about money, and have access to the best of everything—but there's a catch: you must resign yourself to never hearing an interesting comment or idea ever again.

> Like all aristocracies . . . ye shall know them by their imperviousness to ideas and their total lack of interest in them.

> "We can say of [the very topmost classes'] expectations of their children what Douglas Sutherland says of the English gentleman's: 'his offspring are expected to conform in all things, and academic brilliance is not an acceptable deviation from the normal.'"[17]

The top out of sight are not "closeted" so much as "immured" and even self-immured.[18]

Ideas, for Patrick, are simply foibles of other people—Ronnie's magazine, Nicky's job, which he so tiresomely keeps reminding Patrick about—which enable him to manipulate them.[19] If some silly person insists on talking about "ideas" then

---

[16] *Class: A Guide Through the American Status System* (New York: Summit, 1983) pp. 29-30.

[17] *Op. cit.*, p. 33 and p. 139.

[18] Fritz Zorn's *Mars* (German, 1977; English trans. By Robert and Rita Kimber, New York: Knopf, 1982) is a devastating portrait of the similar class on Switzerland's "Gold Coast." Zorn's family shuns all idea and discussion, since that might lead to disagreement, hence unpleasantness. Ideas are for "other people"; people who take ideas seriously are "funny," like Russian novelists. "Funny" not because of wit, like Wilde, but because they are silly and amuse us. His father played only one game, Klondike, the most boring form of the most boring game, Solitaire.

[19] This is paralleled by a disinterest in psychology as such; Patrick is

one just cracks a joke and hopes he gets the message. Otherwise, one calls the attendant and has the bounder ejected from one's club, doesn't one?[20]

Thus, the "action" of the novel, such as it is, is less Nicky's seduction—he succumbs pretty quickly and easily, the whole action of the novel taking place in a week—

> Nicholas had a thoroughly miserable bath. He knew that he couldn't evade Patrick's advances much longer. It was no good pretending that Patrick was going to support him from purely altruistic motives. Patrick wanted his pound of flesh, he was going to make sure he got it. What did sex matter anyway? It was a small price to pay for all the things that Patrick could offer him in exchange.

—but rather, a rather late-developing concern with his intellectual independence.

> Christopher spoke slowly and with difficulty. "Nicholas, you must listen to me. You're an intelligent person. You've a mind of our own. You mustn't sell it. That would be a crime for which later you'd never forgive yourself. There

---

"not interested in discovering what motivates [people]" (p. 108) while himself regarding Michael as having "a nasty habit of looking beyond one's actions and putting his fingers on one's motives." Ironically, Patrick is ultimately defeated when Ronnie's wife (the only woman in the book, other than Patrick's dead aunt from which his fortune derives) points out that "the moment you tell Patrick you don't want his money, he'll be furious. He'll go to any lengths to make you take it" (pp. 206-207). Patrick's obsession with surfaces recalls the English decadent Fr. Rolfe ("Baron Corvo") who was described by a former fellow student of the priesthood as being interested only in surfaces; he wanted to be a priest only because "he saw himself doing picturesque things in a picturesque manner." See A. J. A. Symons, *The Quest for Corvo: An Experiment in Biography* (1932; New York: NYLB, 2001), p. 74.

[20] Needless to say, several scenes take place in London clubs, which, at least in fiction, are usually set up with rules to prevent conversation about "tiresome" ideas—Wodehouse's Drone's Club, Sayer's Egoists' Club, etc.

continually occur moments in one's life when one has to choose between possessions and integrity. . . . But believe me, if you choose possessions today, you'll regret it for ever after."

So the turning point, Nicky's redemption as it were, occurs when he resolves, not to resist Patrick's overtures—that ship, after only the most formal nod to Pamela-like hesitation, has sailed—but when he resolves to keep his own mind.[21]

Of course, there's no tiresome "happy ending"—how middle-class!—and Nicky ignores Christopher's advice, only to find Patrick has already tired of his balkiness and moved on—literally, to Bermuda. Ronnie, however, has a more detailed and consequential epiphany:

> He had dreamed all night about money . . . he was still thinking about money. It was money that had gradually destroyed his integrity. He should never have been a fashion designer. He had given up painting for a quick return. Yet he had never made enough money, probably because he was only capable of spending it. He would have been far happier as a painter. Christopher, in spite of the incredible squalor in which he lived, would ultimately command greater respect. It was a galling thought. (pp. 204-05)

The other characters, all but one homosexual males, some married—to a woman!—or living together or single, most "protégés" that have escaped from Patrick's clutches, all have to work to some degree for their living, and are the better for it; they are the ones who have freed themselves and have ideas.

---

[21] Patrick at one point (p. 166) calls Nicholas "little one" which is what Demian (at least in one English translation) calls Sinclair as he bids him farewell, suggesting Patrick is a kind of anti-Demian, seducing the young from a truly independent life of ideas to the false "independence" of a kept boy. Nicholas later, after Christopher's remonstrance, quotes Jesus on those who cause little ones to stumble as better to have millstones hung about their necks, hammering home the symbolism of his family name, Millstone (pp. 210–11).

Ronnie is apparently based on Cyril Connelly, and it's interesting, in a sour way, to read that

> According to the critics, [Noël] Coward should have faded away long ago. It was one of English theatre's great mantras—his fame was built on gossamer-thin plots and diaphanous characters that doomed his legacy. Not even the slickest epigrams would survive. "One cannot read his plays now," wrote Cyril Connelly, during the war. "For they are written in the most perishable way imaginable. *The cream in them turns sour overnight.*"[22]

I dare say that the reputation of Noël Coward, a man of both wit and ideas, however "slick" his epigrams, has survived considerably longer than overnight, while most of my readers have already asked, "Who's Cyril Connelly?"

Counter-Currents/*North American New Right*
January 20, 2014

---

[22] http://www.huffingtonpost.co.uk/james-ruddick/forty-years-on-why-noel-coward-laugh_b_3246716.html

"THE WILD BOYS SMILE":
REFLECTIONS ON OLAF STAPLEDON'S
ODD JOHN

"Well," said John, "*I'm* thought queer because I have more brains than most children."

After making my way through Olaf Stapledon's *The Flames*, and having read *Last and First Men* already, I decided to press ahead in my Kindle anthology by tackling Stapledon's third novel, from 1935. It's a relatively short novel—Dover packages it with another short novel, *Sirius*—that supposedly pioneers the science fiction subgenre of spooky genetically advanced children, later to be mined by Sturgeon, Heinlein, Lem, and Wyndham.[1]

Blessed Wikipedia has labored to provide a synopsis, using Stapledon's chapter headings, so I don't have to! As you can see there, it's pretty standard for the genre—having established it, after all—until the killing and raping.[2] Now that everyone's (re-)

---

[1] "J. D. Beresford's tale of a child prodigy with superhuman intelligence, *The Hampdenshire Wonder*, was an early entry into the subgenre of sf that explores the next stage of human evolution from *Homo sapiens* to *Homo superior*, the nomenclature coined by Olaf Stapledon for people with superhuman physical or mental abilities. Stapledon was a great admirer of Beresford's book and later paid homage to it in his own novel *Odd John*." See "The Rise of *Homo Superior*," Chapter 2 of The Art of Penguin Science Fiction (http://www.penguinsciencefiction.org/02.html).

[2] http://en.wikipedia.org/wiki/Odd_John%20/%20Outline. Wikipedia says he rapes his mother, which don't think is accurate. Stapledon is rather showily coy about the whole thing, but I think all you can read between the lines is incest. Perhaps the modern, "liberated" editors of the internet are just as "Victorian" as their predecessors, unable to imagine a woman consenting to so monstrous an act. After all, Pax, the mother, did produce this oddity, so it wouldn't be surprising to see them on the same wavelength. Hermann Hesse's *Demian* (1919) is another "Story of a Youth" who represents a new, evolutionary venture

familiarized themselves with the narrative, I'd like to make some comments on some of the more striking features. I think we will find some interesting connections to such topics as initiatory traditions, utopian communities, and even events in the near future of Stapledon's Europe.

What links all this, I think, is that John's advanced genetics results in a prolonged kind of adolescence, while his intelligence advances by leaps and bounds. By the time of his death in his mid-20s, he could be mistaken for a teenager, yet he is part of a group mind contemplating the meaning of the Universe.

John's initial sexual exploits are detailed in an early chapter entitled "Scandalous Adolescence," which hints at a kind of Moll Flanders or even Fanny Hill kind of titillation—we'll see Stapledon's taste for "ribaldry" come up again later—but the activities described—first turning his attentions to the most socially dominant boy in the neighborhood, then using his new-found techniques to rather cold-bloodedly seduce the prettiest girl around, and even the broadly hinted-at relations with his mother—all suggest something more serious: the socializing and ultimately initiatory activities of the *Männerbund*.[3]

---

by Mother Nature. Max Demian is the already-advanced guide who will eventually gather a group of like-minded souls, only to be destroyed by war. Before he dies, the narrator will acknowledge him as "my guide"—in Hesse's German, "mein Führer." Demian's mother is Eve, suggesting both the Garden and the New Eve whose son brings salvation; the schoolboys whisper rumors of incest, or even Islam! Mother, son, and eventually narrator share a connection that is "more like that of lovers, whose this-worldly bonds are incestuous . . . the physical level, homosexual impulses bind Sinclair to *Demian*; *incestuous love binds Eve to both Sinclair and her son, Demian*" (Ralph Freeman, Introduction to the Penguin edition; London, 2013). Evola discusses "philosophical incest" in *The Hermetic Tradition*. All these themes—incest, the evolutionarily advanced group, death, National Socialism—will re-appear as we read *Odd John*.

[3] See my review of Wulf Grimmson's *Loki's Way*, reprinted in *The Homo & the Negro* (San Francisco: Counter-Currents, 2012) and more recently my Kindle Single *A Review of James Neill's "The Origins and Role of Same-Sex Relations in Human Societies"* (Amazon, 2013).

While not necessarily, or exclusively, homosexual,[4] the *Männerbund*, as a band apart, withdrawn though not necessarily hostile to "family oriented" society,[5] is naturally associated with such 'deviance', and both are easily assimilated as metaphors for social and evolutionary advance.

The appropriation of the word 'queer' is relevant here. Although some may carp that a "perfectly good word" has been, well, queered, there is some rationale here.[6]

It is striking, then, that even granting the word "didn't mean that" back then, Stapledon seems to use the word 'queer' almost reflexively, in all kinds of situations. Using my Kindle's handy highlight function, I've taken the liberty of collating his usages, which make for an interesting list.

- This from a queer child to a full-grown man.
- Altogether, his eyes were the most obviously "queer" part of him.

Here, within a single page:

> When I arrived, John was already settled in the corner opposite to the great man, who occasionally glanced from his paper at the queer child with a cliff for brow and caves for eyes.
> "Oh, my name's John. I'm a queer child, but that

---

[4] Jack Donovan's term "androphilic" might be better; Neill, *op. cit.*, regards all humans as "ambisexual."

[5] Evola, in *Men Among the Ruins*, makes a fairly sharp distinction between the State, the affair of men, and above all, of Orders such as the *Männerbund*, the Teutonic Knights, or the SS, and on the other hand, society, the affair of women. See also his disparagement of the idea of the Higher Man producing children, which, in this Kali Yuga, would be unlikely to be worthy successors; an anti-natal theme common to the utopian literature we are examining here.

[6] This is by no means to endorse the sub-Marxist shenanigans of the academic "queer theorists." The distinction of the *Männerbund*, which is outside of society but supportive of it, from the inane anti-social Leftist "gay community" is central to *The Homo & the Negro*, especially the title essay; see also essay therein on Brian DePalma's *The Untouchables* as a tale of the socially useful *Männerbund*.

doesn't matter. It's you we're going to talk about."

We all laughed. Mr. Magnate shifted in his seat, but continued to look his part.

"Well," he said, "you certainly are a queer child." He glanced at his adult fellow travellers for confirmation. We duly smiled.

"Yes," replied John, "but you see from my point of view you are a queer man." Mr. Magnate hung for a moment between amusement and annoyance; but since we had all laughed, except John, he chose to be tickled and benevolent.

"Surely," he said, "there's nothing remarkable about me. I'm just a business man. Why do you think I'm queer?"

"Well," said John," *I'm* thought queer because I have more brains than most children. Some say I have more brains than I *ought* to have. *You're* queer because you have more *money* than most people; and (some say) more than you ought to have."

John uses it himself:

❖ I had a queer notion that if I *pricked* any of you, there would be no bleeding, but only a gush of wind.

More:

❖ But when he was sixteen, and in appearance a queer sort of twelve-year-old, he turned his attention to woman.

As we'll see, some find his kind rather attractive:

❖ Out of the water and played ball with his companions, running, leaping, twisting, with that queer grace which few could detect, but by which those few were strangely enthralled.

John withdraws to the forest, clearly a shamanic, initiatory period:

- There was a pause, then Norton laughed awkwardly, and said, "Well, when one tries to describe it in cold blood over a cup of coffee, it just sounds crazy. But damn it, if the thing *didn't* happen, something *mighty queer* must have happened to *us*, for we both saw it, as clearly as you see us now."
- Certain fungi, too, contributed to his diet on that day, and indeed throughout his adventure. On the second day he was feeling *"pretty queer."*
- Moreover, he coveted the huge material wealth that the slaughter of one stag would afford him. And he had apparently a *queer lust* to try his strength and cunning against a worthy quarry.

After his queer diet of mushrooms, he acquires shamanic, or "mighty queer," powers:

- And I had made queer little visits to events in my own past life. I just lived them again, with full vividness, as though they were 'now.'
- Well, in Scotland, when I began to come into all those *queer powers* that I mentioned just now, I was tempted to regard the exercise of them as the true end of my life.

Using his queer powers, he finds others of his kind — some kind of gaydar?

- I told you before that when I was in Scotland I used to find myself in telepathic touch with people, and that some of the people seemed queer people, or people in a significant way more like me than you.
- Most music, ordinary music invented by *Homo sapiens*, seemed at once to interest and outrage him; though when one of the doctors played a certain bit of Bach, he was gravely attentive, and afterwards went off to play oddly twisted variants of it on *his queer pipe.*
- He stood for a second or two, a *queer little foreigner*, jostled by waiters and a stream of guests.

Even common objects become queer when associated with John and his kind:

- Both Ng-Gunko and Lo had to learn to fly; and all three had to become familiar with the mannerisms of *their own queer aeroplane and their own queer yacht*. ...
- The table was crowded with unfamiliar eatables, especially tropical and sub-tropical fruits, fish, and a *queer sort of bread*

After this semantic flood, it's no surprise to find, fifty years later, in the film *Manhunter*, another freakishly tall albino, taunted in the tabloids with rumors of being "impotent with the opposite sex" and of "having slept with his mother," kidnapping the reporter in question, tying him to a chair, and asking, "Do you imply that I'm queer?" And then deliver this evolutionary rant:

You are privy to a great becoming, but you recognize nothing. To me, you are a slug in the sun. You are an ant in the afterbirth. It is your nature to do one thing correctly. Before me, you rightly tremble. But fear is not what you owe me. You owe me *awe!* [7]

Well, as we've seen, while John may have been born genetically superior, he still needs to withdraw from human society and undergo the "primitive" rites of the shamanic *Männerbund*, albeit alone, complete with mushrooms and stag hunting. The whole point of the queer powers he acquires, however, is to enable him to telepathically contact others of his kind, so as to create a real *Männerbund*.

---

[7] Like John's friend, the reporter is let loose to do his job, report, but only by being burned alive by the Tooth Fairy; John, however, lets his friend live, forcing him to leave the island before he destroys it in an inferno. We'll see that both harelips and being forced to become a serial killer through social pressure are shared by the Fairy and John's queer friends.

"At present I am looking for other people more or less like me, and to do it I become a sort of divided personality. Part of me remains where my body is, and behaves quite correctly, but the other, the essential I, goes off in search of *them*. Or if you like, I stay put all the time, but *reach out* in search of them. Anyhow, when I come back, or stop the search, I get a bit of a jolt, taking up the threads of ordinary life again."

"You never seem to *lose* the threads," I said.

"No," he answered, "The incoming 'I' comes slick into possession of all the past experiences of the residential one, so to speak. But the sudden jump from God knows where to here gives a bit of a jar, all the same."

What John acquires is the awareness of his Higher Consciousness, and the ability not only move from lower to higher and back again, but even to live as both, simultaneously. This experience has been a part of Western esoterica ever since Plotinus,[8] and, as I've noted before, we have our own home-grown and simplified version in the much reviled "New Thought" movement, most recently dumbed down yet further for Oprah's hordes. Prentice Mulford's *Thoughts are Things* provides an excellent summary:

> THERE belongs to every human being a higher self and a lower self — a self or mind of the spirit which has been growing for ages, and a self of the body, which is but a thing of yesterday. The higher self is full of prompting idea, suggestion and aspiration. This it receives of the Supreme Power. All this the lower or animal self regards as wild and visionary. *The higher self argues possibilities and power for us greater than men and women now possess and enjoy.* The lower self says we can only live and exist as men and women have lived and existed before us. The higher self craves freedom from the cumbrousness, the limita-

---

[8] See John N. Deck: *Nature, Contemplation, and the One: A Study in the Philosophy of Plotinus* (Toronto: University of Toronto Press, 1967; Reprinted: Burdett. N.Y.: Larson, 1991).

tions, the pains and disabilities of the body. The lower self says that we are born to them, born to ill, born to suffer, and must suffer as have so many before us. *The higher self wants a standard for right and wrong of its own.* The lower self says we must accept a standard made for us by others—by general and long-held opinion, belief and prejudice.⁹

In light of what we've said about New Thought, it's no surprise that such consciousness, in addition to plugging John into a sort of mental cyberspace allowing him to contact other such minds, past, present and future, also allows him to develop a control over matter that will give him access to a powerful source of fuel, if not exactly "super powers" *à la* Green Lantern.¹⁰ And, as we will see, it will provide John with his own standard of morality.

> By the spiritual mind is meant a clearer mental sight of *things and forces* existing both in us and the Universe, and of which the race for the most part has been in total ignorance.
>
> The higher mind or mind of the spirit *knows that it possesses other senses* akin to those of physical sight and hearing, but more powerful and far-reaching.¹¹

The first contact he makes with a *Homo superior* is, of course, in an insane asylum, and hey, look, it's our old pal Harry Partch!¹²

---

⁹ Chapter One. London: Bell and Sons, Ltd., 1908, and innumerable editions since.

¹⁰ See Chapter One, my "Green Nazis in Space," above.

¹¹ Loc. cit.

¹² See "Our Wagner, Only Better: Harry Partch, Wild Boy of American Music," reprinted in my collection *The Eldritch Evola . . . & Others* (San Francisco: Counter-Currents, 2014). Partch was, in fact, in London in late 1933, reading in the British Museum and later visiting Yeats, where they discussed his ideas for turning his King Oedipus into Partch's first theatre work.

He gave no trouble, they said, except that his health was very bad, and they had to nurse him a lot. He hardly ever spoke, and then only in *monosyllables*. He could understand simple remarks about matters within his ken, but it was often impossible to get him to attend to what was said to him. Yet oddly enough, he seemed to have a lively interest in everything happening around him. Sometimes he would *listen intently to people's voices; but not, apparently, for their significance, simply for their musical quality.*[13] He seemed to have an absorbing interest in perceived rhythms of all sorts. He would study the grain of a piece of wood, poring over it by the hour; or the ripples on a duckpond. *Most music, ordinary music invented by* Homo sapiens, *seemed at once to interest and outrage him*; though *when one of the doctors played a certain bit of Bach, he was gravely attentive, and afterwards went off to play* oddly twisted variants of it *on his* queer *pipe*. Certain *jazz tunes had such a violent effect on him* that after hearing one record he would sometimes be prostrate for days. *They seemed to tear him with some kind of conflict of delight and disgust.* Of course *the authorities regarded his own pipe-playing as the caterwauling of a lunatic.*

These are all recognizable Partch traits — the "monosyllables" refer to what he called "monophonic," his intent to unify voice and music, ideally with one instrument,[14] perhaps a "queer pipe." We also find the violent repulsion from and urge to revamp all music, from Bach to jazz.

And here is John's reaction to the music of those "queer pipes":

---

[13] As did Partch; see Bob Gilmore and Ben Johnston, "Harry Partch (1901–1974)," in Larry Sitsky, *Music of the Twentieth-Century Avant-Garde: A Biocritical Sourcebook* (Westport, Conn.: Greenwood, 2000), pp. 365–72.

[14] *Op. cit.*, and see Brian Harlan's dissertation, *One Voice: A Reconciliation of Harry Partch's Disparate Theories*, cited therein (and available online at Google Books).

"God! it was music," he said. "If you could have heard it! I mean if you could have *really* heard it, and not merely as a cow might! It was lucid. *It straightened out the tangles of my mind. It showed me just precisely the true, appropriate attitude of the adult human spirit to its world.* Well, he played on, and I went on listening, hanging on to every note, to remember it. Then the attendant interrupted. He said this sort of noise always upset the other patients. It wasn't as if it was real *music*, but such crazy stuff. That was why J. J. was really only allowed to play out of doors...."

This was precisely the case I made for Partch's music in my earlier article, that it was based on the Traditional, or true, theory of Music as involving the control and purification of the mind, or soul—straightening out the tangles, as opposed to the deliberate 'entangling' of tonal, and especially "Romantic" music[15]—and bringing them into true alignment with the universe. To do that requires a true, or real, system of notes, with all the so-called "overtones" (i.e., the tones arbitrarily ignored by equal temperament), and

"... yes, that's the starting-point, the very first moment, of what J. J. was working out in his music. If you could hold that always, and *fill it out with a whole world of overtones*, you'd be well on the way to 'us.'"[16]

Later, this will be the music of John's utopia, like Richard Halley at Galt's Gulch. "Presently Tsomotre, the neckless Tibetan, moved to *a sort of harpsichord, tuned to the strange intervals which the islanders enjoyed.*" Like Partch, the islanders have de-

---

[15] "Beethoven managed to put an end to this noble tradition by inaugurating a barbaric U-turn away from an other-directed music to an inward-directed, narcissistic focus on the composer himself and his own tortured soul." See Dylan Evans, "Beethoven was a narcissistic hooligan" in *The Guardian*, June 7, 2005.

[16] "To burn always with this hard, gem-like flame, to maintain this ecstasy, is success in life." —Walter Pater "Conclusion" to *Studies in the History of the Renaissance* (1873).

vised their own instruments, tuned to the natural scale. "He played. *To me his music was indescribably unpleasant. I could have screamed, or howled like a dog.* When he had done, a faint involuntary murmur from several throats seemed to indicate deep approval." True to John's nickname for him, "Fido" can only howl; an all too typical response to a Partch concert!

Partch also insisted that dance and theatre all be present — monophonic! One voice! Integrity! — and so we have a performance not unlike Partch's *Daphne of the Dunes*.

> Shahîn rose from his seat, looking with keen inquiry at Lo, who hesitated, then also rose. Tsomotre began playing once more, tentatively. Lo, meanwhile, had opened a huge chest, and after a brief search she took from it a folded cloth, which when she had shaken it out was revealed as an ample and undulatory length of silk, striped in many colours. This she wrapped around her. The music once more took definite form. Lo and Shahîn glided into a solemn dance, which quickened presently to a storm of wild movement. The silk whirled and floated, revealing the tawny limbs of Lo; or was gathered about her with pride and disdain. Shahîn leapt hither and thither around her, pressed toward her, was rejected, half accepted, spurned again. Now and then came moments of frank sexual contact, stylized and knit into the movement-pattern of the dance. The end suggested to me that the two lovers, now clinging together, were being engulfed in some huge catastrophe. They glanced hither and thither, above, below, with expressions of horror and exaltation, and at one another with gleams of triumph. They seemed to thrust some invisible assailant from them, but less and less effectively, till gradually they sank together to the ground. Suddenly they sprang up and apart to perform slow marionette-like antics which meant nothing to me. The music stopped, and the dance. As she returned to her seat, Lo flashed a questioning, taunting look at John.

Not that any of this makes an impression on our hapless narrator, the appropriately nick-named "Fido":

Later, when I had described this incident in my notes, I showed my account of it to Lo. When she had glanced at it, she said, "But you have missed the point, you old stupid. You've made it into a love story. Of course, what you say is all right—but it's all wrong too, you poor dear."

But let's go back a bit to that "the true, appropriate attitude of the adult human spirit to its world" that J. J.'s music is supposed to inculcate, to which John's colleagues give a "faint involuntary murmur" that "seemed to indicate deep approval." This must be an actual doctrine, or better, account of, the nature of the *Homo superior*'s consciousness, what he sees with that Higher Mind of his. This will require us to first take another look at the encounter with Mr. Magnate, and then jump back to John's next encounter, with what I'll call "Spider Baby."

> Of course, [John] was always either far too brilliant or far too ignorant of life *to play his part* in anything like a normal manner; Mr. Magnate shifted in his seat, but *continued to look his part*.

And here's John describing his encounter with the vapid intellectuals of Bloomsbury:

> The poor little flies find *themselves caught in a web*, a subtle mesh of convention, so subtle in fact that most of them are unaware of it. They buzz and buzz and imagine they are free fliers, when as a matter of *fact each one is stuck fast on his particular strand of the web*.
> This analysis made me feel uncomfortable, for though I was not one of "them" I could not disguise from myself that the same sort of condemnation might apply to me. John evidently saw my thoughts, for he grinned, and moreover indulged in an entirely vulgar wink. Then he said, "Strikes home, old thing, doesn't it? Never mind, *you're not in the web*. You're an outsider. *Fate has kept you safely fluttering* in the backward North."

John's alienation and objectivity, and his precocious, Magic

Christian-like encounters with various social strata and professions, allow him to perceive humans as merely playing roles, within the inter-connected web of the universe. His later shamanic experiences—remember the mushrooms?—would only confirm this insight.[17]

He gets a powerful, negative confirmation with his next encounter, with a deformed, infant-like child whose super-intellect has soured into pure hatred:

> He hated everything, including hate. And he hated it all with a sort of sacred fervour. And why? Because, as I begin to discover, there's a sort of minute, blazing star of *worship* [Stapledon's italics] right down in the pit of his hell. He sees everything from the side of eternity just as clearly as I do, perhaps more clearly; but—how shall I put it?—*he conceives his part in the picture* to be the devil's part, and *he's playing it with a combination of passion and detachment like a great artist, and for the glory of God*, if you understand what I mean.[18] And he's right. It's the only thing he *can* do, and he does it with style. I take off my hat to him, in spite of everything. But it's pretty ghastly, really.

All this sounds remarkably like Alan Watts' description of "the real story" to be found in Hinduism or Zen, or indeed the "secret" Western traditions,[19] and confirmed in mystical experience:

---

[17] For the ancient symbolism of the web, or the puppet, and its counterpart in entheogenic drug experience, see the section on Block-Universe Determinism at Michael Hoffman's website egodeath.com. See also the literature cited in my "The Corner at the Center of the World," reprinted in *Aristokratia I* and *The Eldritch Evola . . . & Others*.

[18] Just as in *Manhunter*, the Tooth Fairy has been "made into a monster" by years of abuse as a deformed outsider, and now identifies himself with Blake's engraving of the great Red Dragon.

[19] See almost any of his books, but especially *Beyond Theology: The Art of Godmanship* (New York: Pantheon, 1964) and "Remembering Alan Watts: January 6, 1915 to November 16, 1973" by Greg Johnson, http://www.counter-currents.com/2011/01/remembering-alan-watts/

So then, here is the drama: My metaphysics, let me be perfectly frank with you, are that there is the central self, you can call it god you can call it anything you like and it's all of us. It's playing all the parts of all the beings whatsoever, anywhere and everywhere and it's playing a game of hide and seek with itself. It gets lost, it gets involved in most far out adventures, but in the end it always finds a way back to itself.[20]

But especially of his way of shoe-horning Christianity into it, as "the most far-out game of them all":

The insides of most Protestant churches resemble courthouses or town halls, and the focal point of their services is a serious exhortation from a man in a black gown. No golden light, no bells, incense, and candles. No mystery upon an altar or behind an iconostasis. But people brought up in this atmosphere seem to love it. It feels warm and folksy, and leads, on the one hand, to hospitals, prison reform, and votes for all, and, on the other, to sheer genius for drabness, plain cooking ungraced with wine, and constipation of the bright emotions—all of which are considered virtues.

If I try to set aside the innate prejudices which I feel against this religion, I begin to marvel at the depth of its commitment to earnestness and ugliness. *For there is a point at which certain types of ugliness become fascinating, where one feels drawn to going over them again and again, much as the tongue keeps fondling a hole in a tooth.* I begin to realize that those incredibly plain people, with their almost unique lack of color, may after all be one of the most astonishing reaches of the divine Maya—the Dancer of the world as far out from himself as he can get, dancing not-dancing.[21]

The "true attitude to life," the sight from the eternal side of

---

[20] Alan Watts, "The Way of Waking Up," http://karmajello.com/mind-spirit/philosophy/alan-watts-way-of-waking-up.html%20/%20_

[21] *Beyond Theology*, Chapter Two, "Is It Serious?"

things, is that of a vast cosmic web; one can in some moods find this comforting; in others, it is the nightmare vision of 'being caught in a web,' or of total determinism. John and his kind, like Watts, seem to find it to be the former.[22]

Watts' notion of "fascinating ugliness" leads us to another important theme: the disquieting or even repulsive "beauty" of John and his kind. Here is Jacqueline:

> But though passably 'human,' according to the standards of *Homo sapiens*, she was strange. Were I an imaginative writer, and not merely a journalist, I might be able to suggest symbolically something of the almost "creepy" effect she had on me, something of its remote and sleepy power. As it is I can only record certain obvious features, and in general that curious combination of the infantile, or even the foetal, with the mature. The protruding brow, the short broad nose, the great distance between the great eyes, the surprising breadth of the whole face, the marked furrow from nose to lips—all these characters were definitely foetal; and yet the precisely chiselled lips themselves and the delicate moulding of the eyelids produced an expression of subtle experience suggestive of an ageless divinity. To me at least, prepared of course by familiarity with John's own strangeness, this strange face seemed to combine idiosyncrasy and universality. Here, in spite of a vaguely repulsive uncouthness, was *a living symbol of womanhood*. Yet here also was a being utterly different from any other, something unique and individual. *When I looked from her to the most attractive girl in the room I was shocked to find that it was the normal beauty that was repulsive. With something like*

---

[22] Watts once lectured at Harvard and invited B. F. Skinner to reply to his idea that Skinner's idea of total control by the environment was depressing only if one assumed, as Christians seem to do, that one was an alien creature trapped in this web, rather than the web and you being part of one, self-determining entity; Skinner supposedly never bothered to show up. See *In My Own Way: An Autobiography, 1915-1965* (New York: Pantheon, 1972), pp. 328-30; more generally, "Zen and the Problem of Control" reprinted in *This is It* (New York: Pantheon, 1960).

vertigo I looked once more at the adorable grotesque.

Jacqueline, unlike J. J. and, in fact, most of John's contactees[23] has found a kind of *modus vivendi*:

> Of course she gave herself for money, like any member of her profession, or of any other profession. Nevertheless, her heart was in her work, and she chose her clients, not according to their power to pay, but according to their needs and their capacity to benefit by her ministrations. She seems to have combined in her person the functions of harlot, psycho-analyst and priest.

This harks back to an old social character, the literate, free-spirited, delightfully risqué (if you go for that kind of thing)[24] salon hostess of the French Enlightenment. Hence, her age, although her large eyes and short hair make her resemble a more recent, less intellectual type, the *gamine, à la* Gigi — she even has an elderly, crusty companion — actually her daughter! — for Hermione Gingold to play. The very American version would be the decidedly anti-intellectual and thoroughly mercenary Holly Golightly. (Capote hated the film in which Audrey Hepburn played her as Gigi.) She also seems to be what lot of modern, college educated prostitutes — or "sex workers" — like to think of themselves as: sort of a hands-on psychotherapist.[25]

Ng-Gunko, John's next contact, also connects with the idea of conventional ugliness becoming a higher kind of beauty,

---

[23] "Save for these, John found nothing but lunatics, cripples, invalids, and inveterate old vagabonds in whom the superior mentality had been hopelessly distorted by contact with the normal species."

[24] As did Jon Lovitz's *SNL* character with his "Tales of Ribaldry."

[25] James Neill notes, *op. cit.*, that the "sacred prostitute" is a typically 'queer' role. One thinks of that typical '90s figure, Terence Sellers, with her criminology degree and weakness for the worst of Huysman's style; her Krafft-Ebbing meets Jack Kerouac pastiche, *The Correct Sadist* (New York: Grove, 1985), compares favorably to Xaviera Hollander's '70s Penthouse Letters-style books, but already seemed dated by the inevitable *Correct Sadist 2: Dungeon Evidence* (The Tears Corporation/Creation, 1997).

through the suggestion of higher realms or dimensions. As Guénon would point out, symbols need to be read inverted — terrestrial ugliness coming celestial beauty, and vice versa.[26]

---

[26] I have alluded to this phenomenon in my essay "From Ultrasuede to Limelight: Aryan Entrepreneurs in the Dark Age" below, in reference to "Anjelica Huston, an actual Halston model whose . . . equally . . . unusual . . . features suggest a beauty that dwells on other planes than ours; superhuman rather than subhuman, elfin rather than bestial." We now have Ms. Huston's own view of the matter: "My earliest impression of great beauty was of blondes with pale eyes, but I realized at a young age that I wouldn't look that way. I was disappointed, but I knew I had to do something with what I had — long legs . . . a chameleon's ability to make myself interesting-looking or plain. Beauty is malleable" (*A Story Lately Told: Coming of Age in Ireland, London and New York* [New York: Scribner's, 2013]).

And consider as well the unmistakable mutant charm of Linda Blair:

> It's worth remembering that, even in the lowliest slasher flick, filmmakers and casting directors in this none-more-patriarchal industry are predisposed to seek out the girls who are flawless and beautiful and charismatic and able to act with, at least, a competent, easily digestible proficiency. Which is not to say that Linda Blair lacks any of those virtues of course, but *we're so used to seeing women on-screen who exemplify this slightly stultifying 'actress ideal' that when someone like Linda, who'd probably get dropped at the first round of auditions for a leading lady role for just being a bit odd lookin', a bit stroppy, a bit UN-actresslike, is able to pull rank based on her childhood notoriety and stomp commandingly across our screens. . . . well it's just a plain beautiful thing to see,* making the grown up Linda (kinda — she was eighteen circa 'Exorcist II') a truly distinctive screen presence. (http://breakfastintheruins.blogspot.co.uk/2010/05/vhs-purgatory-exorcist-ii-heretic-john.html)

And of course, it sometimes works both ways; this aside on bad film legend Ray Dennis Steckler from the same site sounds like it could come out of *Odd John* itself:

> Man, I love this guy so much. I know it's a redundant and cruel thing to say, but *he's just so weird looking.* Every time he's on

He was a grotesque and filthy little blackamoor, and I resented the prospect of sharing accommodation with him. He appeared to be about eight years old, but was in fact over twelve. He wore a long, blue and very grubby caftan and a battered fez. These clothes, we subsequently learned, he had acquired on his journey, in order to attract less attention. But he could not help attracting attention. My own first reaction to his appearance was frank incredulity. "There ain't no such beast," I said to myself. Then I remembered, that, when a species mutates, it often produces a large crop of characters so fantastic that many of the new types are not even viable. Ng-Gunko was decidedly viable, but he was a freak. Though his face was a dark blend of the negroid and the semitic with an unmistakable reminiscence of the Mongolian, his negroid wool was not black but sombre red. And though his right eye was a huge black orb not inappropriate to his dark complexion,

---

screen, it blows my mind. I don't think I've ever seen a human being who looks, or moves, quite the way he does in my whole life. Was Ray Dennis Steckler born somewhere? Did he have a childhood? I'd prefer to think he just walked outta the woods one day, the emissary of a higher race. (http://breakfastintheruins.blogspot.com/search/label/Ray%20Dennis%20Steckler)

And this is in a review of *Wild Guitar*, which features "Bud Eagle, a naïve would-be teen idol played with *boggle-eyed, thug-faced grace* by mighty-quiffed Arch Hall, Jr." Of course, things aren't entirely that simple, and I feel I must insert a warning here, lest anyone think of improving their chances on the dating scene by pulling a Gary Busey on their face. For example, although featuring Meg Foster, herself an excellent example, she's a human collaborator but still human; *They Live* itself contains many more of the wrong kind of alien-ugly:

NADA: You see, I take these glasses off, she looks like a regular person, doesn't she? Put 'em back on . . . [puts them back on] formaldehyde-face!
NADA: That's like pouring perfume on a pig.
NADA: You know, you look like your head fell in the cheese dip back in 1957.
RICH LADY: [into her wristwatch] I've got one that can see!

his left eye was considerably smaller, and the iris was deep blue. These discrepancies gave his whole face a sinister comicality which was borne out by his expression. His full lips were frequently stretched in a grin which revealed three small white teeth above and one below. The rest had apparently not yet sprouted.

Here is John meditating on beauty, during his initiatory period, making some typically disturbing connections:

> From the bottom of his heart he gave thanks for all these subtle contacts with material reality; and found in them a spiritual refreshment which we also find, though confusedly and grudgingly. He was also constantly, and ever surprisingly, illuminated by the beauty of the beasts and birds on which he preyed, *a beauty significant of their power and their frailty, their vitality and their obtuseness.* Such perceived organic forms seem to have moved him far more deeply than I could comprehend. The stag, in particular, that he had killed and devoured, and now daily used, *seems to have had some deep symbolism for him which I could but dimly appreciate,* and will not attempt to describe. I remember his exclaiming, "How I knew him and praised him! And his death was his life's crown."
>
> And suddenly the stag seemed to symbolize the whole normal human species, as a thing with a great beauty and dignity of its own, and a rightness of its own, so long as it was not put into situations too difficult for it. *Homo sapiens,* poor thing, *had* floundered into a situation too difficult for him, namely the present world-situation. The thought of *Homo sapiens* trying to run a mechanized civilization suddenly seemed to him as ludicrous and pathetic as the thought of a stag in the driving-seat of a motor-car.
>
> He himself said that his "discovery of sheer evil" had fortified him. When I asked, "how fortified?" he said, "My dear, it is a great strength to have faced the worst and to have *felt* it a feature of beauty. Nothing ever after can shake one."

And here is another contactee:

> Jelli, a mite said to be seventeen years old. She was no beauty. The frontal and the occipital regions of her head were repulsively over-developed, so that the back of her head stretched away behind her, and her brow protruded beyond her nose, which was rudimentary. In profile her head suggested a croquet mallet. She had a hare-lip and short bandy legs. Her general appearance was that of a cretin; yet she had supernormal intelligence and temperament, and also hyper-sensitive vision.

Most all of John's contactees are physical freaks of some sort, although many seem to sorta grow on one.

> When at last the time came for the visitors to leave the island, I noticed that . . . some who had formerly looked at the young women with disapproval or lust or both, now bade them farewell with friendly courtesy, and *with some appreciation of their uncouth beauty*.

Beautiful or not, the *Homo superior* is known by his smile.[27]

> John's eyes were indeed, according to ordinary standards, much too big for his face, which acquired thus a strangely cat-like or falcon-like expression. This was emphasized by the low and level eyebrows, but often completely abolished by a thoroughly boyish and even mischievous smile.
>
> In the end, however, she [his mother] nearly always adopted John's improvement, with an odd little smile which might equally well have meant maternal pride or indulgence.
>
> John's lips compressed themselves and assumed *a crooked smile*. "You're right," he said. "There's just one possibility that I have not mentioned. If the species as a whole,

---

[27] "Mentats, the human computers; know a Mentat by his red stained lips." —Frank Herbert, *Dune*.

or a large proportion of the world population, were to be divinely inspired, so that their nature became truly human at a stride, all would soon be well."

"Then," said McWhist, "an odd thing happened. The boy's anger seemed to vanish, and he stared intently at me as though I were a strange beast that he had never seen before. Suddenly he seemed to think of something else. He dropped his weapon, and began gazing into the lire again with that look of utter misery. Tears welled in his eyes again. *His mouth twisted itself in a kind of desperate smile.*"

"He stayed still for perhaps half a minute, and silent; then, looking down at us, *he smiled*, and said, 'Don't forget. We have looked at the stars together.' Then he gently lowered the rock into position again, and said, 'I think you had better go now. I'll take you down the first pitch. It's difficult by night.' As we were both pretty well paralysed with bewilderment we made no immediate sign of quitting. *He laughed, gently, reassuringly*, and said something that has haunted me ever since. (I don't know about McWhist.) He said, 'It was a childish miracle. But I am still a child. While the spirit is in the agony of outgrowing its childishness, it may solace itself now and then by returning to its playthings, knowing well that they are trivial.' By now we were creeping out of the cave, and into the blizzard."

At the end he could hardly lift his hands with fatigue, and they were covered with bleeding blisters. But the deed was accomplished. The hunters of all the ages saluted him, for he had done what none of them could have done. *A child, he had gone naked into the wilderness and conquered it*. And *the angels of heaven smiled at him*, and beckoned him to a higher adventure.

Presently James Jones, keeping his eyes on mine, said one word, with quiet emphasis and some surprise, 'Friend!' *I smiled and nodded*. . . . The attendant put the pipe into his hand, closing the fingers over it. He looked blankly at it. Then with *a sudden smile of enlightenment* he put it to his ear, like a child listening to a shell. . . . "The music stopped with a squawk. J. J. looked *with a kindly but tortured smile* at the attendant. Then he slid back into insanity. So complete was his disintegration that he actually tried to eat the mouthpiece."

All these smiles[28] will make for an interesting connection soon, especially their intensification, the Grin (an evil counterpart, like Spider Baby), perhaps busting out into outright laughter:

> John too was a changed being. *His lips were drawn back in an inhuman blend of snarl and smile*. One eye was half closed from Stephen's only successful blow, the other cavernous like the eye of a mask. For when John was enraged, the iris drew almost entirely out of sight.
> He gave a start and a shudder, looked at me with a frown, as if trying to get things straight in his mind, *made a quick movement for the stiletto, checked himself, and finally broke into a wry boyish grin*, remarking, 'Oh, come in, please. Don't knock, it's a shop.' He added, 'Can't you blighters leave a fellow alone?'
> "Then tell me," I said, perhaps rather excitedly, "what *is* the goal, the true life of the spirit?" *John suddenly grinned like a boy of ten, and laughed that damnably disturbing laugh of his*, "I'm afraid I can't tell you, Mr. Journalist," he said, "It is time your interview was concluded."

John is understandably freaked out when Spider Baby turns it on him: "The very sight of the house in the distance gave me the creeps. I couldn't think. *I kept seeing that infantile grin of hate*, and turning stupid again."

Even his eventual companion Ng-Gunko grins creepily:

---

[28] Mulford would have approved: "Thousands live too much in the thought current of seriousness. Faces which wear a smiling expression are scarce. Some never smile at all. Some have forgotten how to smile, and it actually hurts them to smile, or to see others do so." *Thoughts are Thing*, p. 41.

These discrepancies gave his whole face a sinister comicality which was borne out by his expression. *His full lips were frequently stretched in a grin which revealed three small white teeth above and one below.*

Then, projecting his chin above his scarf, he would whip off his glasses and *assume a maniacal grin of hate.*

The last grin belongs to John, however, and like the first signals boyish triumph: "Then one day, grinning with pride and excitement, he summoned the whole company to the laboratory and gave a full account of his work."

And consider this extended meditation:

He looked at me for some seconds in silence, Believe it or not, but that prolonged gaze had a really terrifying effect on me. I am not suggesting that there was something magical about it. The effect was of the same kind as any normal facial expression may have. But knowing John as I did, and remembering the strange events of his summer in Scotland, I was no doubt peculiarly susceptible. I can only describe what I felt by means of an image. It was as though I was confronted with a mask made of some semitransparent substance, and illuminated from within by a different and a *spiritually luminous* face. The mask was that of a grotesque child, half monkey, half gargoyle, yet wholly urchin, with its huge cat's eyes, its flat little nose, its teasing lips. The inner face,—obviously it cannot be described, for it was *the same* in every feature, yet wholly different. I can only say that it seemed to me to combine *the august and frozen smile* of a Buddha with the peculiar creepy grimness that the battered Sphinx can radiate when the dawn first touches its face.[29] No, these images fail ut-

---

[29] One thinks of similar meditations on shape shifting, luminous faces in Hesse, especially in *Demian* or this from *Siddhartha*: "And over everything something thin, inessential yet existing, was continuously drawn, like thin glass or ice, like a transparent skin, a sheath or mold or mask of water. The mask was smiling, and the mask was Siddhartha's smiling face. . . . Thus Govinda saw the smile of the mask, the smile of

terly. I cannot describe the symbolical intention that John's features forced upon me in those seconds. I can only say that I longed to look away and could not, or dared not. Irrational terror welled up in me. When one is under the dentist's drill, one may endure a few moments of real torture without flinching. But as the seconds pile up, it becomes increasingly difficult not to move, not to scream. And so with me, looked at by John. With this difference, that I was bound, and could not stir, that I had passed the screaming point and could not scream. I believe my terror was largely *a wild dread* that John was about to laugh, *and that his laugh would annihilate me*. But he did not laugh.

Before explicating those smiles, let's ask ourselves why John wants to contact, and indeed bring together, all these fellow mutants. Once more, our old Yankee philosopher has the answer:

> If thought was visible to the physical eye we should see its currents flowing to and from people. We should see that persons similar in temperament, character and motive are in the same literal current of thought. . . . [E]ach one in such moods serves as an additional battery or generator of such thought and is strengthening that particular current.
> The more minds so working in the same vein, the quicker came the desired result.[30]

John and his fellow freaks use their advanced mental powers to find an uncharted island, create a source of unlimited power, repel the curious and dangerous outsiders, and devote themselves at first to eugenic experiments, then, when the outsiders become too insistent, to their most important activity, group meditation. A utopia, in short.

---

unity over the flowing forms, the smile of simultaneity over the myriad births and deaths. The smile was exactly the same, resembled exactly the still, refined, imperetrable, perhaps-kind-perhaps-disdainful, wise, thousandfold smile of Gotama the Buddha. . . . So Govinda knew, this is the way the Perfect One smiles."

[30] *Thoughts are Things*, pp. 33, 38.

And why? Well, because their super-intellects just happen to have informed them that *homo sapiens* is through, finished, washed-up, out of time. John once again appropriates Harry Partch's condemnation of modern Western music for a metaphor embodying our epitaph:

"Well, if we could wipe out your whole species, frankly, we would. For if your species discovers us, and realizes at all what we are, it will certainly destroy us. And we know, you must remember, that *Homo sapiens* has *little more to contribute to the music of this planet, nothing in fact but vain repetition. It is time for finer instruments to take up the theme.*"

Bitter music indeed, for *Homo sap.*[31] Let's cheer ourselves up by going back to all that smiling.

It may seem like a trivial point—but will prove quite otherwise—but smiling is one of several links to more recent work, the "queer utopia"[32] of William S. Burroughs' *The Wild Boys*.

Now, while Burroughs' utopia is certainly "queer" in the modern sense, we've seen that John and his group are repeatedly described or associated with the "queer" in the sense of strange or uncanny, a different species in effect while at the same time comprising both genders and all the various shades of what James Neill has called human "ambisexuality." However tempting it may be for today's "queer theorists," Burroughs' utopia should also be seen in the same inclusive way:

Burroughs has never demanded the subordination of the feminine to the masculine, as many heterosexual male chauvinists have; he has argued, rather, for the total sepa-

---

[31] Harry Partch, *Bitter Music: Collected Journals, Essays, Introductions, and Librettos*, ed. Thomas McGeary (Urbana: University of Illinois Press, 2000).

[32] James Grauerholz gives this as the title of the relevant section of *Word Virus: The William S. Burroughs Reader*, ed. James Grauerholz and Ira Silverberg (New York: Grove Press, 2000). See also Jamie Russell's *Queer Burroughs* (New York: Palgrave MacMillan, 2001) which discusses his "queertopias."

ration of the masculine from the feminine, as befits his theory that men and women *are actually separate species that cannot be united under the rubric of an expanded, and therefore abstracted, definition of "humanity."* In light of this, it seems more fruitful to view the project of *The Wild Boys* not simply as "the occlusion of women" but as an attempt to take sexual difference as a point of departure for political transformation, rather than seeing it as a problem to be overcome. Though his own viewpoint is unrepentantly androcentric, Burroughs said at that time that "I certainly have no objections if lesbians would like to do the same" from a gynocentric point of view. (Burroughs, *Rolling Stone* Interview, p. 52.)[33]

"Queer theorists" will also be disappointed that Burroughs does not indulge in the cult of the Beautiful Boy.[34] Like John's colonists, the Wild Boys are hard on the eyes, starting with Audrey, described by neighbors as "looking like a sheep-killing dog," to, in the last chapter, the boy we spend the most time getting to know, presumably typical, known as The Dib: "His face had been beautiful at some other time and place now broken and twisted by altered pressure, the teeth stuck out at angles the features wrenched out of focus body emaciated by distant hungers" (WB p. 172). A veritable Ng-Gunko, complete with jellaba and fez.

We'll get back to those teeth, but let's note that the colonists, of both genders, share these emaciated bodies that they do

---

[33] Timothy J. Murphy, Wising Up the Marks: The Amodern William Burroughs (Berkeley: University of California Press, 1998), p. 147. Cf. Alain De Benoist: "I am not against feminism. There is a good kind of feminism, which I call identitarian feminism, which tries to promote feminine values and show that they are not inferior to masculine values." The *American Renaissance* Interview, http://www.amren.com/features/2013/11/we-are-the-end-of-something/

[34] Perhaps because Burroughs associates physical attractiveness with reproduction? Is it a coincidence that the chief modern theorists of The Boy are Camille Paglia, "The Beautiful Boy as Destroyer" in *Sexual Personae* (New Haven: Yale, 1990) and Germaine Greer, *The Beautiful Boy* (New York: Rizzoli, 2003)?

nothing to hide:

> As soon as my baggage and some cases of books and stores had been transhipped in the *Skid's* dinghy, we got under way. Ng-Gunko and Kemi promptly divested themselves of their clothes, for it was a hot day. Kemi's fair skin had been burnt to the colour of the teak woodwork of the *Skid*.
> Looking at the *slight naked figures of various shades* from Ng-Gunko's nigger-brown to Sigrid's rich cream, all seated round the table and munching *with the heartiness of a school treat*, I felt that I had strayed into an island of goblins.
> The invaders were fluttered by the sight of naked young women, several of whom were of the white race.
> [John] was an uncouth but imposing figure, with his dazzling white hair, his *eyes of a nocturnal beast*, and his *lean body*. Behind him the others waited, a group of unclad boys and girls with formidable heads. One of the *Viking's* officers was heard to exclaim, "Jesus Christ! What a troupe!"

A pack of Wild Boys indeed. The Dib explains the rugged practicality here: "'Clothes no good here. Easy see clothes. Very hard see this.' He pointed to his thin body" (WB, pp. 175-76).

Just as John's colonists are biological freaks (born this way, as Lady Gaga would say), the Wild Boys are at least partially made that way, again for practical reasons; as Murphy expounds:

> "Each group developed special skills and knowledge until it *evolved into humanoid subspecies*" (WB, p. 147), like the Warrior Ants, handless boys who screw steel implements into their stumps; cat boys who wear poison-clawed gloves; Snake boys, who handle (and *even become*) *venomous reptiles*; and lycanthropic wolf boys. Other boys deterritorialize themselves through technology, attaching themselves to gliders, roller-skates, and other weapons systems in order to battle the state apparatus (WB, pp. 147–48, 150–

54). . . . Burroughs calls these Wild Boys "biologic adaptives" (Burroughs, *Port of Saints* 101).

We'll soo get back to that "biological adaptive" bit.

The Warrior Ants remind us that the colonists are good with knives: "Fortunately Shahîn wore a sheath-knife . . ."[35] As was John in his (wild) boyhood:

> He sprang into a crouching posture, clutching a sort of stiletto made of the largest tine of an antler. McWhist was so startled by the *huge glaring eyes and the inhuman snarl* that he backed out of the cramping entrance of the cave. . . . . He gave a start and a shudder, looked at me with a frown, as if trying to get things straight in his mind, *made a quick movement for the stiletto*, checked himself, and finally *broke into a wry boyish grin*, remarking, 'Oh, come in, please. Don't knock, it's a shop.' He added, 'Can't you blighters leave a fellow alone?'

Boyish indeed. We're back in the *Stalky & Co., Boy's Own Mag* world Burroughs would mine for both *Wild Boys* and his *Dead*

---

[35] David Bowie had already noted the connection between Stapledon's "*Homo superior*" and Burroughs' Wild Boys, along with spiders and knives: "It was the era of *Wild Boys*, by William S. Burroughs. That was a really heavy book that had come out in about 1970, and it was a cross between that and *Clockwork Orange* that really started to put together the shape and the look of what Ziggy and the Spiders were going to become. They were both powerful pieces of work, especially the marauding boy gangs of Burroughs' *Wild Boys* with their bowie knives. I got straight on to that. I read everything into everything. Everything had to be infinitely symbolic." David Sinclair, "Station to Station," *Rolling Stone*, June 10, 1993. When Bowie met Burroughs in 1974, at *Rolling Stone*'s behest, he claimed "No, I didn't know that was their weapon. The name Bowie just appealed to me when I was younger. I was into a kind of heavy philosophy thing when I was 16 years old, and I wanted a truism about cutting through the lies and all that." I suppose at some point Burroughs must have pointed out to the former David Jones that actually it's "boo-ie" not "bow-ie" ("Beat Godfather Meets Glitter Mainman," *Rolling Stone*, February 28, 1974).

Roads Trilogy.

> In *The Wild Boys,* the image of a smiling wild boy becomes a hugely popular media icon which spreads the wild-boy virus across civilisation, causing more and more youths to join the wild boys.[36]

> Tío Mate, the Chief, and Old Sarge—the antiauthoritarian figures of the first three routines [i.e., chapters]—share with the Wild Boys *a peculiarly beatific way of smiling*; indeed, the chapter's titles and closing lines draw attention to it. Skerl sees in these smiles "that invite comparison with the smile of Dante's Beatrice and of the Mona Lisa—two hallowed female icons that embody traditional Western values" evidence that the Wild Boys and their allies "exist in a state of ecstasy" (Skerl 83). Perhaps, *like Beatrice, the Wild Boys are to be our guides to/through the lands of the dead*; perhaps as well, like Dante, we will not be subject to any of the perils and delights to be found there—but perhaps we will. At any rate, the smiles of the Wild Boys and of the characters who anticipate them do not bode well for those "traditional Western values."[37]

The smiles are not only advertising and recruitment devices, they are weapons as well. We'll explore those odd and interconnected features in a bit. For now, let's note that while smiling a lot, the colonists don't talk much at all, which just adds to their creepiness.

> One of the most disconcerting features of life on the island was that much of the conversation of the colonists was carried on telepathically. So far as I could judge, vocal speech was in process of atrophy. The younger members still used it as the normal means of communication, and even among the elders it was often indulged in for its own

---

[36] Phil Hine, "Zimbu Xototl Time," http://www.philhine.org.uk/writings/flsh_zimbu.html

[37] Murphy, *op. cit.*, p.161.

sake, much as we may prefer to walk rather than take a bus. . . . . Speech was but an obbligato to the real theme. Serious discussion was always carried on telepathically and in silence. Sometimes, however, emotional stress would give rise to speech as a spontaneous but unconsidered accompaniment of telepathic discourse. In these circumstances vocal activity tended to be blurred and fragmentary like the speech of a sleeper. *Such mutterings were rather frightening to one who could not enter into the telepathic conversation.* At first, by the way, *I had been irrationally disturbed whenever a group of the islanders, working in silence in the garden or elsewhere, suddenly began to laugh for no apparent reason though actually in response to some telepathic jest.* In time I came to accept these oddities without the "nervy" creepiness which they used to arouse in me.

As for the Wild Boys, "What unifies their agenda is the refusal of *talk*, of representation in the form of religious belief ('priest talk') and social or political ideology ('mother talk, father talk . . . country talk *or* party talk')" (Murphy, p. 164).

"Fido" the narrator was right to be concerned:

The Wild Boys themselves do not speak much, and when they do, they speak in performatives, like the lies they tell to lead the American forces sent against them into a trap in the desert. . . . They use the representational structure of the socius against itself by sending out false calls for help to police units and by impersonating the police themselves to undermine their authority;

Just as the colonists psychically brainwash intruders into madness or suicide, or simply to make false reports, the absurdity of which lead to their public disgrace.

The Wild Boys do not demonstrate or denounce; *they simply seduce and destroy*, leaving others to explain their work.

John: "You will laugh when I tell you I want you to come and use your journalistic prowess upon us. In fact I want you to write that threatened biography after all, not for our sakes but for your own species."

This is consistent with the imperative to forget rather than to consolidate power. Even their methods are parodies of representation, based as they are on Burroughs's viral theories of language: they kill by spreading "trained killer viruses" (WB 133), literally *contagious forms of laughter,* sneezing, hiccuping, and coughing that render their victims helpless and defenseless before the Wild Boys' killer legions. (Murphy, pp. 165-67)

Remember this odd freak-out from John's biographer? "I had passed the screaming point and could not scream. I believe my terror was largely *a wild dread* that John was about to laugh, and that *his laugh would annihilate me.*"

Since, as we've suggested, the two utopias, one of genetic sports and the other of runaway boys, can be linked by their mutual "queerness," it's no surprise that both manifest an intense interest in eugenics. John's colony is a kind of cross-breed of Huxley's dystopia *Brave New World* (from near-contemporary 1932) and his later Buddhist utopia, *Island* (1962), as if the one's Savage had run away to an island, taking Our Ford's technology with him and combining it with his native religion:

I was shown a series of thirty-eight living human embryos, each in its own incubator. These startled me considerably, but the story of their conception and capture startled me even more. Indeed, it filled me with horror, and with violent though short-lived moral indignation. The eldest of these embryos was three months old. Its father, I was told, was Shahîn, its mother a native of the Tuamotu Archipelago. The unfortunate girl had been seduced, brought to the island, operated upon, and killed while still under the anaesthetic. The more recent specimens, however, had been secured by milder methods, for Lo had invented a technique by which the fertilized ovum could be secured without violence to the mother. In all the more recent cases the mothers had yielded up their treasure unwittingly, and without leaving their native islands. They were merely persuaded to agree to comply with certain instructions given by the supernormal father. The technique apparently combined physical and psychical methods, and was imposed upon the girls as a sublime religious ritual.

We note the casual use of human material, which will come up again. Burroughs' approach, oddly enough, is far more genteel; apart from their smiling recruitment posters and other means of seducing the young, the Wild Boys make use of black market surrogates—presumably no more involuntary than any other transaction in the "corrupt border towns" (WB, 153-54)—cloning themselves, and ultimately, purely mental power:

> A boy with Mongoloid features steps onto the rug playing a flute to the four directions. As he plays phantom figures swirl around him taking shape out of moonlight, campfires and shadows. He kneels in the center of the rug playing his flute faster and faster. The shape of a boy on hands and knees is forming in front of him. He puts down his flute. His hands mold and knead the body in front of him pulling it against him with stroking movements that penetrate the pearly grey shape caressing it inside. The body shudders and quivers against him as he forms the buttocks around his penis stroking silver genitals out of the moonlight grey then pink and finally red the mouth parted in a gasp shuddering genitals out of the moon's haze a pale blond boy spurting thighs and buttocks and young skin. The flute player kneels there arms wrapped tightly around the Zimbu's chest breathing deeply until the Zimbu breathes with his own breathing quivering to the blue tattoo. The attendants step forward and carry the pale blond Zimbu to the blue tent. (WB, 160)

Although John's colonists do not abandon their technological experiments to concentrate entirely on such group contemplative efforts until the outside world begins to encroach, this scene already resembles the musical/dance gathering previously described: "But you have missed the point, you old stupid. You've made it into a love story. Of course, what you say is all right—but it's all wrong too, you poor dear."

We have again the "queer pipes"—flutes this time—and while Burroughs does not discuss music specifically, the North African setting and his own involvement with the Master Musicians of Joujouka, whose "Pipes of Pan" were described by his friend Brion Gysin as "a four thousand year old rock and roll band," suggests that like Traditional Indian and Chinese music discussed in my essay on Partch, both John and Burroughs' utopias call upon the *literally creative power* of authentic, Traditional music.[38]

Of course, this only works in the hands of a Realized individual, or in John's case, a *homo superior*. Thus we find in John's gatherings the same stone language we've seen before in such context, but now having an even more appropriate relation to the ithyphallic symbolism Evola discusses:

> The library and meeting-room was *a stone erection* which had evidently been built to last, and to delight the eye.
>
> There was silence. Having had some experience of Quaker meetings, I was not at first ill at ease. But presently a rather terrifying absolute stillness came upon the company. Not only gross fidgetings, but even those almost imperceptible movements which characterize all normal living, ceased, and became noticeable through their absence. I might have been in a roomful of stone images. On every face was an expression of intent but calm concentration which was not solemn, was even perhaps faintly amused.

But what after all is the point of John's utopia, how do they live from day to day? It's hard to pin down, which is likely the best strategy for fiction. Again, it seems like a combination of *Brave New World* and *Island*, but with the cosmic consciousness

---

[38] See the remarkable material quoted in Alain Danielou's *Music and the Power of Sound: The Influence of Tuning and Interval on Consciousness* (Rochester, Vt.: Inner Traditions, 1995).

(though drug-free)[39] and Polynesian free sex of the latter combined with a positive—i.e., utopian—view of eugenics.[40]

More generally, Stapledon seems to imagine some kind of post-Communism:

> "Yes," said John, laughing, "Comrades, you have the wrong approach. Like you, we are Communists, but we are other things also. For you, Communism is the goal, but for us it is the beginning. For you the group is sacred, but for us it is only the pattern made up of individuals. Though we are Communists, we have reached beyond Communism to a new individualism. Our Communism is individualistic. In many ways we admire the achievements of the New Russia; but if we were to accept this offer we should very soon come into conflict with your Government."

As we noted before, Stapledon is your typical '30s British academic com-symp, but, as also noted before, he shows odd little touches of pro-German and pro-National Socialism that I don't know how to explain biographically, but only, as in *The Flames*, due to his remarkable freedom of imagination—perhaps the

---

[39] "They are poisoning and monopolizing the hallucinogen drugs—learn to make it without any chemical corn"—William S. Burroughs, *Nova Express* (New York: Grove Press, 1964), Preface.

[40] "[T]he Wild Boys themselves, bands of young homosexuals who reproduce by a kind of fantasmatic parthenogenesis...."—Murphy, *op. cit.*, p. 146. Perhaps Burroughs himself is a genetic experiment? "Kim Carsons, as an amalgam of trace elements gathered here and there, also represents the successful result of breeding, like a eugenic model. In Burroughs's early work ... the protagonist was someone much like Burroughs himself: a hard case, cynical and grimly humorous, with the junkie's agelessness and the con man's radar. In *The Wild Boys* (1971), this figure gradually receded in the face of the tidal wave: teen-aged homosexual guerrillas, precivilized, preliterate, parthenogenetic, like an all-male version of the Primal Horde. Afterward, the aging con man became available only for walk-on parts. The wild boy had triumphed, and he rides through *Ah Pook is Here, Port of Saints, Cobble Stone Gardens, Cities of the Red Night,* and the present novel" (Luc Sante, "The Invisible Man," *New York Review of Books*, May 10, 1984).

"objectivity" his super-humans practice, which is the "inhumanism" Lewis condemned.[41]

Here, for instance, he might be trying some kind of Trotskyite anti-Stalinism (which became neo-conservatism) or proto-New Leftism (which became post-'60s liberalism), but "our Communism is individualistic" also sounds like the kind of fascism Maurice Bardèche defined, in which threats to society were ruthlessly dealt with, while leaving a wide margin of freedom in the purely personal arena.[42]

It's those threats, as well as the way they are dealt with, that makes John's island seem rather National Socialist. For one thing, the threats come from Britain and the Soviet Union; now, this is certainly an accurate depiction of the Great Powers of the Pacific in the '30s, but it also recalls the NS view of Germany's encirclement.

There's also the remarkably casual "racism" even for the '30s. John may mock South Africans but then there's that Africa baby they claim for themselves, "who somehow acquired the name Sambo," Ng-Gunko is described by the narrator as "niggerbrown" (and earns a warning from an Amazon reviewer to those of delicate PC sensibilities), and a Japanese diplomat casually referred to as a "Jap" like one of Dr. Seuss's war propaganda cartoons.

While the Super Humans are of various races, even African, they are mostly blue-eyed and fair-haired (even Ng-Gunko has one blue eye and red hair, like a Nation of Islam nightmare), mostly Asians, and the original mutation is traced to Central Asia.

---

[41] Like the narrator of Stapledon's *The Flames*, Jacqueline performs her own kind of "relief work" in Germany: "During the war of 1914-18 she was drawn into overstraining herself once more. So many tragic cases came her way. And after the war, being wholly without national prejudices, she moved to Germany, where the need was greater." See my essay on *The Flames*, "A Light Unto the Nations," in *The Eldritch Evola*.

[42] See "The Fascist Dream," http://www.counter-currents.com/2013/10/the-fascist-dream-part-1/ and Greg Johnson's "Remembering Maurice Bardèche: October 1, 1907–July 30, 1998," http://www.counter-currents.com/2013/10/remembering-maurice-bardeche-3/

Above all, Jews are conspicuous by their absence from this utopia of "super intellects." Stapledon, by intention or not, has done the same thing he did in *The Flames*. There, the grand symbol of our time, Judaics burning in furnaces, is traduced, like Joseph K: an alien race lives unscathed in our stoves, plotting takeover by mind control. Here, the intellectual elite take over someone else's country, massacre the natives, and plan their benevolent world rule; and it's the *goyim*!

OK, I've mentioned "dealing with threats" and just now the ethnic cleansing of their island, so let's finally deal with perhaps the most telling similarity to NS Germany: the eugenics goes along with a most casual attitude to killing, mass and otherwise. John murders a policeman while committing a burglary at age 10, and by the time he and his crew, essentially pirates now,[43] have set sail they will be machine-gunning the survivors of a shipwreck (lest they reveal their mission) and exterminating the aborigines of their uncharted island.

> I did not hear about these original inhabitants till much later, when I visited the island. "They were simple and attractive creatures," said John, "but, of course, we could not allow them to interfere with our plans. It might have been possible to obliterate from their minds every recollection of the island and of ourselves, and then to transport them. But though I had learned much from Langatse, our technique of oblivifaction was still unreliable. Moreover, where could we have deposited the natives without rousing protests, and curiosity? We might have kept them alive on the island, as domestic animals, but this would have wrecked our plans. It would also have undermined the natives spiritually. So we decided to destroy them. One bit of hypnotic technique (or magic, if you like) I felt sure I could now perform successfully on normal minds in which there were strong religious convictions. This we de-

---

[43] The colony is more like D'Annunzio at Fiume in 1920 than Brook Farm; see Hakim Bey's "March on Fiume" at http://www.countercurrents.com/2012/03/march-on-fiume/ and more generally, his *Pirate Utopias* (New York: Autonomedia, 2003).

cided to use. The natives had welcomed us to their island and arranged a feast for us. After the feast there were ritual dances and religious rites. When the excitement was at a climax I made Lo dance for them. And when she had done, I said to them, in their own language, that we were gods, that we needed their island, that they must therefore make a great funeral pyre for themselves, mount it together, lie down together, and gladly die. This they did, most gladly, men, women and children. When they had all died we set fire to the faggots and their bodies were burnt.

The machine-gunning in particular recalls typical British anti-Hun propaganda. Once more one wonders how a British Communist academic could write this without having some kind of ulterior agenda.

John's biographer and lifelong friend struggles to make the reader understand and perhaps . . . approve:

I must make it clear that in reporting John's behaviour at this time I do not seek to defend it. Much of it seems to me outrageous. Had it been perpetrated by anyone other than John, I should have unhesitatingly condemned it as the expression of a self-centred and shockingly perverted mind. But in spite of the most reprehensible incidents in his career, I am convinced that John was far superior to the rest of us in moral sensibility, as in intelligence. Therefore, even in respect of the seemingly disgraceful conduct which I have now to describe, I feel that the right course is not to condemn but to suspend judgement and try to understand. I tell myself that, if John was indeed a superior being, much of his conduct would certainly outrage us, simply because we, with our grosser sensibility, would never be able to apprehend its true nature. In fact, had his behaviour been simply an idealization of normal human behaviour, I should have been less disposed to regard him as of an essentially different and superior type. On the other hand it should be remembered that, though superior in capacity, he was also juvenile, and may well have suffered in his own way from the inexperience and crudity of the juvenile mind. Finally, his circumstances were such as to warp him, for he found himself alone in a world of beings whom he regarded as only half human.

And another time:

> I cannot defend this act. But I may point out that, had the invaders been members of the normal species, they would probably have baptised the natives, given them prayer books and European clothes, rum and all the diseases of the White Man. They would also have enslaved them economically, and in time they would have crushed their spirits by confronting them at every turn with the White Man's trivial superiority. Finally, when all had died of drink or bitterness, they would have mourned for them.

And yet again:

> Perhaps the only defence of the psychological murders which the supernormals committed when they took possession of the island would run as follows. Having made up their minds that at all costs the island must be theirs, and unencumbered, they did not shirk the consequences of their decision. With open eyes they went about their task, and fulfilled it in the cleanest possible way. Whether the end which they so ruthlessly pursued did in fact justify the means, I simply do not feel competent to decide. All my sympathies lie with the view that murder can never be justified, however lofty the end at stake. Certainly, had the killing been perpetrated by members of my own kind, such a deed would have deserved the sternest condemnation. But who am I that I should judge beings who in daily contact with me constantly proved themselves my superiors not only in intelligence but in moral insight?

One can't help but be reminded of Savitri Devi's defenses of National Socialism at various times: Thou hypocrite! And: Get thee behind me, Satan! You kill innocent animals for food, for shoes and belts, even for sport, and perform horrifying, usually unnecessary experiments on them; above all, you fight the largest and bloodiest and most "inhumane" wars of all time; and yet, you would deny to us the opportunity to rid our society of the genetically inferior "humans" that perhaps not deliberately but inevitably coarsen our society and contaminate our race, as well as those aliens among us that directly seek to harm us. Who among us, forced to live in cities overrun with the former, and conscious of the alien elite above us, has not had similar thoughts respectively?

The same must be our answer to those who promote ideas of "color-blind" America and bemoan "past racial violence [white on black]." In reality, such "violence," wildly exaggerated anyway, was simply the means of ensuring a country built by White people would stay White, and not become what it is now: Black Run America (BRA),

> . . . dominated politically by "color-aware" black people, while "color-blind" white people moan and cry over their displacement ("collectivism is racism," they'll shout, on their way to Galt's Gulch); demand 'justice' and 'fairness' all you want, but the black District Attorney is shopping for his next hoodie.
>
> "Color-blinded" into oblivion, doomed to walk a country their ancestors created without a territory to call home; A fitting epitaph for white Americans.[44]

After all, if we are "White-guilty" for acts we haven't done, then nothing should stop us from acts involving any additional "real" guilt.

Above all, and in the end, the island resembles NS Germany, because, like most utopias, it must be destroyed at the end. Of course, like tragic lovers, this obviates any anti-climactic peter-

---

[44] "Black Knockout Game Attacks (Flash Mob Violence) are Politics by Other Means," *Stuff Black People Don't Like*, November 25, 2013, http://stuffblackpeopledontlike.blogspot.com/2013/11/black-knockout-game-attacks-flash-mob.html

ing out in reality; ending on a high note, as it were; better to burn out than fade away. The Savage in *Brave New World* commits suicide, the Island of Pala is invaded by oil interests backed by a local tyrant, Kurtz's command is terminated to the tune of the Doors "The End."

But the destruction of John's island goes even further, utterly annihilated and sunk by some kind of deliberate super-reactor explosion, an act of fiery mass suicide (again, an inversion of accepted history, where the "good" Allies used atomic weapons homicidally against the "bad" guys) that inevitably calls to mind the *Götterdämmerung* chosen by Hitler. "From our point of view it is better for our colony to be destroyed than to be enslaved by any alien Power."

And reverting to Burroughs' utopia again, here is how Timothy Murphy describes the denouement there:

> The novel concludes with a chapter entitled "The Wild Boys Smile," which is also the last line of the text. In it, an unidentified narrator (perhaps Audrey, who is pronounced dead in the penultimate Penny Arcade Peep Show, or Rogers from "The Chief Smiles") joins the Wild Boys in their struggle for the streets. . . . At the conclusion of the chapter, the narrator and his companion, confronted by policemen and photographers at the "time barrier" (*WB* 181) that separates the Wild Boys' "dead" world from our "live" historical world, escape by throwing a film grenade at them; this grenade, like the novel itself, is meant to blow a hole in the ideological "reality film" that controls social reproduction (as well as the producers) under the existent socius. After it goes off, we are left with the final fading images in the Penny Arcade Peep Show—naked boys fucking, laughing, and gaming—as the Peep Show (and the novel itself) burns out: "The silver screen is exploding in moon craters and boiling silver spots. 'Wild boys very close now.'
>
> Darkness falls on the ruined suburbs. A dog barks in the distance. Dim jerky stars are blowing away across a gleaming empty sky, *the wild boys smile.*" (*WB* 184)

Murphy then points out the usefulness of such apparently cataclysmic endings:

> Since they must forget power if they are to avoid duplicating it, the Wild Boys cannot smile in triumph over their enemies. Instead *they smile in invitation to the reader*; such an invitation is precisely what the book of the dead must offer if it is to be a viable subject-group fantasy.[45]

Again, one thinks of Savitri Devi; the National Socialists may not have been able to triumph, in the conditions of the Kali Yuga, but their example remains to inspire our own efforts.[46]

The National Socialist angle may bring to mind another book, Thomas Mann's *Dr. Faustus*. Mann's work is also a fictional biography, written by a childhood friend whose love for his subject almost makes up for a considerable intellectual disparity — Serenus Zeitblom might have better reason to be called "Fido" than John's narrator. While John stages his *Götterdämmerung* in 1935, Adrian Leverkuhn dies in 1941, but only after a Nietzschean decade of mental collapse. The latter is the result of a "devil's bargain" — hence the title — in his youth, in which he deliberately acquires syphilis from a prostitute so as to supercharge his musical creativity.[47]

---

[45] Murphy, *op. cit.*, pp. 166-67. As we have said before, Guenon frequently points out that symbolism must be applied in an inverted fashion: the "defeat" of the ideal is its real triumph.

[46] See, for example, *Gold in the Furnace: Experiences in Post-War Germany*, ed. R. G. Fowler, Kindle ed. (San Francisco: Counter-Currents, 2013).

[47] The idea of his 12-tone system being appropriated, to say nothing of being attributed to a syphilitic madman, did not sit well with Mann's fellow LA exile Arnold Schoenberg. Things must have been pretty tense around the poolside, until Mann agreed to add a prefatory note acknowledging Schoenberg as the owner of the system. Partch, of course, despised Schoenberg and the other "avant-garde" academics; he would have counseled Adrian that he was on the wrong track altogether, and would not have been surprised at his fictional crack-up. The Mann-Schoenberg kefuffle seems as silly as the time Columbia Pictures sued the maker of *The Incredibly Strange Creatures Who Stopped*

John and his kind need no such aid, being in a sense born infected, but the result is the same—prolonged adolescence, uncanny creativity, and a moral sense that several characters, and even the narrator, call "satanic" and "devilish." There is the same eerie music-making.

Above all, Leverkuhn's career is intended by Mann as a typically heavy-handed allegory for Germany's fall (or rise, as some of us might prefer) into Nazism. As we've seen before (e.g., *Green Lantern*) to the Christian—even a lukewarm "lover of the humanities" such as Zeitblom or Mann himself—the Superman can only be seen as Satanic. As Mann says, theology inevitably becomes demonology.[48]

And yet, Mann, like Stapledon, has to resort to the favorite meme of the Satanic Nietzsche or Hitler, namely genetics, race, the Superman. Is it possible, that one must inevitably avail oneself of such language, if on wishes to speak at all?

Lester Bangs once wrote that Lou Reed was constantly lying because he took so much speed that he'd run out of things to say if he stuck to the truth. Perhaps that's the function of political correctness—a concept invented by Stapledon's beloved Soviets—to keep thought from its . . . um . . . *natural, genetically sound* paths.

Counter-Currents/*North American New Right*,
November 12, 2013

Living and Became Mixed-Up Zombies because the original title, *The Incredibly Strange Creature: Or Why I stopped Living and Became a Mixed-up Zombie*, was "too similar" to Kubrick's upcoming *Dr. Strangelove or: How I Learned to Stop Worrying and Love the Bomb*. The filmmaker was: Ray Dennis Steckler!

[48] See Chapter One, "Green Nazis in Space," above, and the literature cited there.

FROM ODD JOHN TO STRANGE LOVE

Dr. Strangelove, or: How I Learned to Stop Worrying and Love the Bomb
Director: Stanley Kubrick; written by Peter George, Stanley Kubrick, Terry Southern
Columbia Pictures (1964)

> GENERAL "BUCK" TURGIDSON: Hmm . . . Strangelove? What kind of a name is that? That ain't no Kraut name is it, Stainesey?
> MR. STAINES: He changed it when he became a citizen. Used to be "Merkwürdigliebe."
> GENERAL "BUCK" TURGIDSON: Well, a Kraut by any other name, uh Stainesey?

The German word *"Gemeinschaft"* means "A spontaneously arising organic social relationship characterized by strong reciprocal bonds of sentiment and kinship within a common tradition." In this context the discussion of the post-apocalypse society living in mine shafts at the end of the film presents an interesting double-entendre. Dr. Strangelove's remarks about the participants in the new society spontaneously accepting new social norms and having "bold curiosity for the adventure ahead" is especially germane. Also, General Turgidson's admonition to "not allow a mine shaft gap" at the end is a particularly vivid pun.[1]

Toward the end of my reflections on Olaf Stapledon's queer utopia, *Odd John*, Stanley Kubrick's *Dr. Strangelove or: How I Learned to Stop Worrying and Love the Bomb* put in a brief appearance. I think a closer look at how the movie appears in the light of our reflections would be interesting.

I would suggest that despite its status as a classic "black comedy," and whatever the intentions of its creators to reveal the mod-

---

[1] An anonymous bit of "Trivia" at the Internet Movie Database, http://www.imdb.com/title/tt0057012/trivia?ref_=tt_trv_trv

ern world as a dystopia, the film can be seen as presenting a series of increasingly perfected—though somewhat claustrophobic—utopian *Männerbünde*.[2]

Each is a group of men (with one small exception to the rule[3]), cut off from the rest of the world, operating by its own rules. As we'll see, the B-52 is a closed tube in the upper atmosphere, with oxygen masks for emergencies; we only see it open up when Maj. Kong forces open the bomb bay doors to his doom. Burbleson Air Force Base is, cinematically, nothing but Gen. Ripper's office—even his *en suite* bathroom is unseen—with some second unit cutaways to show the storming attack. Then there's Gen. Turgidson's motel room, followed by The War Room, which is obviously sealed off and perhaps underground; Turgidson freaks when the Russian Ambassador enters ("He'll see the Big Board!"); then Strangelove's mine shaft vision.

Each unit includes one outsider, like "Fido" at John's colony: RAF Captain Mandrake, Turgidson's female "assistant," James Earl Jones as the anachronistic black pilot,[4] and the Russian Ambassador whose appearance in the War Room freaks out Turgidson.

Additionally, each utopian segment ends with a symbolic ejaculation, a destructive opening to the outside: the iconic scene of Maj. Kong riding the bomb down; "Bat" Guano shoots the Coke

---

[2] Each of the main three would have featured Peter Sellers, playing the "Only Sane Man" each time, "but a sprained ankle prevented him from getting into and out of the B-52 set, so Slim Pickens was added to the cast to play 'King' Kong," http://tvtropes.org/pmwiki/pmwiki.php/Main/ActingForTwo%20/%20http:/tvtropes.org/pmwiki/pmwiki.php/Main/ActingForTwo

[3] "Precisely one female character appears in this movie. General Turgidson's mistress and secretary, heard in one scene and seen in a bikini in another. She is also a *Playboy* centerfold," http://tvtropes.org/pmwiki/pmwiki.php/Main/FanService%20/%20http:/tvtropes.org/pmwiki/pmwiki.php/Main/FanService

[4] Like the "Tuskegee Airmen," black pilots are a modern Liberal myth; see Paul Kersey's *Stuff Black People Don't Like*, *passim*, such as "Black History Month Heroes—Sky Marshal Tehat Meru of *Starship Troopers*," http://stuffblackpeopledontlike.blogspot.com/2010/02/black-history-month-heroes-sky-marshal.html.

machine and gets a spurt of soda in the face; Turgidson's last words in the motel room are "Blast off!"; a climactic pie-fight was cut from the War Room scene, which now ends with the compulsively saluting Strangelove rising erect from his wheelchair; his utopian vision ends with the equally iconic montage of phallic mushroom clouds.

Each, in some sense, fails, but as we've seen with *Odd John*, this is just a genre convention of utopian writing; the final group will succeed beyond its own imagination. And each climaxes with a big smile.[5]

For once, TV Tropes has got it exactly wrong:

> World Gone Mad: Every single group of people are various sorts of insane, incompetent, and/or incapable of focusing on the important subject at hand. Except for the bomber crew, who are all well-trained and manage to adapt to the various obstacles in their path. Too bad they're the one group that desperately needs to fail.[6]

1. Burpleson Air Force Base

> **Group Capt. Lionel Mandrake:** Colonel! Colonel, I must know what you think has been going on here! [...]
> **Colonel "Bat" Guano:** I think you're some kind of deviated prevert. I think General Ripper found out about your preversion, and that you were organizing some kind of mutiny of preverts. Now MOVE!

Or in practice, the executive office of Base Commander Gen. Jack D. Ripper. Apart from a couple cutaways during the Army's attempt to retake the base, and the business with the Coke ma-

---

[5] Kong's "yippe-yi-ay" on the bomb, Turgidson's "Blast off!" to his secretary, Strangelove's iconic *Risus sardonicus*. Ripper's suicide would not seem to fit; this is why, as noted, the segment has two endings. When "Bat" Guano takes the Coke stream to the face, the audience can be expected to laugh—it's a "black comedy" after all—and this ties in with what Murphy said about the Wild Boys' smiles—they invite the audience into participation.

[6] http://tvtropes.org/pmwiki/pmwiki.php/Main/WorldGoneMad

chine and the telephone booth in the corridor, we are entirely within Gen. Ripper's private realm. Although the rugby balls and Greek grammars have been replaced with bombs, rifles, and bullets...

> GROUP CAPT. LIONEL MANDRAKE: Shoot it off! Shoot! With a gun! That's what the bullets are for, you twit!

... the atmos' is more like a British public school. Gen. Ripper commands not men but "my boys."

> GENERAL "BUCK" TURGIDSON: [reading Gen. Ripper's last communication] "My boys will give you the best kind of start, 1,400 megatons worth, and you sure as hell won't stop them now."

There's even intra-mural rivalry: "General Turgidson, with all due respect for your defense team *my boys* can brush them aside without too much trouble."

And while the base troops do eventually surrender — "My boys let me down"[7] — we'll see that at least one plane in the Attack Wing will get through.

> GENERAL "BUCK" TURGIDSON: Mr. President, if I may speak freely, the Russkie talks big, but frankly, we think he's short of know-how. I mean, you just can't expect *a*

---

[7] "A Father to His Men: When the base falls Ripper feels let down and remarks that the soldiers were like his children. It rings as true as anything else he says. Mandrake manages to obliquely mock him.

> MANDRAKE: I'm sure they all died thinking of you, every man jack of them... Jack."

http://tvtropes.org/pmwiki/pmwiki.php/Main/AFatherToHisMen%20/%20http:/tvtropes.org/pmwiki/pmwiki.php/Main/AFatherToHisMen

On the contrary, I would suggest that "man jack" suggests the utopian union of Jack Ripper and his boys, symbolized by Mandrake, as does Mandrake's fake nostalgia for earlier helping Ripper with the machine gun: "'You said, 'feed me' and I fed you Jack...'"

bunch of ignorant peons to understand a machine like some of *our boys*. . . . if the pilot's good, see, I mean, if he's really . . . sharp, he can barrel that baby in so low [he spreads his arms like wings *and laughs*], you oughtta see it sometime, it's a sight. A big plane like a '52. VRROOM! There's jet exhaust, fryin' chickens in the barnyard.

PRESIDENT MERKIN MUFFLEY: Yeah, but has he got a chance?

GENERAL "BUCK" TURGIDSON: Has he got a chance? Hell, Ye . . . ye . . .

So Peter Sellers' role as Group Captain Mandrake, ex-RAF pilot, is quite appropriate here. He's a slightly slow on the uptake senior boy, getting some private tutoring from the Headmaster;[8] it's a reversal of the *Boy's Own Mag* world of *Stalky & Co.*, where the playing fields of Eton have simply *become* the theatre of war.

BASE COMMANDER JACK D. RIPPER: Mandrake, in the name of Her Majesty and the Continental Congress come here and feed me this belt, *boy*!

The lesson Ripper imparts is, of course, his famous "purity of essence" meme, the original "conspiracy theory."[9] Along the way,

---

[8] And we know where that's going: "No Sense of Personal Space: As Ripper gets drunk, he starts getting uncomfortably close and hands-on toward Mandrake, suggesting a possible explanation for his sexual issues," http://tvtropes.org/pmwiki/pmwiki.php/Main/NoSenseOf Persona Space%20/%20http:/tvtropes.org/pmwiki/pmwiki.php/Main/NoSenseOfPersonalSpace

[9] At the time a well-known hobby horse of the Right, it's surprising how it continues to be a kind of cargo cult on the Left. Concern about using early PR techniques "after the war" as Ripper correctly notes, to convince local governments to allow a poisonous industrial waste product into the water supply, seems tailor made for the Left, especially after all the Rachel Carson business and modern concerns with GMOs etc. Apparently, the "commie plot" angle led it to become a shibboleth, like the "innocence" of Hiss or authenticity of "folk" music, constantly invoked as a test of loyalty (oddly enough, the Right had the same idea about loyalty tests). Only Alexander Cockburn, Stalinist that he was, seemed to have the guts to challenge the Left. Indeed, good-

though, he gives Mandrake a history lesson that will become important at the end:

> GENERAL JACK D. RIPPER: Mandrake, do you recall what Clemenceau once said about war?
> GROUP CAPT. LIONEL MANDRAKE: No, I don't think I do, sir, no.
> GENERAL JACK D. RIPPER: He said war was too important to be left to the generals. When he said that, 50 years ago, he might have been right. But today, war is too important to be left to politicians. They have neither the time, the training, nor the inclination for strategic thought. I can no longer sit back and allow Communist infiltration, Communist indoctrination, Communist subversion and the international Communist conspiracy to sap and impurify all of our precious bodily fluids.

As Trevor Lynch has noted on several occasions: in the modern world, only madmen are allowed to articulate the truth.[10]

Burpleson is ultimately taken back by the Army, and General Ripper, true to the public school ethos, "does the right thing, old chap" and commits suicide.[11] This is the darkest utopia (note the cinematography) but even so, it's, as we've said before, only a genre convention, not an admission of defeat.[12] Indeed, we'll see

---

thinking sites like HuffPo now attack anti-GMO activists as "creationists of the Left"; GMOs, fluoridation, and even circumcision, if not climate change, seems to be one of those "scientific facts" only known to American Leftists, puzzling the rest of the world.

[10] "Dangerously Genre Savvy: General Ripper may be demented but he knows his trade; he's shown as an experienced and competent leader who invokes, anticipates and discusses very relevant tropes," http://tvtropes.org/pmwiki/pmwiki.php/Main/DangerouslyGenreSavvy

[11] Even a light-hearted romp by a Catholic author ends with Lord Peter himself recommending, successfully, suicide to the club bounder in *The Unpleasantness at the Bellona Club* (1928), http://en.wikipedia.org/wiki/Bellona_Club

[12] The bathroom suicide recalls the one in *Advise and Consent* which I discussed in my "*Mad Men* Jumps the Gefilte Fish" articles in *End of an*

that Ripper's vision—rule by the elite—will come to pass.

To lighten the mood, and provide the real ending, we have Mandrake's monkeying around with the pay phone, and "Bat" Guano's encounter with the Coke machine. It's the audience that can be expected to smile when "Bat" fires his rifle and gets a Coke facial in return—"a Coke and a smile," as the ad would say a few years later.[13] Meanwhile, the utopian, anti-economic scarcity note is again sounded as Mandrake doesn't have enough money for the phone, and "Bat" sneers at the idea of "going into combat with loose change in my pocket."

1A. THE MOTEL ROOM

The Motel Room is an odd little scene, that does little but show us Gen. Turgidson being summoned to the War Room in the midst of a tryst with his "assistant." It's as much a closed environment as Ripper's office—later we'll see Ripper enter the bathroom to shoot himself, here Turgidson enters the scene from the bathroom. More connections: Premier Kissoff will be caught in a similar tryst during the War Room scene, and the General's "assistant" will turn up in the *Playboy* centerfold viewed by a crew member onboard "The Leper Colony" (her ass covered with an issue of *Foreign Affairs,* nudge nudge) and presumably is the unwanted caller to Turgidson in the War Room . . .

> GENERAL "BUCK" TURGIDSON: I told you never to call me here, don't you know where I am? . . . Well look, baby, I c-, I *can't* talk to you now . . . my president needs me!

. . . but otherwise it has little to do with the rest of the film. I suspect it's here to establish Gen. Turgidson's, and by extension the rest of the "boys'" hetero cred; otherwise we might be suspicious, since he contemns Kissoff for his tryst as a "degenerate" (another

---

Era: Mad Men *& the Ordeal of Civility* (San Francisco: Counter-Currents, 2015).

[13] The comedy is so deliberate that "the actor's head was too high when the stream began to spew toward him, and he can be seen lowering his face down into it to produce the full comedic effect." —IMDb, http://www.imdb.com/title/tt0057012/goofs?ref_=tt_sa_1

"prevert" for the "Leper Colony" no doubt) and other than shouting "Blast off!" he doesn't seem to have much interest in Miss Foreign Affairs, preferring to answer the call of his President.

2. "THE LEPER COLONY"

> The men will cheer and the boys will shout
> The ladies they will all turn out
> And we'll all feel gay
> When Johnny comes marching home.

The B-52 and the War Room are the most famous segments. I say "the" B-52 since although Ripper clearly orders a "wing attack," and we see dozens of vectors on The Big Board,[14] but only one plane is ever shown. The B-52 is code-named "The Leper Colony," which "designates the crew as incompetent, even degenerate,"[15] but also sounds *Odd John*'s themes of island utopias of physically deformed social outcasts that seem retarded but get lots of high-tech things done.

> **MAJOR T. J. "KING" KONG**: Stay on the bomb run *boys*, I'm gonna get those bomb doors open if it harelips everyone on Bear Creek.[16]

As IMDb noted above, the crew is actually quite competent, even heroic and self-sacrificing; an ideal *Männerbund*. It's impossible not to be rooting for them, and unlike IMDb, I think Counter-Currents readers, at least, will find their goal quite admirable.

---

[14] "Bombers on the Screen: The primary purpose of The Big Board," http://tvtropes.org/pmwiki/pmwiki.php/Main/BombersOnTheScreen%20/%20http:/tvtropes org/pmwiki/pmwiki.php/Main/BombersOnTheScreen

[15] "Dark Roots: Humor and Tragedy in Doctor Strangelove" by Caran Wakefield, http://www.nyu.edu/cas/ewp/wakefielddark05.pdf

[16] No one since seems to understand WTF Kong is talking about, but I note the connection to the harelipped "Tooth Fairy" in *Manhunter*, which I referenced before in discussing the ugliness and deformity of Odd John's horde.

And what Aryan male wouldn't want to go out riding an ICBM onto Laputa?[17]

The precise function of Plan R, and the CRM 114 coding device, which is *not* to be able to receive, recalls *Odd John*'s use of psychic techniques to confuse anyone—as here, both Soviets and Brits—nosing around the island. We can't tell from the angle but he might be taking his iconic bomb ride on the one designated "Dear [Odd?] John."

3. THE WAR ROOM

The culminating utopia, in many senses, is of course the War Room. Several of the themes we've noted are tied together here. It's a macho environment where women only intrude from the outside: first, Gen. Turgidson receives an unwanted call from (presumably) the woman—his secretary, not his wife—we saw him with earlier (in another closed environment—a motel room—where another unwanted call sends him to the War Room).

> **GENERAL "BUCK" TURGIDSON:** I told you never to call me here, don't you know where I am? ... Well look, baby, I c-, I *can't* talk to you now ... *my president needs me*!

Then, to bring the Russian premier to the Hot Line requires the Ambassador to reveal his secret rendezvous:

> **RUSSIAN AMBASSADOR:** Our Premier is a man of the people, but he is also ... a man, if you follow my meaning.

Gen. Turgidson erupts with outrage at the Premier being a "degenerate atheist commie!" which is odd, since, apart from the hypocrisy, the Ambassador's comment should be lessening the homoerotic implications of Turgidson's spurning his girlfriend to serve his President's needs.

Perhaps he is offended by the implication of Kissoff (note the

---

[17] "La puta" of course is "the whore," in line with the obsessive sexual symbolism of the film, but also a reference to Swift's airborne utopia of scientific cranks; as we'll see next, taking out Laputa will make way for Strangelove's very different, solidly based ge-mineshaft utopia.

name) actually consummating the act, since Turgidson never seems to:

> GENERAL "BUCK" TURGIDSON: I know how it is, baby. Tell you what you do: you just start your countdown, and old Bucky'll be back here before you can say *"Blast off!"*

Maj. Ripper earlier clarified the code of the *Männerbund*:

> BASE COMMANDER JACK D. RIPPER: Women, er, women sense my power, and they seek the life essence. *I do not avoid women, Mandrake . . . but I do deny them my essence.*

Only in the "modern world" would this be construed as madness or, heavens, "repressed."[18]

But don't get them wrong; when needed, under the appropriate conditions, these boys can get the job done!

> PRESIDENT MERKIN MUFFLEY: Is there really a chance for that plane to get through?
>
> GENERAL "BUCK" TURGIDSON: Mr. President, if I may speak freely, *the Russkie talks big, but frankly, we think he's short* of know-how. I mean, you just can't expect a bunch of ignorant peons *to understand a machine like some of our boys.* . . . if the pilot's good, see, I mean, if he's really . . . sharp, he can *barrel that baby in so low* [he spreads his arms like wings and laughs], you oughtta see it sometime, it's a sight. A big plane like a '52. VRROOM! There's jet exhaust, fryin' chickens in the barnyard.
>
> PRESIDENT MERKIN MUFFLEY: Yeah, but has he got a chance?
>
> GENERAL "BUCK" TURGIDSON: Has he got a chance? Hell, Ye . . . ye . . .

---

[18] See Andy Nowicki's meditations on the demeaning subtext of the macho "Game" theorists; for example, "Trouble in Twilight," http://alternativeright.com/altright-archive/main/blogs/untimely-observations/trouble-in-twilight

And a good thing, because they will be called on to perform heroic service. That's because despite all the cheers and smiles all around, the recall efforts end in failure, and "The Leper Colony" gets through. But wait, this isn't the end, really; there's more! This leads us to the Final Utopia, Strangelove's "post-war future."

4. Strangelove's "Astonishingly Good Idea"

As all the Gloomy Guses sit around waiting for the Doomsday Machine to blanket the Earth in a "radioactive shroud," something remarkable takes place. Despite "acting as cartoonishly evil as possible," Strangelove is suddenly revealed as the smartest, and sanest, man in the room.

> [T]here's a brief scene with the president demanding to know who would create a doomsday device; the camera lingers on Strangelove, calmly smoking in the shadow, the president off-screen. A few minutes later, Strangelove casually suggests *the mine shaft survival plan, a new system of government, including who lives and who dies. For all intents and purposes, he takes over the US government right then and there, in front of its actual leaders, who are oblivious.* Nobody said the Only Sane Man has to be a good person.

Just like Odd John, "He looks and speaks like a Looney Tunes character, but everything he says is coldly rational." Strangelove's dark glasses recall John's "eyes like caves." Although his mechanical arm with a life of its own references both Rottwang and Robot/Maria from *Metropolis* (another curdled utopia); not only mad scientist but like Robot/Maria he seems to have two natures, embodied in the mechanical arm, not unlike Odd John's ability to operate on two levels of consciousness, personal and communal.[19]

While we might imagine his arm was injured in an experi-

---

[19] "Evil Hand: Dr. Strangelove has one, which seems to act on Strangelove's violent and Nazi subconscious. The portrayal was so influential that the real life condition "alien hand syndrome" is also known as "Dr. Strangelove Syndrome," http://tvtropes.org/pmwiki/pmwiki.php/Main/EvilHand%20/%20http:/tvtropes.org/pmwiki/pmwiki.php/Main/EvilHand

mental accident, like Rottwang, or that he was crippled in the war, like Baron Evola, none of this is made explicit; Strangelove, like one of the freaks in John's troupe, could have just been born that way. In any event, the prospect of nuclear annihilation—"brighter than a thousand suns"—literally erects him, just as Baron Evola asked to be wheeled to a window so that he could die like his Aryan ancestors, upright and facing the rising sun.

But is it the end; death and destruction? Before that climax, Strangelove has narrated his seemingly well-rehearsed utopian dream, which deserves to be quoted in full:

> **DR. STRANGELOVE:** I would not rule out the chance to preserve *a nucleus of human specimens*. It would be quite easy ... heh, heh ... at the bottom of ah ... some of our deeper mineshafts. Radioactivity would never penetrate a mine some thousands of feet deep, and in a matter of weeks, sufficient improvements in dwelling space could easily be provided.
> **MUFFLEY:** How long would you have to stay down there?
> **DR. STRANGELOVE:** Well let's see now ah ... cobalt thorium G. ... Radioactive halflife of uh, ... I would think that uh ... possibly uh ... one hundred years.
> **MUFFLEY:** You mean, people could actually stay down there for a hundred years?
> **DR. STRANGELOVE:** It would not be difficult, Mein Führer! Nuclear reactors could, heh ... I'm sorry, Mr. President. Nuclear reactors could provide power almost indefinitely. Greenhouses could maintain plant life. Animals could be bred and slaughtered. A quick survey would have to be made of all the available mine sites in the country, but I would guess that dwelling space for several hundred thousands of our people could easily be provided.
> **MUFFLEY:** Well, I, I would hate to have to decide ... who stays up and ... who goes down.
> **DR. STRANGELOVE:** Well, that would not be necessary, Mr. President. It could easily be accomplished with a computer. And a computer could be set and programmed to accept factors from *youth, health, sexual fertility, intelligence, and a cross-section of necessary skills*. Of course, it

would be absolutely vital that our top government and military men be included to foster and impart the required principles of leadership and *tradition*. Naturally, they would breed prodigiously, eh? There would be much time, and little to do. Ha, ha. But ah, with the *proper breeding techniques* and a ratio of say, ten females to each male, I would guess that they could then work their way back to the present Gross National Product within say, twenty years.

MUFFLEY: But look here doctor, wouldn't this nucleus of survivors be so grief-stricken and anguished that they'd, well, envy the dead and not want to go on living?

DR. STRANGELOVE: No, sir . . . excuse me . . . When they go down into the mine, everyone would still be alive. There would be no shocking memories, and the prevailing emotion will be one of nostalgia for those left behind, combined with a spirit of bold curiosity for the adventure ahead! [involuntarily gives the Nazi salute and forces it down with his other hand] Ahhh!

TURGIDSON: Doctor, you mentioned the ratio of ten women to each man. Now, wouldn't that *necessitate the abandonment of the so-called monogamous sexual relationship, I mean, as far as men were concerned*?

DR. STRANGELOVE: Regrettably, yes. But it is, you know, a sacrifice required for the future of the human race. I hasten to add that since *each man will be required to do prodigious . . . service along these lines, the women will have to be selected for their sexual characteristics which will have to be of a highly stimulating nature*.

RUSSIAN AMBASSADOR: I must confess, you have an astonishingly good idea there, Doctor.

It's all there, the whole National Socialist utopia, complete with self-selected elite and selective breeding.

While Strangelove is conventionally seen as a "black comedy" in which the post-war doctrine of "mutual assured destruction" (MAD) is ruthlessly satirized, we can see, in the light of our earlier reflections on the utopian genre, that once Kubrick or his co-writers settled, likely unconsciously, on the multi-utopian structure, he was committed to the fact that the logic of utopia leads to an apparently — but only apparently — disastrous conclusion.

The final segment then, is not really a fiery *Götterdämmerung*, at least not for Strangelove and Co.[20] It is not Strangelove's comeuppance, but his triumph.

We Will Meet Again: The memorable final montage plays the song of the same name over images of atomic explosions, implying the two superpowers are destined to trade blows ever after.[21]

A sappy WWII Brit tune; we've met the Nazis again; we [today] will all meet again — this time the "Allies" will wipe out each other, and the only German ("a Kraut by any other name") in the room is the only one still standing.

We don't know how much time passes from Strangelove's exultant "Mein Fuhrer, I can walk"[22] and his initial baby steps,[23] to the Doomsday machine going off. Strangelove & Co. are presumably already protected in the War Room, and may have had time to put together some version of Strangelove's mineshaft utopia.[24]

If so, Kubrick's film has foreshadowed Pynchon's *Gravity's Rainbow* (which returns the favor by ending with a hapless soldier riding a V-2) which Dale Carter has analyzed[25] as presenting the

---

[20] Cf. the iconic boys' book, Kipling's *Stalky and Co.*

[21] http://tvtropes.org/pmwiki/pmwiki.php/Film/DrStrangelove?from=Film.DoctorStrangelove

[22] Strangelove's lapse into German links him to the equally deceptive failure at the end of Hesse's *Demian*: "In the very last sentence of the novel Sinclair addresses Demian, his recently departed friend and mentor, as 'mein Führer'." Mark Harmon, review of Gunnar Decker's *Hesse: Der Wanderer und sein Schatten* in the *TLS*, September 14, 2012, available here: http://www.gss.ucsb.edu/projects/hesse/documents/Harman-Decker-2012-2.pdf

[23] "Physicist Isidor Rabi noticed Oppenheimer's disconcerting triumphalism: "I'll never forget his walk; *I'll never forget the way he stepped out of the car . . . his walk was like High Noon . . . this kind of strut*. He had done it" (http://en.wikipedia.org/wiki/J._Robert_Oppenheimer).

[24] Itself an obviously phallic notion: satirizing the "missile gap" — a lie about the aged Eisenhower that helped put virile Kennedy in the White House; Turgidson demands that "Mr. President, we must prevent a mineshaft gap!"

[25] Dale Carter, *The Final Frontier: The Rise and Fall of the American*

posthumous triumph of the Third Reich in the form of the Kennedy-led space race:

> In this book, Carter draws on Thomas Pynchon's novel 'Gravity's Rainbow' to define the post-World War Two period as the 'Rocket State', a social form salvaging elements of the defeated Nazi 'Oven State' to create a totalitarian capitalist order. The rocket, based on Nazi military technology, is a central element of this as the launch vehicle for both nuclear weapons of mass destruction and the Apollo programme, highest point of the propagandist spectacle or, as Carter calls it 'the Orpheus Theater' where at the conclusion of *Gravity's Rainbow* the spectators watch the screen as the rocket heads towards their destruction.[26]

Much as Strangelove & Co. must have watched the Big Board, we watch the final montage. Muffley himself recognizes the ominous parallels:

> **MUFFLEY**: I refuse to go down in history as the greatest mass murderer since Adolf Hitler.
> **TURGIDSON**: Perhaps it might be better, Mr. President, if you were more concerned with the American people, than with your image in the history books.

Each utopia has superficially failed, but each sets up the final one (the final solution?) which has succeeded, although the logic of the utopian genre requires, as we saw, that this one too apparently fail, spectacularly.

Ever tried. Ever failed. No matter. Try again. Fail again. Fail better.[27]

Fail Safe?[28]

Rocket State (New York: Verso, 1988).

[26] An outdated webpage at http://www.oocities.org/redgiantsite/moon.html which also includes an excerpt from Carter's book.

[27] Samuel Beckett, *Worstward Ho* (1983).

[28] In a replay of the whole "Incredibly Strange Creatures" kerfuffle that we referenced before, "*Fail-Safe* and *Dr. Strangelove* were both pro-

In a final, ironic—or rather, utopian—reversal, the bombs are dropped on the Allies, and after this new "holocaust" all the messy aspects of eugenics—exterminating the unfit—are left behind, leaving only the pleasurable eugenic tasks of *Kraft durch Freude*, with the males called upon to perform heroic services on specially selected females. Everyone is smiling in anticipation, and even Ambassador de Sadesky joins in:

> **RUSSIAN AMBASSADOR:** I must confess, you have an astonishingly good idea there, Doctor.

See, if you squint at *Dr. Strangelove* through the utopian lens we've provided, where the apocalypse is just a genre convention, it's clear that the Nazis come back, and this time they win![29] I like to think this would bring a smile to Savitri Devi herself.[30]

Counter-Currents/*North American New Right*
December 23, 2013

---

duced by Columbia Pictures. . . . Director Stanley Kubrick, adapting Peter George's novel *Red Alert*, insisted the studio release his movie first (in January 1964). "Fail-Safe" so closely resembled *Red Alert* that George filed a plagiarism lawsuit. The case was settled out of court." (http://en.wikipedia.org/wiki/Fail-Safe_%281964_film%29#Lawsuit).

[29] Albeit an underground triumph, which does fit in with many "Nazi survival" mythologies.

[30] Although she wouldn't like that bit about "animals raised and slaughtered."

FROM ULTRASUEDE TO LIMELIGHT:
HALSTON & GATIEN, ARYAN ENTREPRENEURS IN THE DARK AGE

Ultrasuede: In Search of Halston (2010) Director: Whitney Sudler-Smith

Limelight (2011) Director: Billy Corben

Party Monster (2003) Directors: Fenton Bailey, Randy Barbato

"I love America."

— Peter Gatien

"All-American kid from the Midwest. This is a great American."

— Liza on Roy Halston Frowick

Fashion and dance clubs may seem to "the Right" to be odd places to look for icons of America, to say nothing of being embodiments of Aryan archetypes. Well, too bad for them; they're losing anyway, and that lack of imagination is why.[1]

The first generation of Traditionalists knew that the Tradition they defined and defended was precisely that which manifested itself in all parts of so-called "traditional" societies; conversely, even the smallest, most "irrelevant" part of a Traditional culture could serve as a vehicle of metaphysical principles; hence the importance, especially to Coomaraswamy and Daniélou, of art and music.[2]

---

[1] Trevor Lynch shows the right approach. Reviewing Jan Counen's *Coco Chanel and Igor Stravinsky*, he points out that "Stravinsky and Chanel . . . were both highly talented individuals in their own rights, but they also interest me because they combined *avant-garde* aesthetics with archaic, conservative, even reactionary tastes and convictions." See *Son of Trevor Lynch's White Nationalist Guide to the Movies*, ed. Greg Johnson (San Francisco: Counter-Currents, 2015).

[2] As Baron Evola says: "'Tradition,' in the complete sense, is a feature of the periods which Vico would call 'heroic ages' — where a sole forma-

These two films, *Ultrasuede* and *Limelight*, each tell the tale of a White man from the North American heartland who, imbued with the Faustian Spirit, came to New York to make his dreams come true, only to be torn down by the undermen. And if that seems too depressing, you can watch *Party Monster* for a (perhaps unintentionally) comic take on the whole thing.[3]

They also display quite different documentary styles. *Ultrasuede* is typical of the modern, "guerilla" filmmaking school; the director, in this case one improbably named Whitney Sudler-Smith, makes himself part of the show, gonzo-style, sort of a less uptight Michael Moore but more serious than Sasha Baron Cohen.[4] *Limelight* is the more traditional, National Film Board of Canada style, but both are cobbled together from news footage and *vérité* clips, with present-day interviews added in for commentary, backstory, and reflections, all held together with contemporary music as grout.[5]

---

tive force, with metaphysical roots, manifested itself in customs as well as in religion, in law, in myth, *in artistic creations, in short in every particular domain of existence.* Where can the survival of tradition in this sense be found today? And, specifically, as European tradition, great, unanimous, and not peasant or folkloric, tradition? It is only in the sense of the levelling "totalitarianism" that tendencies towards political-cultural absolute unity have appeared. In concrete terms, the 'European tradition' as culture has nowadays as content only the private and more or less diverging interpretations of intellectuals and *scholars in fashion* . . ." —Julius Evola, "Spiritual And Structural Presuppositions of The European Union" in Greg Johnson, ed. *North American New Right*, vol. 1 (San Francisco: Counter-Currents, 2012).

[3] It's like *Rosenkrantz and Guildenstern are Dead* to Gatien's *Hamlet*. If, as I will suggest, Gatien found himself in the role of Wotan, Michael Alig would be his Loki.

[4] Halston turns out to have had a . . . friend . . . who seems to have been the real-life inspiration for Baron's Borat—it's easy to imagine him in Borat's yellow slingshot bikini—not that Sudler-Smith ever makes the point.

[5] *Limelight* is, after all, about a dance club entrepreneur, while *Ultrasuede* veers off, like its subject, into an infatuation with the Judaic-run Studio 54. Bizarrely, the latter film makes considerable use of Wild Cherry's "Play that Funky Music, White Boy" but keeps cutting out the words "White boy" in the chorus (perhaps using a version, similarly cut, that

Whether you like the first kind of documentary is largely a function of whether you like the filmmaker. As someone once explained tenure decisions to me, would you want to have lunch with this person for the next 20 years? Sudler-Smith starts off rather irritating, but damn if he doesn't kinda grow on yah.

Detroit, when I grew up there in the '60s and '70s, was not just mostly White but specifically a mixture of second or third generation Irish, recent European immigrants, mostly Polish, as well as internal immigrants from Appalachia, hillbillies, in short; the ones sung about, and singing, Bobby Bare's country hit "Detroit City."[6]

So one has to smile—well, our kind of people would—at his cherry red Pontiac Firebird with its Confederate license plates, and especially how his interview with *Vogue*'s Head Negro in Charge, Andre Leon Talley, is interrupted not just by his cellphone but his "Dixie" ringtone.[7]

All this seems to be based on some kind of Southern connection in his upbringing,[8] although his mother is more debutante than Daisy Duke, and her more recent marriage to a Tribesman—Arthur Goodhart Altschul—is more relevant, as we'll see. Smith even starts by bringing his mother on to try to explain his fascination with the '70s, and all they can come up with is his love of watching *Smokey and the Bandit* on TV. Hence, the car, the porn moustache, the vaguely but not oppressively "Southern" attitude.[9]

Like many immigrants, internal or otherwise, he calls on his "heritage" selectively; mostly, to annoy his interviewees. Wheth-

---

was used for airplay in Boston—banned in Boston?)—an interesting choice, given the Aryan themes we will find in Halston's life and work.

[6] Not for nothing did the Federal Court system link together Michigan, Ohio, Kentucky, and West Virginia into one district.

[7] And love Andre's smooth reaction: "Can somebody get me another cappuccino, puh-leeze?"

[8] One wishes he would wind up interviewing Hannibal Lecter, so that the good Doctor could tell him that "Good nutrition's given you some length of bone, but you're not more than one generation from poor white trash, are you . . . ? And that accent you've tried so desperately to shed: pure West Virginia."

[9] Though he does not "way over-southern it" as MST3k finds the actors in *Squirm*.

er this is a conscious strategy, or just Judaic/hillbilly bumptiousness, is unclear.

What soon becomes clear is that the whole thing is something of a vanity project. His childhood fascination with the '70s has become a grown-up obsession with great periods of decadence, from Babylon to Weimar, and he has become "interested" in Halston as the great symbol of '70s sleaze.

It's easy to imagine him simpering "Divine decadence" like Sally Bowles, so it's appropriate that his first stop is to interview Liza Minnelli. She patiently instructs the hapless Smith to "do some research" and stay away from the gossip, but Smith is incapable of really "getting" what Halston was or what he meant to the fashion world, despite all the people he interviews, so eventually, having run out of content, he circles back to his personal obsessions and devotes a great deal of time, and news footage, to Studio 54 and Halston's rather gruesome boy toy. He even finds time to interview Billy Joel, whose expertise on Halston is based on one line in one of his dumb songs. But he's rich, and famous, and a Tribesman, so enjoy![10]

It is interesting, though, to see juxtaposed interview subjects recalling all kinds of sex and drugs in the Studio 54 basement, with Liza's deadpan "I never saw anything like that." Allowing for selective memory, it's still a testament to Aristotle's dictum that poetry is truer than history.[11] We'll see soon what relevance, tiny though it is, Studio 54 may have to Halston.

Even within the wreckage of Smith's wretched film, there's enough material to suggest the real significance of Halston.

HALSTON: FASHION FASCISM, FASHION FUTURISM

Using simple shapes and luxe fabrics, Halston helped cast

---

[10] For more on Billy see James Holbeyfield, "Billy and Alexa Ray Joel," http://www.counter-currents.com/2013/02/billy-and-alexa-ray-joel/

[11] To anticipate our proposal of the correct way to view Halston, Smith's fixation on Studio 54 as the "key" to Halston reminds one of Pasolini's *Salo*, where the last days of Mussolini's Social Republic are recast as a reenactment of Sade's *120 Days of Sodom*. Of course, there is otherwise no similarity between the two auteurs.

off the hippie look in the '70s, and he was America's celebrity designer. Designer Ralph Rucci, whose first job was toiling in Halston's workshop, described the feeling at the time of the designer's influence, "It was going to be a new history. You knew it. Working on the clothes, you had never seen patterns like these before. You . . . had to think in different dimensions." *Vogue*'s Talley emphasized the American-ness of Halston's clothing, and its sense of post-war industriousness: "Ultimate quality for the American woman, or the international woman, with style glamour and class is his legacy."[12]

In order to understand the significance of Halston, I suggest we need to see him as an embodiment of the Faustian Man, Spengler's term for the spirit of Western, White civilization—or rather, culture, a significant difference for Spengler, as we shall see. Moreover, by looking at the contradictory advice by Spengler and the Italian Futurists to Faustian Man at the end of his culture's lifecycle, we can see how Halston's career trajectory instantiated the Futurist option that Spengler rejected as heroic, but inevitably doomed.[13]

SIMPLICITY, SPACE, LIGHT

The "prime symbol" of the Faustian is "pure limitless space."[14] We see this manifested in several ways throughout Halston's career.

Although his life was associated with excess, from sex and drugs to his six-figure orchid habit, Halston's clothes were characterized by elegant simplicity. As Rucci fondly recalls, "Nobody looked tasteful anymore."[15]

---

[12] "Disco's Not Dead; the Return of Halston," review of *Ultrasuede*, *Interview Magazine*, http://www.interviewmagazine.com/film/ultrasuede-in-search-of-halston%20/%20_

[13] For information on Spengler and the Futurists I am indebted to Kerry Bolton's "Faustianism and Futurism: Analogous Primary Elements in Two Doctrines on European Destiny" in *Aristokratia* (Manticore Press, 2013), pp. 82–114.

[14] Spengler, *Decline of the West*, vol. 1, p. 183.

[15] Sam Adams January 19, 2012, http://www.avclub.com/articles/

Not only his designs—simple, elegant mathematical expanses of pure fabric—but even his work methods manifested the same effortless command of space:

> None tells the story of his talent as well as one-time design assistant and now-famous couturier Ralph Rucci. One night, Halston startled him by throwing a bolt of purple chiffon on the floor and *cutting a dress out of a single piece of fabric, no seams necessary*. "It wraps around the body *in one piece* and it catches at the top of the neck. As a woman walks, it opens a bit at the leg and she almost becomes naked in this vapor of chiffon," Rucci says. "Do you know anybody who can *think in three dimensions* and cut it right there on the floor? I don't."[16]

The story is repeated in the film, and seems to be the basis of a kind of fashion myth—one inevitably thinks of the cloak Mary sewed for Jesus, without seam. As we'll see, eventually lots will be cast over the ownership of Halston's empire.[17]

We also find pure, limitless space, and its accompaniment, pure light, in Halston's workspace and living space. As his career skyrocketed, he moved from a small boutique to the 21st floor of Olympic Towers in New York's Midtown.

"THE KING NEEDED A CASTLE"

The showroom/offices, which Smith visits today to interview Halston model Pat Cleveland, are one, contiguous space, bisected by floor to ceiling pocket doors (costing 500k or 5 million in today's money, we are breathlessly informed). The walls are mirrored. "It was like being in a glass box" Cleveland recalls, adding that she used the World Trade Center, visible through the floor to ceiling glass of one wall, "as my focal point" when

---

ultrasuede-in-search-of-halston,67879/

[16] "Halston we hardly knew ye," http://www.thedaily.com/page/2012/01/20/012012-arts-movies-review-halston-1-3

[17] When the ultimate ownership of Halston's empire was decided, the new owners sent security guards—centurians—to effect the return of every item of clothing Halston had ever given a model or celebrity.

applying makeup.

"He called me the moth. I was always flying to the light."

"Always had big windows and sun."

—Liza

And something else could be seen more closely: Halston's "insolent boast" (Spengler): "I don't have to go to church. [St. Patrick's] is right across the street." —Halston

The same marshaling of vast amounts of space and light occurs in Halston's equally famous townhouse, at the time the only contemporary house built in New York since the war. With 30-foot ceilings and a 60-foot living room, it was the scene of legendary dinners and parties, which of course is all that Smith is interested in. More importantly for us, the carpet and furnishings are monochromatic grey, a color we'll be seeing again in significant places, with candles everywhere. After tearing himself away from reminiscing about "decadent parties" at the townhouse, we return to the offices so that we can see Smith get a delusory compliment from Cleveland about looking like Halston, while we get the more important fact that "he always wore black." The theme of monochromatic uniforms will become important in our reflections here.

HARNESSING TECHNOLOGY

But if Halston had merely been a skilled dress-cutter he would have earned nothing but the scorn of Spengler or the Futurists. Spengler regarded the "artsy craftsy" obsessions of many Conservatives as a dead end, a confession of defeat, like—as we shall see—pacifism. Faustian Man, to be true to himself, must harness the latest technology to his ends.

Halston did this most famously with his realization that simple, flowing designs would be perfectly realized by a new synthetic fabric, Ultrasuede. Typically, Smith gloms onto the word for his very title, but says nothing about it. So, courtesy of Wikipedia, here's a quick rundown:

> Ultrasuede is the trade name for a synthetic microfiber fabric invented in 1970 by Dr. Miyoshi Okamoto, a scientist

working for Toray Industries. In Japan it is sold under the brand name Ecsaine. It was the world's first ultra-microfiber. It is often described as an artificial substitute for suede leather. The fabric is multifunctional: it is used in fashion, interior decorating, automotive and other vehicle upholstery, and industrial applications, such as protective fabric for electronic equipment. It is also a very popular fabric in the manufacture of footbags (also known as hacky sacks).

Warfare/Uniformity/Democratizing Fashion

For Spengler, the very dynamism of Faustian Man's nature prevents him, even in the Winter of his culture, from simply surrendering to the inevitable decline; rather, he will harness his technological achievements and hurl himself full steam ahead.[18] Pacifism was impossible, short of senility; the race's will to power, expressing itself in all aspects of life, from personal interaction to vast cultural enterprises to, indeed, literal warfare, must inevitably lead to conflict and struggle for supremacy. As Kerry Bolton says, "The aesthetic of the new Western will to power is ushered by both Spengler and the Futurists by struggle."[19]

Here, however, Spengler and the Futurists diverge, in a way relevant to our look at Halston. For Spengler, art, including presumably fashion, was dead, fit only for museums. "Artists" today are just kidding themselves at best; at worst, poisoning our culture, or what's left of it, with their decaying "ideas." The best White brains should be directed to science, and in particular, engineering — interestingly, Evola's field of study.

"Art, yes, but in concrete and steel."

—Spengler

The Futurists seem to take Spengler's challenge but invert it; they would attempt to make art *out of* concrete and steel.[20] "There

---

[18] Bolton, pp. 84–86.
[19] Bolton, p. 89.
[20] "Appear" because, as Bolton makes clear, neither Spengler nor the Futurists seems to have even heard of each other, much less been influ-

is nothing for us to admire today but the dreadful symphonies of the shrapnel and the mad sculptures that our inspired artillery molds among the masses of the enemy."[21]

Of course, although the Futurists contributed much to the public monuments and graphic propaganda of Fascist Italy, they never actually shot up any enemy troops—just as the Surrealist Breton never fired a gun into a crowd. Their struggle, like Halston's, took the form of what Nietzsche called *Geisterkrieg*, comparable to the European New Right's—and the North American New Right's—notion of metapolitics.

The struggle originates with one, charismatic individual—a Marinetti, a Halston, a Warhol, or a Chávez—who seeks to impose his vision—his will to power—on society.

> It is from these differentiated individuals that influence is exerted upon society in the wider perspective—[forming] *the loci and focal points* of the causal power structure. Individualism is followed by the formation of groups and organs, related tendencies join together . . . ; between these centres of power friction, recognition of one another's forces, [etc.] Every Aristocratic Radical maintains the central position within their respective collective as the creative principle until eventually society is presided over by a new aristocracy of creators.

In this "optimistic" version of Spengler,

> Culture, therefore, will return when the people work together to place value upon producing single individuals who are capable of creating and shaping the current to produce great works. . . . Nietzsche's *Geisterkrieg* has no need of garnishing votes, no need of propaganda or money—all it needs to be enacted is to win the hearts and the minds of the people—which is why it is a "war of the spirit" against the "cultural philistine."[22]

---

enced. The same, of course, with them and Halston.

[21] Marinetti, "War: The Ultimate Hygiene," quoted in Bolton, p. 90.

[22] Gwendolyn von Taunton, "Aristocratic Radicalism: The Political

"All it needs"? This seems like the kind of "optimism" that Spengler decried as unrealistic, in an essay defending himself from the corresponding charge of "pessimism."[23] The experience of Futurism, Fascism, and, as we shall see, Halston, suggests he has a point.

Although it may seem a bit of a stretch to construe the "struggle" of, say, an Andy Warhol to impose his vision on every aspect of society in terms of warfare, in the case of Halston the image imposes itself, again and again.[24]

Halton's first *triumph*—and is this not already a military term?—occurred when, still only a milliner at Bergdorf's, he was selected to design a hat for Jackie Kennedy to wear to the inaugural. The result, the famous "pillbox" hat, was an instant fashion craze and remains a fashion icon. And of course, in name and form, it's entirely military.[25]

Then, striking out on his own as a designer, Halston scores his greatest triumph when he is one of five American designers selected, for the first time, to exhibit in France.

Philosophy of Friedrich Nietzsche," in *Aristokratia*, pp. 11–49; quotes on pp. 28, 40, and 48.

[23] See his "Pessimism?" from 1921.

[24] As Greg Johnson writes: "If the moral life is rooted in a plurality of different cultures and ways of life, this also implies the existence of real conflicts of interest. These conflicts can always become existentially *serious*: peoples can fight over them; men can kill and die over them; in short, there can be war. And the potential for war is the origin of the political in Schmitt's sense," in "Leo Strauss, the Conservative Revolution, and National Socialism," *North American New Right*, vol. 2, ed. Greg Johnson (San Francisco: Counter-Currents, 2016).

[25] According to Wikipedia: "Historically, the pillbox was also military headgear, often including a chin strap, and can still be seen on ceremonial occasions in some countries, especially former members of the Commonwealth. For example, the Royal Military College of Canada dress uniform includes a pillbox hat. A pillbox cap, also referred to as a kilmarnock, is a modern manufacture of the traditional headdress worn by members of virtually all Gurkha Regiments. During the late Roman Empire, the pillbox, then known as the pilleus or 'Pannonian cap' was worn by Roman soldiers," https://en.wikipedia.org/wiki/Pillbox_hat

Versailles '73 tells of an EPIC—people usually use this word for non-epic moments, but this is one that's deserving—fashion show that would put five well-known French couturiers against five, then less globally recognized and respected, American fashion designers . . . the end result of what happened that night would forever change fashion, the lives of the designers involved, and the models that served as muses that night; especially the African American models who came onto stage and dazzled the predominantly French audience like nothing they had ever seen before.[26]
. . . These designers put ready-to-wear on 'the map', and took fashion in a new direction, away from the elaborate haute couture that only the noble and, well, rich could wear, and opened everyone's eyes to a new way of dress, that was

---

[26] Halston's use of so-called "African-American" models had nothing to do with modern multi-culti notions or affirmative action. "I wanted the best girl I could get, the best girls in America." That included Midwestern blondes as well, even from Detroit. Partly based on his pro-Americanism, which we'll discuss soon, it is mostly due to his Aristocratic Radicalism, itself fully in line with American ideas of "natural aristocracy," promoted by Jefferson and Emerson (one of Nietzsche's favorite authors, by the way). See von Taunton, pp. 21ff. The model interviewed for the film, Pat Cleveland, like Andre Talley, clearly belongs to what W. E. B. Dubois would call "the talented tenth."

Spengler incurred the wrath of NS Germany when, in *The Hour of Decision*, he mocked biological notions of race and emphasized the far more important notion of "having race": a mestizo like Hugo Chávez is a man of race, unlike a nominally White globalist; the former can be our ally, the latter is the enemy. Evola also contrasted "zoological" notions of race with his own ideas of physical, psychological, and spiritual race, for which he too was declared *persona non grata* in NS Germany.

Interestingly too, the contemporary work von Taunton relies most on for her discussion of Nietzsche's Aristocratic Radicalism is "The Challenge of Aristocratic Radicalism" by N. A. Tobias, a black scholar at the University of Michigan. Also, Halston's personal disinterest, contrary to the stereotype of "fashion designers," is what enabled him to field a group of Halstonettes that was, despite the uniformity of dress, quite "diverse" for its time; it is the heterosexual, homophobic Judaic "porn" producers that have eventually created the truly uniform, plastic "bimbo" as a "model" for women.

fit for all.[27]

"The Battle of Versailles," as *Women's Wear Daily* called it, was a rout for the French. Supremely confident—"The French didn't consider America as anything," fellow designer Stephen Burrows recalls. The *ancien regime* put up the whole creaking machinery of their high "culture," including . . . ballet dancers. Really?[28]

"They had scenery and staging . . . it was really kind of corny."

—Stephen Burrows

For once, Sudley-Smith gets it right, saying to Minnelli, "So, the Americans whipped the French again." Or as Yves Saint Laurent had to admit, "We've learned something."
Learned what? As Minnelli recalls: "We did it like Americans. We did it like Halston. Direct, to the point, effective."
Or as Marinetti might say, ballet dancers are no match for bullets.
Simplicity, whether cutting a dress without a pattern[29] or employing a high-tech fabric that could be used for anything by anyone, this was the purest expression of Faustian Man, the fit weapon to combat the cultural philistines.
We'll get back to that bit about "Americans" and clothing "fit for all" in a moment, but first let's finish the chronicles of Halston by looking at his next triumph: Halston went to China—like Nixon—ostensibly to open up Chinese manufacturing for American clothing makers. Actually, it was another field for Halston to im-

---

[27] Sharontina, "The Runway Battle of Versailles '73: A Story That Needed to be Told," *The Runway Times*, September 13, 2012 (http://therunwaytimes.com/the-runway-battle-of-versailles-73-a-story-that-needed-to-be-told/). The author says the story of the event "is finally being told" which seems like a fitting response to Sudley-Smith's earlier yet trivializing film.

[28] "Nietzsche's primary task is to create a transition point which shifts the emphasis from the old regime towards a new and eminently more useful cultural stratification." —Von Taunton, p. 15.

[29] "We are not given patterns to imitate" —Spengler, "Pessimism."

pose his will: "Can the designs be changed? Is that such a problem?"

But although Halston's more colorful designs and models win over the dour Chinese bureaucrats, we also notice that there's not that much difference between the two groups. Next to the Chinese officials, Halston's own monochromatic clothes fit right in, and when two officials give approval to one of the models' outfits—"Nice color"—we notice the color, at least in the washed-out news footage, matches their own suits.[30]

In fact, we've seen these models at various earlier scenes, as Halston's constant entourage, known variously as the Halstonettes (*WWD*) or Ultraettes (Talley), making grand entrances on yachts—another military image—all, including Halston, attired in the same color, which would change on schedule throughout the day, even in China. And remember the pillbox hat?

Indeed, what better expression of the modern, technological age than the uniform, especially for a designer known for simplicity, monochromatic, uniformity ('natch)?[31]

Reflecting on the China trip, model Pat Cleveland muses, "He did it for America. Everything he did was for America."

And America, as Minnelli told us earlier, "did it like Halston."

So it becomes clear that what Halston wanted to do for America was provide it with a uniform—not so obvious and forced as the Mao suit, but a wardrobe simple, affordable, and flattering on all. America's true nature, expressed in its clothing, just as Tradi-

---

[30] It appears to be the same grey as the furniture in the famous townhouse; when asked about it by a talk-show audience member, he says it "brings people out." We'll revisit that guest in a moment.

[31] The Halstonettes' landing by yacht at the celebration of Halston's contract to design Braniff's uniforms and planes, with its conjunction of black uniforms, sea, and air recalls the quasi-Futurist and Italian air ace D'Annunzio's pirate republic of Fiume, whose black naval uniforms—designed by D'Annunzio himself—were the clear inspiration for the famous SS uniforms, right down to the Death's Head. See Hakim Bey's "March on Fiume" (http://www.counter-currents.com/2012/03/march-on-fiume/). Fiume is one of the historical instantiations of Bey's concept of "Temporary Autonomous Zones," and is obviously related to the Nietzschean *Geisterkrieg*, just as is Peter Gatien's club scene to be discussed in the next section.

tion is manifested in the Hindu *sari* or the Arab's *thawb*. Exactly what a man whose talent lay in fashion design could give to—or impose upon by sheer will—a still majority White nation facing the coming struggle to the death against what Spengler called "the colored world revolution." "I always wanted to reach a wider America. When you're able to produce a dress—that a woman can wear to work, wear out, that's machine-washable—for $75, that's magic."

Things did not quite work out, but before turning to Halston's decline and fall, let's ask ourselves, what with this America bit? Who cares? Why on Earth did Halston care?

As we saw in discussing the necessity of struggle, cultures are rooted in real communities, not any abstract "humanity."[32] The task, as the Futurists realized, was that, "Western technics must be harnessed for the great deeds to be undertaken by the West, *or at least by Italy*, and not in the service of democratic and humanistic doctrines in the service of a nebulous 'mankind.'"[33]

The task, then, having overthrown the French hegemony and pacified China with trade, was to clothe America. But how?

Here was Halston's last great idea—his last temptation, as it were.[34] Halston inked a licensing deal—worth, he said, a billion dollars—in the '70s!—with down-market mass-marketer J. C. Penny's. Such deals are fairly common today, but the fashion industry was not ready for them back then. Trying to lead the masses, Halston got too far out in front of his industry peers, and lost control of them. He lost his flagship position at Bergdorf, had his

---

[32] As Greg Johnson writes: "The core of a culture is a set of ideals or norms. To participate in a culture is to feel that one is part of the culture and the culture is part of oneself. It is an experience of *identity*. It is also an experience of *commitment* to the culture's ideals, the feeling that they are *obligatory*, that they demand that one change one's life. This obligation is experienced as a kind of vitalizing tension between the ideal and the reality of one's life, leading one to master one's passions and mobilize one's energies toward *living up* to the ideal. The moral life, in short, requires cultivation within a normative culture," "Leo Strauss, the Conservative Revolution, and National Socialism."

[33] Bolton, p. 86, my emphasis.

[34] Did the Prince of the Air bring Halston to the heights of Olympic Towers in order to display the world before him, as in Matthew 4: 8–10?

name diluted by being attached to too many and too poorly thought-out products—basically, anything that could have Ultrasuede tacked onto it, in line with our idea of the creator imposing his vision on every aspect of a culture—and after a number of corporate shifts and buy-outs, wound up with the ultimate indignity of losing control of his own name. "Halston" was now the registered trademark of a mayonnaise company.

So what ultimately happened to what Mel Brooks might call "Halston: the Label"?

> In 2007, *Harvey Weinstein* curated a team of people, including ex-Jimmy Choo scion Tamara Mellon and *Rachel Zoe*, to revive the Halston label. . . . Zoe, an avid Halston collector, dissociated herself from the revival not long after she signed on. (Sudler-Smith approached her about participating in the film around the time she was dismantling her contract, so she didn't participate.) The team was plagued with unstable management and *halfhearted investors*, who seemed to have good intentions but *did not want to invest the necessary energy and resources to see them through.* That revival fizzled not long after *Sarah Jessica Parker* practically *sneaked out of her contract* as creative director of the more affordable Halston Heritage line—which will endure without the pricier Halston line in her wake. (Halston hired Parker after shooting for *Ultrasuede* wrapped, but she lent her support by attending its Tribeca Film Festival premiere in 2010.) Now Halston Heritage is run by ex-BCBG president Ben Malka, and owned by him and Hilco Consumer Capital, which bought Weinstein and Parker's contracts out. Though BCBG is a *watered-down, mid-market mass label* that can hardly be thought of as fashion-forward, it's unclear what Malka will do with Halston.[35]

A veritable gathering of the Elders of Zion, to fiddle and fuss over the corpse of an Aryan talent they coveted but now have no

---

[35] Amy Odell, "From the Disco to JC Penney: The Enduring Tragedy of Halston," *New York*, http://nymag.com/thecut/2011/12/halston-from-the-disco-to-jcpenney.html

Earthly clue what to do with!³⁶ Harvey Weinstein (a.k.a. Les Grossman of *Tropic Thunder*), Rachel Zoe (née Rosenzweig), Sara Jessica Parker,³⁷ and even apparently the Talmudic sage Ben Malka—a dead ringer for Jerry Orbach—who, to answer *New York*'s question, plan to run Halston the Brand as "an American fashion legacy."

"Legacy"; Zoe as an "avid Halston collector"; as with everything else, what White culture creates winds up in one of the famous international Judaic "collections."³⁸ And get this:

> How ironic that *Sudler-Smith's stepdaddy, Arthur Altschul,* was part of the corporate takeover phenomenon that crushed Halston and made a bad name for licensing. In fact, daddy's company, Goldman Sachs, was pretty much the nexus of the takeover phenomenon: remember folks, it's all about who can get the credit.³⁹

Getting back to the "optimistic" Futurists, it seems clear that

---

³⁶ As James Holbeyfield puts it: "These people, adapted to the white brain instead of to a piece of this beautiful earth, truly know the price of every continent and the value of none." See his review of Werner Herzog's Antarctic odyssey *Encounters at the End of the World*, http://www.counter-currents.com/2013/03/werner-herzogs-encounters-at-the-end-of-the-world/

³⁷ Parker has been pushed for decades by the Judaic media as some kind of sex symbol—despite looking more equine than aquiline—or role model for modern "liberated" women—apparently, be like promiscuous gay men—as if they were Dolly Levi promoting an unpromising spinster. She makes an interesting contrast with Anjelica Huston, an actual Halston model we see in archival footage and interviews. Her equally . . . unusual features suggest a beauty that dwells on other planes than ours; superhuman rather than subhuman, elfin rather than bestial. Like Meg Foster, it would be possible to imagine a production of LOTR where she plays Galadriel, while Parker suggests nothing more otherworldly than a wicked witch or stepmother. Only Ed Wood, appropriately enough, would cast her as the Angel of Peace.

³⁸ And should any White group try to "loot" them, all must be tracked down and "restored" to them, even after almost a hundred years.

³⁹ A. Nolen on *Ultrasuede*, http://anolen.com/tag/ultrasuede-in-search-of-halston/

the "pessimistic" Spengler foresaw Halston's error. The fatal flaw in the Faustian and Futurist visions was that The West was not liberated from plutocracy, and Western technics remains firmer than ever in the grasp of Money.

Indeed, the recent "credit crisis" (i.e., the Greater Depression) only shows that Goldman Sachs is indeed even more the Master of the Universe than ever before.[40] We must wait until that changes before our culture will be "presided over by a new aristocracy of creators."[41]

Until then, what the global financiers want is not the "chaotic" world of competing cultures unified by their own styles under their various cultural elites, but one "world culture" unified as merely as interchangeable humanoids under the finan-

---

[40] The Left has never understood how different at least some German bankers were in the '30s, and even today talks about "bankers supporting Hitler" and comparing it to today's so-called "corporate fascism." As Bolton remarks, German bankers were "conscious of a national and cultural mission" unlike today's globalists. See Bolton, p. 101.

[41] On a related note, one thing Spengler warned against was "noisy self-advertisement." It is in this light that we should view Halston's legendary hard-partying lifestyle, which Sudler-Smith seems to think reveals his essence. On the contrary, it was a fairly deliberate marketing strategy, creating an indelible connection in the public mind between fame, celebrity, and Halston's clothes, which he would be very happy to sell you down at Penny's. It also serves as a release from the immense tension felt most acutely by the creator type: "The gap between the ideal and the real is bridged by a longing of the soul for *perfection*. This longing is a tension, like the tension of the bowstring or the lyre, that makes human greatness possible" (Greg Johnson, "Postmodernism, Hedonism and Death," http://www.counter-currents.com/2013/03/postmodernism-hedonism-and-death/); see also his remarks on the "*vitalizing tension* between the ideal and the reality of one's life, leading one to master one's passions and mobilize one's energies toward *living up* to the ideal" in "Leo Strauss, the Conservative Revolution, and National Socialism," cited above). As we'll see, Peter Gatien would try a better strategy, controlling his partying by limiting himself to occasional, secretive binges in locked hotel rooms, but would eventually be counseled to "be seen more" to create a more welcoming atmosphere; once again, the marketing strategy wins out, fatally.

ciers' rule.[42]

As Evola said, discussing Spengler's contrast of culture and "civilization" (meaning, among other things, rule by Burnham's "managerial elite" and other financial types):

> If it is absurd to pursue our higher ideal in the context of a *'Zivilisation'*, [as Halston unknowingly did] *because it would become twisted and almost inverted*, [as Halston's vision was subverted into what we have today] we can still recognise, in the overcoming of what has precisely the character of *'Zivilisation'*, the premise for every really reconstructive initiative.[43]

Thus Halston's end is tragic, because, like Faust, he was unable to overcome his fated environment.[44]

But as several voice-overs tell us as the film fades out, there would not be this tragic end if the work hadn't been good. And the work remains: still seen, still worn, still, as Rucci says, untouchable.[45]

---

[42] "When a culture is eviscerated of its *defining worldview*, all integrity, all *unity of style is lost*. Cultural integrity gives way to multiculturalism, which is merely a pretentious way of describing a shopping mall where artifacts are bought and sold, *mixed and matched to satisfy emancipated consumer desires*: a wax museum jumping to the pulse of commerce" (Greg Johnson, "Post Modernism, Hedonism and Death"(http://http/www.counter-currents.com/2013/03/postmodernism-hedonism-and-death/) [my emphases]). See also René Guénon, "Unity versus Uniformity" in *The Reign of Quantity*.

[43] "Spiritual and Structural Presuppositions of the European Union."

[44] Ted Sallis writes: "We can project a future High Culture that is based on the ultimate and successful [eventual] achievement of what was previously considered to be 'unattainable.' I would argue that the Christian foundation of the Faustian High Culture is responsible [for this inevitable failure of men becoming as Gods]. . . . The full development of Western Man has been restrained by an alien religion that has placed shackles on his mind and soul [Gatien will attempt to revive ancient pagan rites]" — Ted Sallis, "The Overman High Culture: the Future of the West," *North American New Right*, vol. 1.

[45] See my review of de Palma's *The Untouchables* for a discussion of

Smith seems incapable of learning to appreciate Halston through his interviews. At best, he winds up appreciating that Halston was not just the ultimate decadent of the '70s of Smith's teenage fantasies, but "had a lot of friends." Sheesh.[46]

Perhaps inevitably, Smith ends his movie with a credit sequence that layers a montage of Halston sketches over The Trampps "Disco Inferno." It really kind of works, suggesting a kind of fashion *Götterdämmerung* for this most Aryan of fashionistas.[47]

The real end of Halston was more subtle; after moving to San Francisco, he bought an 800k Rolls Royce and had himself driven through redwood forests in Northern California, a perfect image of archeofuturism.

Ultrasuede is ultimately a failure, due to Smith's vanity and ignorance ("Who's Diana Vreeland?"). Despite himself, the story he tells has enough elements to suggest that Halston deserves a full-scale treatment of his role as an Aryan fashion entrepreneur. Smith, however, is just not the White Guy to do it.

No matter; the Poet who will sing the tragic legend of Halston will someday appear:

> The Poet reminds us that we were not born yesterday. He restores the foundations of our identity, the paramount expression of an ethical and *aesthetic inheritance* that is "ours," that he held in trust. And *the principles that he brought to life in his models* never cease to reappear to us, proof that the hidden thread of our tradition could not be broken.[48]

---

the true, aristocratic meaning of "untouchable"'" in *The Homo & the Negro: Masculinist Meditations on Politics and Popular Culture*, ed. Greg Johnson (San Francisco: Counter-Currents, 2012).

[46] Sudley-Smith doesn't even have a clear idea of what friendship itself means; having heard Liza was at Halston's funeral, he naively asks her what she sang; she coolly informs him that "it wasn't about me."

[47] James Hawes recent *Excavating Kafka* (London: Cuercus, 2008) suggests that even Kafka got the Weinstein treatment from Brod, Buber and company; both he and Halston might have been better off burning their sketches rather than leaving it for the vultures of Kazakhstan.

[48] Dominique Venner, "Homer: The European Bible," in *North American New Right*, vol. 1.

"The scandal involved Crowley's Abbey of Thelema in Sicily where he reportedly held Satanic type rituals of quite depraved character, and where shortly one of his acolytes died apparently from bad water."

— Kerry Bolton[49]

While *Ultrasuede* presented us with the White Entrepreneur undone by the forces of Judaic Big Business, *Limelight* presents the parallel spectacle of the White Entrepreneur up against the forces of Judaic Big Law.

Limelight, despite its name, is an altogether darker film. Halston's bright, sunny '70s are a thing of the past.[50]

Peter Gatien, though born and raised in semi-rural Canada, presents an image of the Ultimate '80s New Yorker — black clothes, black (at least back then) hair, and a unique touch, black eye-patch, the significance of which we'll soon see. If we did not already know from the newspapers, we can sense Gatien is doomed, though unlike Halston, even now he lives — although, like the punishment Athens offered Socrates, it is a living exile.

His world is not the bright world of Halston's window-walled skyscrapers and runway shows. Gatien's clubs are dark, actual tunnels and abandoned churches. Here though there is a kind of link, for while Halston at his peak looked down from Olympic Towers on St. Patrick's Cathedral, here Gatien makes his greatest splash by taking over an abandoned Episcopal church, creating the legendary Limelight. While Halston set up an alternative home of the gods, from which he could look down on the Christian peasants, Gatien moved right in, reversing the historic trend of Christians taking over pagan temples and holy places (a favor returned by Islam). This would prove to be his greatest crime: defiling churches to provide spaces for kids to re-enact ancient Mystery rites of drugs, sex, music, and dance.[51]

---

[49] Bolton, "Political Aspects of Crowley's Thelema," p. 237.

[50] See Michael Hoffman's "Loftiness of Rock: The Authentic Popular Mystery-Religion of the Late 20th Century" at his site, egodeath.com. The former "Episcopal Church of the Holy Communion" was indeed an appropriate site.

[51] See my "Fashion Tips for the Far-from-Fabulous Right" in *The Ho-*

Being set almost a generation later also means that unlike Smith and his TV-derived image of Halston and "decadence," I actually had some experience of my own to judge the portrayal of New York City club life in *Limelight*. Of course, my club life was very much among the anti- or rather simply non-Gatien circles, such as Jackie 60 and the other events held at the alternative club Mother, inspired more by Warhol's Factory than Halston,[52] and at a time when Gatien's clubs were, as documented here, already invested with the "bridge and tunnel" crowd that The Tunnel, despite its name, was never supposed to cater to.

On the other hand, Giuliani's attack on Gatien was known to be only the symbol of a widespread attack on nightlife in general, so when Jackie 60 took Gatien's trial as one of its weekly themes I found myself there, attired in ironically worn "New York City Black" and with black eye-patch; that I was actually mistaken by more than a few people for Gatien himself that night was due more to bad lights and too many drugs, especially since I did not alter what was then a full head of blond hair.

Of Gatien's own clubs — there were eventually four, including of course Limelight — I remember only attending Limelight once, and then only when a friend was DJ-ing some Gothic night off in one of the many little ex-chapel spaces. For some reason, although the idea of setting it in a church seemed genius, it never really appealed to me in actuality; considering what happened to Michael Alig, and the people around him — the subject of *Party Monster* as well as some parts of *Limelight* — that's probably all for the best.

We shift, then, from Halston among the California redwoods to another Aryan region, the Great White North of Canada. Little Peter is playing the implicitly — or not so implicitly — White game of hockey, when a puck or a stick cost him an eye. The settlement money — it's not clear who or what was the party at fault, but one suspects a school system or public arena — provides Gatien with the stake he needs to start his first club.

Is it too much to find here the archetypal Aryan legend, Wotan

---

mo & the Negro.

[52] "Everything was just sunny and perfect then" — MST3k on the opening scenes of *The Starfighters*, an early '60s Air Force epic starring future Congressman Bob Dornan.

trading his eye to the Well of All Knowing for its wisdom?[53] We will see.

Speaking of Wisdom, his first club, still in Canada, opened with an early incarnation of Rush, the *Über*-White rock band. Rush, of course, is an extremely, though implicitly, White band, and while its relatively literate lyrics are more associated with Neil Peart's Objectivist interests, they actually operate on a deeper level as explorations of the drug-induced Mystery experience that Gatien's clubs would latter provide on a more massive scale.[54]

Like many Canadians, after making a little money, Gatien traded symbolic but hostile polar regions for the more effectively sunny realms, opening the first Limelight club in Florida, then another in Atlanta, which quickly became known as "the hottest club in the South."

But Gatien knew that you're never on top of an industry until you succeed in New York. Here we see the most important of Gatien's Aryan characteristics, his desire to excel in his chosen field, and the willingness to do whatever hard work it took to get there.

"I figured I had paid enough dues to compete with Studio 54."

"You need to be the best, you need to be innovative, you need to be the best in your industry."

"I want to be the best at what I do."[55]

---

[53] Kris Kershaw, *The One-eyed God: Odin and the (Indo-)Germanic Männerbünde* (Washington, D.C. Institute for the Study of Man, 2000). If configuring Gatien as Wotan due to his eye patch seems a stretch, several people in the documentary explicitly point out how the eye patch functioned to make him the perfect tabloid victim.

[54] See Hoffman again, "Rush Lyrics Alluding to Mystic Dissociative Phenomena," http://egodeath.com/rushlyrics.htm

[55] The Aryan code, right from the beginning: "Homer does not conceptualize, as philosophers later did. He makes visible; he shows living examples, teaching the qualities that make a man a '*kalos k'agathos*,' noble and accomplished. 'Always be the best,' Peleus told his son Achilles, 'better than the rest' (*Iliad*, VI, 208)." Venner, "Homer: The European Bible."

> "The only way to run not just one but 4 of the best clubs is to work 16 hour days, 6 day weeks."
>
> —Gatien

To compete with the post-Halston Studio 54, Gatien needed to be different. First, he'd play rock not disco. And he decided that "chrome and neon" had gone as far as it could be taken, so he made an archeofuturist move—"art and architecture" were the way to go—"If you could find me a church," he told his agents, "that would be perfect."

Thus Gatien acquired the obsolete Church of the Holy Communion, a fitting setting for a club scene that would not only evoke the pre-modern pinnacle of White civilization, the era of the great cathedrals—yes, I know, it's an Episcopal church from 1846, but good enough for an allusion, especially if you're high already—but also, going even further, the drug-infused Mystery cults of the West and Tantric rites of the East.[56]

AIDS, of course, put a damper on things for a few years, but by the '90s, nightlife, and Gatien, were on the rebound.

But at this point, Nemesis appeared, in the form of two shady characters who approached Gatien with cunning plans for taking his clubs to the next level. I suggest we continue the mythological approach and designate them as Loki and Fafner.

Loki was Michael Alig, who arrived in New York with the idea of "being the next Andy Warhol"—although, as pointed out to him at the time, Warhol was still alive. Despite having bankrupted every club he's been associated with, Gatien decides to give him a dead, unfashionable night. Inexplicably, his "Disco 2000"

---

[56] "It was pagan Rome with acid." Although at this time the drug of choice was the *white* powder known as cocaine—Gatien's security director points out that in New York, until then, "we were *traditionalists*—just heroin and cocaine"—eventually, "ecstasy punch" would be "handed out from the DJ booth like communion wine," an allusion to the "mixed wine" used not only in Greek mystery cults and Christian "love feasts" but even socially, as in Plato's *Symposium*. See Hoffman's "Wine and Sacred Meals" (http://egodeath.com/WineAndSacredMeals.htm). Nightlife at that time, the mid-'80s, "had no rules"—unlike today, of course, when everything from smoking to "sugary drinks" is banned—and was essentially "a secret society."

party becomes a hit.⁵⁷

Fafner is one "Lord Michael," described as a "wannabe gangsta" and, several times, a "Staten Island scumbag." He epitomizes the shaved-headed Negro-worshiping "White" Youth of Today. Lord Michael's night, 'Future Shock" — anti-archeofuturism defined — introduced a new drug — Ecstasy — and a new crowd — unfashionable "bridge and tunnel" types from the "outer boroughs" — think, *Saturday Night Fever* — a mixture of "soccer rioters and ravers." Everyone someone notes with pleasure, "on the same level."⁵⁸

Typically, this moment of Nemesis appears to be that of apotheosis; Wotan's entry into Valhalla triggers what will eventually become *Götterdämmerung*. If I still seem to be hitting the Wotan theme too hard, consider how Gatien was portrayed at the time,

---

⁵⁷ James St. James, who I like to think of as my *Doppelgänger* in Gatien's world, sneers in *Party Monster* that "Somehow, his dopey language [dividing the world into Skrinks and Scrots, a crude and arbitrary attempt to emulate a true hierarchy] caught on, like his stupid parties. . . . Suddenly, the hateful little twerp was the king of the club kids." Alig is the Anti-Gatien; while Gatien is praised for the essential ability to "know what makes a party good or bad," the credits to *Party Monster* as set to what might well be Alig's credo: "Everything bad is good."

⁵⁸ The "democracy" of the mystery cults is often misunderstood, perhaps deliberately. While theoretically open to all, regardless of social station or caste, initiation itself had its own qualifications. While Gatien originally envisioned Limelight as having "10% of everybody" in the crowd, this is altogether different from the almost "open door" policy of raves and other examples of a more Christian, slave-morality inspired "promiscuity" as Evola calls it in discussing the decline of Rome. In a more specifically initiatory context, he discusses the famous "paradox" than an initiated murderer would gain immortality, while an ordinary good citizen would wind up in Hades or worse; see Julius Evola and the Ur Group, *Introduction to Magic: Rituals and Practical Techniques for the Magus*, trans. Guido Stucco, ed. Michael Moynihan (Rochester, Vt.: Inner Traditions, 2001), pp. 182–83, where he notes that in the unqualified subject, "the power of initiation would either fail to take hold or could act in a negative, distorted or even destructive manner on the subject." This is essentially what happened in Gatien's clubs with the introduction of "E." As one of the interview subjects says, this is always what happens — Woodstock becomes Altamont.

from news reports—"A single cool, watchful eye looks over all. The eye of Peter Gatien, the Lord of Nightlife"—to rap songs: "Running New York's night scene/with one eye closed like Peter Gatien."

And of course, it was the manic Alig who put him forward as the Face of Nightlife, insisting that he shouldn't be "just this shadowy figure who would occasionally show up" but rather drag him out "to be seen to have fun!"

Instead, Gatien ran smack dab into Rudolph Giuliani and his Neocon inspired program to "clean up" New York by focusing not on "real" crimes but on "quality of life" violations.[59]

Here another mythological figure steps in: Alberich, in the person of one Sean Markham. Thrown out of Limelight for selling drugs, Markham will take his revenge by becoming a DEA informant, to prove Gatien . . . was selling drugs.

The idea was to use New York's "nuisance abatement" law; all Markham had to do was make a call, arrange a drug buy, and after two or more re-iterations, another Gatien club would be shut down as a public nuisance.[60]

Various people, including even King Koch of the NeoCons, are quoted expressing puzzlement over the "Get Gatien at all costs" and "scorched Earth" tactics of the city, state, and ultimately Fed-

---

[59] Gatien notes that, ironically, he had contributed to Giuliani's re-election campaign. While the Left generally understands that "quality of life" issues are "implicitly White," Gatien didn't realize that only certain Whites have immunity—namely, ones like Mike Bloomberg and his rich pals. Contrary to the Left's fantasies of "White skin privilege," the NeoCon plan is to create multi-culti hellholes of violence, which Judaics will "need" to be called in to run, less due to their high IQs than to their reputation as the classic social "middlemen" (White but not rednecks). People like Gatien will be targeted as a "problem" to be "solved"; later, we'll see how the champions of "open borders" moved Heaven and Earth to deport . . . Peter Gatien.

[60] The FBI uses a similar technique to manufacture "terrorists"; interestingly, Bradley would later be accused of trying to sell information to the London police on the 7/7 bombing. At his most disgusting, he invokes "the Nuremberg defense": he was just doing his job. As if his sleazy little action had anything to do with the greatness of the European Revolution of 1933!

eral governments. This was "an irrational hatred" that went beyond Giuliani's moral crusade. But the answer would require Koch to exert too much self-awareness of what drives the Neocon mentality.

I suggest that Gatien was simply too White to be tolerated. His successful businesses, fueled by his perfectionism and hard work, his promotion, however unknowingly, of outlets for atavistic pagan rituals, and topping it all off, his mythological appearance, made him a target so tempting the Judaics lost all control in their lust to tear him down.[61] To quote Michael Alig: "When you have an eye-patch [as well as] a face it makes an even more attractive person to target ... an evil, sinister, eye-patched figurehead."[62]

In August 1995, they got just what they needed: some kid, whose family knows the Governor of New Jersey, winds up dead after visiting a club. Somewhat lost in the excitement was the actual death certificate: suicide. And the method? Hanging, of course. What other method would be associated with an attempt to take down Wotan?

And who do the Feds get to conduct the prosecution? From the people who brought you, not so much the Marx Brothers as the Three Stooges: Michele Adelman, Lisa Fleishman, and Eric Friedberg.[63]

For those inclined to buy into the NeoCon's "anti-crime" notions, assuming "there must be something to it," consider the absurdity of the case: that Peter Gatien had personal control over everything happening at every moment in four separate nightclubs; or that anything happening in them was any different from what went on all over the New York streets.[64]

---

[61] Gatien's attorney notes that one day he saw a big picture of Gatien in the office of one of the prosecutors — a woman — and told her "This is not healthy. Get a life."

[62] So much for "people want to see you having fun." Thanks, Mike.

[63] "I was beginning to wonder if there was an Anglo-Saxon name left in the Department..." (William S. Burroughs, *Naked Lunch* [London: Flamingo, 1993], p. 171]).

[64] Gatien notes wryly that although prisoners are "strip searched nine times a day," he saw more drug sales in his overnight stay in jail then in his entire nightlife career.

In fact, of the hundreds of people Gatien employed over the years, not one, despite the considerable amount of force the Feds could apply, could be found as a witness.

Instead, the Feds mounted a "rogues gallery of Staten Island scumbags" (there's that slander, I'm sure, against Staten Island).

There was Alig, in jail for murdering his dealer—Feds would take him out occasionally for "questioning" so he could buy drugs. There was Lord Michael, who, when questioned about the "suicide" of his "houseboy" broke down in tears and begged the jury to believe "I'm not a murderer!" And there was Markham, who was now also claiming to have been hired as an escort—by the male prosecutor.

The case against Gatien seems to have been yet another example of the classic Judaic technique of Projection: the unbelievably corrupt Feds[65] fielded an array of drug dealers, perjurers, and murderers to convince a jury that Gatien was . . . a drug-dealing scumbag.[66] They refused to go along and delivered eleven not-guilty verdicts.

In the end, Gatien was saved by his Aryan rectitude. As Alig says, Gatien was making money hand over fist, why would he risk it all for a few thousand more? "Peter was a businessman but he wasn't extraordinarily greedy"—i.e., not a Judaic New York businessman, "counting his shekels."

Indeed, asked by his lawyer what he would do now, Gatien replied: "I'm going to church." Meaning, of course, reopening his clubs and earning an honest living.

But the government was not done with him yet. The Empire struck back, in the form of a state prosecution for sales tax fraud, pursued this time by another tribesman, one Morgenthau. Yet another Judaic inversion, this time of the Fed's famous attempt to get Capone for Federal tax fraud.[67]

---

[65] One example from many: DEA agents would take Alig out of jail, ostensibly for "questioning," so he could buy drugs, which he would take in the back seat of their car.

[66] As if he was holed up in his office "counting his shekels" as Alig puts it. As the Polish proverb says, "The Jew cries when *he* hits *you*."

[67] See my study of reversals and other Shamanic tropes in de Palma's *The Untouchables* in *The Homo & the Negro*.

"I thought they got their *pound of flesh*."

—Gatien[68]

Gatien paid a fine for some technical violations and went about his business. But the government Shylocks had one more trick up their sleeves. Despite having given Gatien a "Certificate of Relief" after the failure to convict, two years later they decided to use their unsuccessful prosecution as itself evidence of fraudulent activity, and thereby deport the Canadian citizen as an undesirable alien.[69]

Gatien notes with some well-earned irony that he left the USA with less money than he entered with 30 years before. But he actually took more back with him than that. The club scene has been dead since he left, and, as several voices in the film emphasize, nightlife is the matrix from which art and culture arise.[70] Not unlike Gatien's Toronto when it was known, mockingly, as "Toronto the Good," New York is now just a tourist trap and an international joke, presided over by its Judaic Mayor for Life, who has extended Giuliani's no-nightlife crusade into every taxable and regulatable area of business and even personal life.

Judging from viewer reactions on, for example, Amazon[71] or

---

[68] At least, did prosecutor Lisa *Fleish*man (i.e., "butcher")?

[69] This from a government that still welcomes Mexican scumbags, drug dealers, and killers, with open arms, and even provides them with free weapons ("Operation Fast and Furious"). Speaking of disgusting hypocrisy, Gatien's most recent, yet again denied, petition for a pardon was denied by New York's Governor David Paterson, an adulterous, drug-using Negro, who is also, interestingly enough, legally blind in both eyes. Now there's an upright citizen!

[70] The Classical World was awash in hallucinogenic drugs and other, more authentic kinds of "ecstasy"; see Hoffman, as well as D. C. A. Hillman's *The Chemical Muse* (New York: St. Martins, 1988).

[71] For example, "Here was a man who fulfilled the American dream. Peter Gatien was an immigrant from Canada who came here, worked 16 hour days, and duly became rich and famous. . . . He's back in Canada now, and I can't blame him if he never sets foot in the US again. The government hated this fellow and would not accept anything less than his destruction. The film—and what I've read about him in the days since I saw it—leaves me convinced of his innocence. . . . The last thing

the Internet Movie Database,[72] the makers of *Limelight* have, unlike Sudley-Smith, managed to craft a film that gets their message across to, and accepted by, its audience. Gatien and even New York in the '90s come over as stylish and sympathetic,[73] while Halston and the '70s seem to remain just a vaguely creepy childhood obsession of Smith's.

Even so, while the film, being an accurate record, necessarily contains the Aryan themes we've been highlighting, it seems unaware of them. Halston clearly still needs a film documentary,[74] while it would be fascinating to see what someone like Ken Russell, or one of the great Germans, like Lang or Harlan, could have done with Gatien. (Or Harlan on Halston?)

In fact, what the whole film industry, as well as our culture in general, needs is a wholesale return to White standards.[75] Only then could justice be done to the lives of Halston and Gatien.

Counter-Currents/*North American New Right*
March 19 & 20, 2013

---

we need is a huge state apparatus that can be used against us based on the personal likes and dislikes of a few functionaries. If this doesn't sell you on libertarianism, nothing will."

[72] For example, "It is patently clear that Mr. Gatien was served up as a sacrificial lamb to those in state and federal politics at the time. . . . Whatta disgrace. . . . I'm disgusted."

[73] In the film's new interviews, Gatien has abandoned the cursed eyepatch for dark glasses; in looks and sound, he now seems to be channeling Anthony Bourdain, ex-junkie, "celebrity" chef and reputed scumbag, apparently a more sympathetic look for New Yorkers today. Although Dylan McDermott does a fine job portraying him in *Party Monster,* it's a shame James Woods wasn't cast; he's a dead ringer, and his work in *Videodrome* would give an interesting edge to the Canadian dealing with altered states theme.

[74] The book industry hasn't done much better; Halston is the subject of a couple of coffee-table photo books — one an oddly small size — and a tabloidesque biography.

[75] See *Trevor Lynch's White Nationalist Guide to the Movies,* ed. Greg Johnson (San Francisco: Counter Currents, 2012), and especially Kevin MacDonald's "Foreword," for an idea of what's needed.

REFLECTIONS ON
SARTORIAL FASCISM

"I like killing guys when I'm wearing a tux. Makes me feel like James Bond."
— Brock Samson, *The Venture Bros.*

JOEL: You can bet that anybody seriously interested in world domination is going to end up looking like a real snickerdoodle.
DR. FORRESTER: (*wearing a pirate costume/fruit hat*) What's *that* supposed to mean? I'll deal with you later, back to the drill, Frank. You will bow down before me, Son of Jor-El! Bow down!"
— *MST3K* on *The Castle Of Fu Manchu*

Americans, who tend to be either uneducated and therefore ignorant, or educated and therefore brainwashed,[1] are wont to ask questions like "How could the most educated and civilized society in Europe fall for a madman like Hitler?" So great is their puzzlement over this apparent anomaly that, though a thoroughly respectable question itself — indeed, constitutive of respectable discourse — the answers tend to spill out past the bounds of respectable discourse, winding up in such otherwise verboten areas as UFOlogy, black magic, and perhaps plain old hypnotism.[2]

Those of us reading Greg Johnson's "Remembering Sir Oswald Mosley"[3] and the articles recommended there, or the series of paperbacks and kindles being put out by Black House Publishing Ltd. on and by the British Union of Fascists, have a simi-

---

[1] "The educated are the most heavily indoctrinated" — Noam Chomsky.

[2] The *locus classicus* of this meme is likely found in "Mario and the Magician," by the traitorous propagandist Thomas Mann.

[3] http://www.counter-currents.com/2014/11/remembering-sir-oswald-mosley-3/

lar, but very different question: how on Earth did Mosely fail?

Hitler and Mussolini, after all, actually came to power, and it took the entire world to drive them from power; Franco died in his bed; Salazar was done in by his deck chair. But Mosely never came within a country mile of holding power in Britain.

How could this man, with so much charisma,[4] and with all the right answers to the nation's problems (ideas already successful in NS Germany, and still relevant today[5]) fail so completely? How could Britain entrust its fate to that bloated, drunken buffoon, Churchill?[6]

And even more generally: Why was there no significant "fascist" movement in the UK or (especially) the USA? After all, aren't we constantly being told these are "fascist" states?[7]

The answer, I think, is the uniforms.

Now, Germany, Italy, even France, these are all countries that respect the uniform. Think Emil Jannings as the washroom attendant in Murnau's *The Last Laugh* (1924). Brits and Americans

---

[4] A more suitable subject for Clay Shaw's no doubt ironic statement to Jim Garrison: "In fact, I admired President Kennedy. A man with true panache and a wife with impeccable taste." — *JFK* (Oliver Stone).

[5] See, for example, Alexander Raven's *The Coming Corporate State* (1936; reprinted London: Black House, 2012) and discussed by Alisdair Clarke in his "ARYAN FUTURISM" speech, delivered to the New Right meeting in central London on May 28, 2005 (http://aryanfuturism.blogspot.com/2006/03/aryan-futurism-vision_28.html). See also *Spring Comes Again* by Jorian Jenks (Uckfield, Sussex: Historical Review Press, 2011), an early contribution to organic agriculture (https://secure.counter-currents.com/spring-comes-again/).

[6] See Mark Weber's "An Unsettled Legacy," reviewing David Irving's *Churchill's War: Triumph in Adversity*: "Churchill, writes Irving in the introduction, 'won the war in spite of himself. . . . Britain, in short, surrendered her own empire to defeat a chimera conjured up by Winston Churchill, a putative danger from Nazi Germany — a threat which never existed except when Churchill needed to call upon it. He sacrificed the substance to defeat the myth'" (http://www.ihr.org/jhr/v20/v20n4p43_Weber.html).

[7] Christopher Hitchens, I think in the *New Left Review*, not *Vanity Fair*, mocked the absurd notion that Britain had tried to appease Hitler because the post-WWI leadership was "pacifist" by pointing out that would have come as a surprise to Gandhi.

are prone to find such things laughable, or sinister, muttering about "Prussian martinets"[8] or comic operas[9] set in places called Ruritania.[10]

Probably the most devastating, long running (1938–1974) and, I suggest, archetypal attack on Mosely came from P. G. Wodehouse, of all people, in the shape of Roderick Spode, 7th Earl of Sidcup, known as Spode or Lord Sidcup.[11] Wikipedia says:

> Spode is modelled after Sir Oswald Mosley, leader of the British Union of Fascists, who were nicknamed the *blackshirts*. Spode was at first an 'amateur dictator' who led a farcical group of fascists called the Saviours of Britain, better known as the Black Shorts. Spode adopted black shorts as a uniform because, according to Gussie Fink-Nottle in *The Code of the Woosters*, "by the time Spode formed his association, there were no shirts left" — alluding to various fascist or right-radical groups: Mussolini's Blackshirts, Hitler's brownshirts, the Irish Blueshirts and Greenshirts, the South African Greyshirts, Mexico's Gold shirts, and the American Silver Shirts.
> Bertie Wooster believes that wearing black shorts is an extreme social and sartorial *faux pas* (shorts being inappropriate for a grown man outside a sporting context) and

---

[8] "All manly peoples today have a bad name; the Prussians are the prototype." (Alle männlichen Völker sind heut in Verruf; die Preußen sind der Prototyp). Ernst Jünger in *Ernst Jünger – Carl Schmitt: Briefe 1930–1983*, ed. Helmuth Kiesel (Stuttgart: Klett-Cotta, 1999).

[9] "There were Fascists all around his Italian villas. Though he initially saw them as not much worse than a bad comic opera whose chorus was prone to fisticuffs." Clive James, "Huxley Then and Now," http://www.clivejames.com/aldous-huxley

[10] Someone once described Himmler's *Annenerbe* as "like someone gave the anthropology department at the New School uniforms and guns."

[11] Strangely, David Mamet has apparently written — that is, handwritten and illustrated — a children's book [!] called *The Trials of Roderick Spode* ("*The Human Ant*"). It appears to be quite dreadful, but I haven't found any explanation for his use of the name.

uses it to make fun of Spode:

> The trouble with you, Spode, is that just because you have succeeded in inducing a handful of half-wits to disfigure the London scene by going about in black shorts, you think you're someone. You hear them shouting "Heil, Spode!" and you imagine it is the Voice of the People. That is where you make your bloomer. What the Voice of the People is saying is: "Look at that frightful ass Spode swanking about in footer bags! Did you ever in your puff see such a perfect perisher?" — Bertie Wooster in *The Code of the Woosters* (1938)

Before Spode inherited the title of Earl of Sidcup on the death of his uncle, he made a living as the "founder and proprietor of the emporium in Bond Street known as Eulalie Soeurs," a famed designer of ladies' lingerie.[12]

Wikipedia adds this interesting detail:

> In the television series *Jeeves and Wooster*, the Black Shorts are portrayed as a tiny group of around a dozen men and teenage boys. They comprise the small, but enthusiastic, audience to whom Spode makes loud, dramatic speeches in which he announces bizarre statements of policy, such as giving each citizen at birth a British–made bicycle and umbrella ["At birth, every citizen, as of right, will be issued with a British bicycle and an honest British-made umbrella. Thus assured of a mobile workforce adequately protected against the elements, this great country can go forward once more to glory!"], widening the rails of the entire British railway network, so sheep may stand sideways on trains, the banning of the import of foreign root-vegetables and the compulsory, scientific measurement of all male knees. ["Not for the true-born Englishman the bony angular knee of the so-called intellectual, not for him

---

[12] http://en.wikipedia.org/wiki/Roderick_Spode

the puffy knee of the criminal classes. The British knee is firm, the British knee is muscular, the British knee is on the march!"]

We should note, for future reference, the insinuations of homosexuality: Spode's audience pointedly includes "teenage boys," he is, we learn in "Jeeves and the Feudal Spirit," an expert on jewelry, and above all, the lingerie business.[13]

> Out of embarrassment, Spode had long attempted to keep his ownership of the business a secret, though Jeeves discovered the fact in the Junior Ganymede Club's official Book, where one of Spode's former valets had inscribed it.

"Former" valet? Junior Ganymede Club, eh?

> In *The Code of the Woosters*, this discovery allowed Bertie to threaten Spode with public embarrassment and prevent the threatened "jellying process." As Bertie says, "You can't be a successful Dictator and design women's underclothing. One or the other. Not both." Indeed, whenever Spode sees Bertie after the point where Bertie mentions the name "Eulalie," Spode instantly becomes meek and acquiescing.

This instinctive, visceral mockery of Spode is especially interesting, since Wodehouse himself, though "apolitical" in that typically ga-ga way of the Brits, found himself, during the War, not only in occupied France, but was gently coerced by the Germans to give a series of radio "chats" aimed at the United States, detailing how jolly much fun the occupation was. Unlike Ezra Pound and William Joyce, Wodehouse was never prosecuted

---

[13] The Fascist, for the many reasons we've listed in the past, always types on the Homo end of the Homo/Negro spectrum; thus, the thoroughly Judaified populace is easily swayed by the epithet, which the Left always reached for first. By today, any "expertise" is suspect. "Niggers proud to be ignorant" —Chris Rock.

(being, apparently, ga-ga, after all),[14] though now and again some busybody tried to smear him as a "Nazi."[15] The real irony is that Wodehouse himself was quite Jew-wise:

> [A]s far as Wodehouse in his novels and short stories was concerned the Jews were an objectionable, shady, traitorous, money-obsessed lot who exercised an inordinate amount of influence in the city of London and had the entire British and American industry in their hands.[16]

Of course, being Jew-wise does not necessarily make one a fascist (nor, given the example of Franco and Mussolini, *vice versa*) but I mention this to show that Wodehouse's antipathy does not arise from some modern, "post-Holocaust" mentality ("Fascism leads to Auschwitz").[17]

Now, before delving further into this "shorts" business, let me step back again and make the general point that the Anglo-Americans seem to have a bug up their ass/arse when it comes to authority, government, and its tool, the armed forces. Both countries, for example, pat themselves on the back incessantly as abhorring "standing armies," though this hasn't prevented them from fighting each other twice, fighting the bloodiest civil war in history, creating and running the largest empire in history (na-

---

[14] It has been suggested that Wodehouse actually performed a great service for the Allies, by convincing the Germans that his Drones Club was an accurate depiction of the British as dopey, ineffectual phebes.

[15] Hence, I suspect, the long running anti-Spode campaign; as long as Mosley was alive, Wodehouse (Spode = Wode?) was in peril.

[16] See "P. G. Wodehouse on the Jews," http://semiticcontroversies.blogspot.com/2014/11/p-g-wodehouse-on-jews.html

[17] In the good old days of free speech, antipathy to the Chosen was common; take, as an example we'll return to, the ultimate Empire figure, Kipling; as Andrew Hamilton says: "Rudyard Kipling is out of favor, in large part because his work was so politically and racially incorrect. In a letter written from Jerusalem to his only surviving child, Elsie, Kipling reportedly observed that 'many races are vile but the Jew in bulk on his native heath is the Vilest of them all,'" http://www.counter-currents.com/2013/07/rudyard-kiplings-the-burden-of-jerusalem/

vies are OK, I guess), and being in a constant state of war since 1941.

So, even if you libertarian or anarchist types like the "anti-military" hype, not only is it hypocritical, it's also just a manifestation of a generalized attitude of social slackitude.[18]

Now, my Gentle Reader, being likely of the Anglosphere himself, is also likely muttering to himself, "Who need a bunch of closet cases marching around like Nutzis anyway?"[19] So let's back up even further.

Traditional societies are above all *integral* societies; every aspect of the society is derived from, or refers back to, one or more metaphysical Principles (*viz*, Tradition), and since these principles are an integral whole, so are the various aspects of the society. This includes such "minor" or "irrelevant" aspects as clothing, or music.[20]

Traditional societies have traditional clothing, and vice versa; moreover, we can say that traditional societies produce, as a kind of natural by-product, traditional clothing, and vice versa as well: traditional clothing *produces* a traditional society.[21]

---

[18] America's ultimate religion, pipe-smoking suburban salesman/dad J. R. "Bob" Dobbs' Church of the Sub-Genius, has officially deified slack. "Every man a king, and every child and dog a slave," http://www.subgenius.com/bigfist/answers/faqs/X0040_What_is_all_this_Sla.html

[19] If he fancies himself a Chestertonian, he's likely to be pounding his fist on the pub table, spewing cheese and cracker crumbs from his beer-soaked moustache and shouting "I'll stand for no damned nonsense!"

[20] See my essays on Wagner ("worth the price of the book alone!" raves an Amazon reviewer) in *The Eldritch Evola . . . & Others* where the doctrinal formulations of Guénon, Daniélou, and Coomaraswamy are cited.

[21] Well, tends to; it's not a magic panacea. Thus, the regrettable fanaticism of Taliban, and the more media-friendly Amish. By contrast, consider the absurdity, obvious even to the secular eye, of Ashkenazi Jews dressed up like 17th-century Polish merchants in thick black wool and beaver fur hats, impudently pretending to be "the true inhabitants" of Palestine. As for vice versa, Alan Watts praised the Japanese kimono, and wore them himself; when a modernized Japanese objected

With this in mind, when the modern Anglo Saxon proudly states, and correspondingly wears, his vaunted "independence" and "originality" and "individualism," as opposed to the supposed "repression" and "conformity" of the uniformed, we need to point out to him the difference between "unity" and "uniformity."[22]

Traditional society, as we have said, is integral, i.e., characterized by Unity, which, being aligned with Quality, is characterized by precisely differentiations: caste, rank, guild, corporate body, etc.

To these correspond various appropriate types of clothing, or a similar style of clothing, often with some indication of rank or order: the uniform.

Modern society is indeed characterized by an opposite principle, but it is the pseudo-freedom of mere atoms, indiscernible and interchangeable, with clothing to match. It is unfortunate for our purposes that Guénon calls this other principle Uniformity; in this context, we would better call it by its most salient characteristic: Conformity. In the 1820 the European (and hence relatively still traditional) De Toqueville had already discerned that the American's much vaunted "freedom" actually produced, unlike the stratified, articulated societies of Tradition, a dull conformity of opinion (and hence, of dress, or fashion).

Furthermore, we can trace the decline of a society, or culture, or civilization, by the decline of its clothing, a process that, with Spenglerian inevitability, traces a path between the archetypes we have identified as the Homo and the Negro—a somewhat tendentious version of Guénon's Quality/Quantity and Evola's Solar/Telluric.[23]

Thus, to reenter our discussion, the uniform, despite its "uniformity," can be seen—and is seen, by the modern prole—as es-

---

that one couldn't run for a bus in one, Watts replied suavely that "No gentleman should ever run for a bus." In general, see "Mad *Männerbund*" in *The Homo & the Negro* and *End of an Era*.

[22] See René Guénon, *The Reign of Quantity and the Signs of the Times*, 4th ed. (Ghent, N.Y.: Sophia Perennis, 2001), chapter 7, "Uniformity versus Unity."

[23] See, of course, *The Homo & the Negro*.

sentially of the pole of Tradition, integrity, unity (as defined just now), and thus always an implicit insult, and threat, to all the prole stands (or lies around) for.

Fascism, as Evola noted, was the attempt to shore up a disintegrating (i.e., a de-traditionalizing and modernizing) society under emergency conditions—hence, its rather unfortunate tendency to rigidity and, well, uniformity.[24]

Fascism, with its ranks, orders, and corporations, is the modern analogue of traditional society, and thus can, with sufficient reason, be symbolized by the uniform itself;[25] conversely, the uniform is feared and loathed as the very symbol of fascism, which is itself loathed and feared—by the prole—for its attempt to restore tradition.

With that in mind, consider that Wikipedia adds that, "The flag of the *Black Shorts* as devised for the *Jeeves and Wooster* television series [was] modelled on the Flash and Circle of the British Union of Fascists."

The "flash-in-the-pan," as Mosley's mockers called it. Which reminds us of Jef Costello's "The Flash in the Pan": Fascism & Fascist Insignia in the Spy Spoofs of the 1960s."[26] Here, Costello

---

[24] Fascism, and especially National Socialism, thus had a regrettable "prole" aspect to themselves which prevented Evola from entirely endorsing the movements. As Chris Rock said about O. J., Evola didn't say they were right, but he . . . *understood.* See his *Fascism Viewed from the Right*, trans. E. Christian Kopff (London: Arktos, 2013) reviewed here: http://www.counter-currents.com/2013/04/fascism-as-antimodernism-julius-evola-fascism-viewed-from-the-right/ and *Notes on the Third Reich*, trans. E. Christian Kopff (London: Arktos, 2013), reviewed here: http://www.counter-currents.com/tag/notes-on-the-third-reich/.

[25] Even without its various insignia further distinguishing internal rank, the uniform symbolized hierarchy as such, in its clear delineation from civilian wear. Armies are known only by the most basic character of their uniforms—redcoats, blues vs. grays; also men in blue (police), the red and black of Stendhal's novel, etc. Thus Jef Costello is right, as we'll see, to assimilate the lab coat wearing elite of Flynt to his fascist groups. The white lab coat, presumably without any distinguishing marks of rank, still denotes separation from the profane masses.

[26] In *North American New Right*, vol. 1, *op. cit.*

looks at Hollywood's James Bond rip-offs of the '60s, rather than genteel comic literature from the '30s, and, corresponding to the decline of society in the ensuing decades since the defeat of Fascism, we can see that the Wooster/Spode dialectic is updated and replayed as the laid-back secret agent of Yankee-style "liberty" vs. the Worldwide Fascist Conspiracy.[27]

But much more interesting is what these American spy spoofs reveal about the modern American soul. Let's focus just on Matt Helm for the moment, as paradigmatic of the genre. It's discipline, order, duty, and iron will (the villains) . . . against hedonism, debauchery, and selfish abandon (the hero). (I didn't mention this earlier, but Matt Helm always has to be talked into taking a break from chasing tail so that he can save the world.) The conflict between America and fascism in World War II was presented as the conflict between freedom and slavery. In Matt Helm, however, the truth is laid bare and the conflict revealed for what it really was. *The freedom of Matt Helm is mere license. He's out to make the world safe not for democracy and individual rights, but for boozing and boinking and sleeping till noon. That's the American Dream, and he is living it. And so when those handsome, uniformed, lock-step, lightning-bolted troops in their spotless lairs are blown to kingdom come we can all cheer. Who did they think they were, anyway?*

[Flint's] Galaxy is a bit different from [Helm's] B.I.G.O., however. They are headed by three *white-coated, idealistic scientists* who aim to pacify the world and create a conflict-free utopia.[28] Ideologically, this actually puts them further to the left, but there are strongly authoritarian overtones to

---

[27] As always with Judaic propaganda, ideas like "liberty" and "fascism" are hyped up to 11, exactly when both are quite non-existent.

[28] Wodehouse's Spode, when challenged, spouts things like "It's been scientifically proven!" As Costello notes, the scientist angle plays more Left than Right—"bad" planning is always fascist, unlike the Left's "good" planning, but the lab coats as uniforms definitely tip the balance toward fascism. For the difficulty Leftists have imagining a "fascism" that doesn't wind up being built from elements of their own Leftism, see my "The Fraud of Miss Jean Brodie," above.

Galaxy *(nifty uniforms, a "Führer Prinzip" of absolute loyalty to the three leaders, etc.).* At the climax of the film, as Flint is poised to destroy the weather machine, one of the mad scientists pleads with him to desist: "Ours would be a perfect world!" he cries. "Not my kind of world," Flint responds, as he proceeds to demolish their handiwork. Again, *everything here is on personal terms. Our hero goes on his mission because his life is adversely affected; he foils the villains' scheme because their vision is not his. No conception of duty is at work in Flint, and no high-minded ideals. He is just looking out for number one.* (It is noteworthy that on its release, *Our Man Flint* received a positive review in Ayn Rand's journal *The Objectivist*.) . . . Us vs. them foreign interllectuals with their books and their high-minded ideals. (The villains in the Helm films are always foreign and often — interestingly — *aristocratic*. What a delight it is to see the noble and the dignified toppled by the hometown boy!)

And that, of course, is the "delight" of seeing batty Bertie besting beastly Spode.[29] As Costello sums it up:

The American versions of Bond jettison all that is noble about the character and turn him into a grinning lothario, a self-involved hedonist, a perpetual adolescent, a vulgar operator always on the make. And please keep squarely in mind that this was done so that American audiences would have a character they could more easily identify with and root for. The American soul is rotten to the core.

Though Bertie — who's really more infantile than adolescent, less afraid of marriage than of women in general, especially his Aunt Julia — has been reconfigured as a surprisingly effective spy (just as the Anglo-American public had to be "toughened up" and frog-marched into the Second World War and the Cold

---

[29] In Huxley's *Point Counter Point* (1928), The Brotherhood of British Freemen (BBF) is known on the streets as the "Bloody Buggering Fools."

War[30]) his heart's still in the right place: fighting for the right to sleep late against all those tightly uniformed meanies.

America was always more slovenly ("rotten to the core"), but standards of dress have sunk since Matt Helm to levels that would have been impossible to imagine back then; you need only look at a random photo or movie scene from no further back than the '50s to observe adults dressed like adults, with suit, tie, and hat, even at sporting events; today, "sportswear" — simultaneously childish (though sized for ever-increasing girths) and shoddy — is *de rigueur* for all events, indeed all public appearances, part of the negrofication of American, and ultimately world, society, the fruit of the much hullabalooed fascist defeat, which we've commented on for some time now.

Negro society, to the extent that the term "society" can even be used,[31] is, as a result of its relative lack of intelligence, characterized precisely by an overwhelming conformity, of both dress and opinion — any signs of intelligence or originality being immediately stomped out as being "acting white" or "being gay," which are equivalent terms here; while clothing must adhere to the loose, baggy "style" of the prison, where the most authentic negro males spend most of their time.[32]

As society becomes more uniform, more negroid, clothing becomes duller, uglier, and baggier.

So it is incorrect to simply say that "clothing has become

---

[30] I describe the change in the image of "the real boy" in "Welcome to the Club," above.

[31] As Guénon notes, "pure" Quantity can never actually exist; rather it is a logical endpoint for the decline and quantification of pure Quality.

[32] Today, at the Times Square station, I heard a ringing bell, and inferring the start of the Salvation Army kettle-Santas, I turned to behold a Negro who, apart from bell, kettle, and some kind of apron emblazoned with the Salvation Army emblem, was indistinguishable from any other homeless skell. Only some white suburban faggot like Clark Griswold would be so un-cool as to bother to "dress up" (a term used by drag queens) as Santa, even to make money. The attack on Santa has been one of the main prongs of the "progressive" assault on White culture, with the drunken, child molesting white bum becoming the standard Santa impersonator.

more casual" since "casual" styles of the past would be considered ridiculously fussy and "uptight" today. As what little Quality has declined further into Quantity, "casual" has itself declined into "slob."

How appropriate, then, that "shorts" should be the chosen vehicle of mockery. As Wikipedia says, the crux of Wodehouse's derision is that, "wearing black shorts is an extreme social and sartorial faux pas (shorts being inappropriate for a grown man *outside a sporting context*)."

Ironically, today wearing "footer bags" anywhere at all would actually be a seen as faggy in itself — the recent World Cup games led to a predictable orgy of homosexual panic among the usual suspects on the Manly Right (e.g., Steve Sailer). While shorts have spread (like American asses) from sports to everyday wear, the *kind* of short has mutated.

Once again, *Mystery Science Theater* provides us with a useful index of what educated, white middle-class people in America's upper Midwest — the theoretical "White People" that White Nationalists would supposedly convert to supply the population of the White Homeland — think; and of the Stuff these White People don't Like, shorts is/are high on the list.

When the cast view old movies, which by definition are of the past (even "sci fi fantasies" take place in the "lost future"[33]), whiteness is always noticed — it's rare today — and more importantly, mocked. Exclusively white casts are puzzling; the occasional menial black character, though culturally accurate, is an embarrassment. When white bodies — "white, white, bodies" — are unclothed, the guys groan at the "fish belly white" display.

But it's shorts, plain old jean shorts, and especially swim trunks, that elicit the greatest cries of horror: "Tiny, disturbing shorts."

"Mike, look, his batch, it's horrible!"

"At this point the swim trunks are just a formality, right?"

---

[33] For example, the relentless mockery of the Seattle World's Fair promo, Century 21 Calling: "Isn't it great there's only white people?" "Who directed this, Leni Riefenstahl?" "The Führer will like this."

"We'll be right back to 'Men with Little Pants.'"

Remember, we're talking about films made by, for, and starring *ordinary American people*, at a time when America was, by population, *almost totally white* (but, as we know, already negrofying in culture) — *The Boggy Creek Monster* ('70s), *The Revenge of the Creature* ('50s), *The Undersea Kingdom* ('30s) — not gay porn.

This mutation has been usefully diagnosed and analyzed by Mark Simpson in his epoch-making essay, "Speedophobia: The American Fear and Loathing of Bedgie Smuggling."[34]

> Bathing and swimming are undoubtedly pagan passions. The ancients invented the seaside resort and spent a great deal of gold on, and time in, their blessed public baths, where the men bathed and swam naked. Not because they were indifferent to nakedness, but because they esteemed virility.
>
> Medieval Christianity, with its ghastly suspicion of the body, rendered water — the sensual cleanser of limbs — suspect. As late as the 16th century, bathing was thought to be wicked, unhealthy, and, er, filthy.
>
> [I]t was in Australia, a warm country where most of the population tenderly hug the coastline and pay little attention to busybodies — perhaps because Australia began as a convict colony — that the bodily freedom of the modern beach lifestyle ("surfers rather than serfs!") was invented, anticipating by decades the sexual revolution of the 1960s.
>
> Up until the early 1980s, Speedos were a common sight here, both on the beach and at the pool. Everything was lovely and snug and nicely outlined. *But then something horrifying happened.* Sometime in the late '80s men's swimsuits began to grow in length and bulk. Year by year they crept down the thigh toward the knee-and beyond — all the while billowing clownishly outward. Now U.S. men wear, *of their own volition,* not even the knee-length woolen knickers that the Australian men of Manly heroically pro-

---

[34] February 11, 2007, http://www.marksimpson.com/blog/2007/02/11/speedophobia/

tested in the early 20th century, but bloomers—a voluminous form of female attire last seen in the 1850s (and *generally regarded as ridiculous back then*). In the water, today's Speedophobic males are half-man, half-jellyfish.

"Something happened"; "Of their own volition." Although he doesn't see the larger implications (not having read this book) Simpson is on the right track:

> In the '70s basketball *shorts were skimpy (almost like Oz football shorts)* [that is, Wodehouse's "footer bags"], but *Michael Jordan popularized sexless long shorts* in the NBA in the late 1980s. . . . *Because Jordan was Jordan, others copied, and thus baggy shorts became fashionable.* It seems that this evil trend spread to male swimwear.

"Because Jordan was Jordan"; meaning, we live in a thoroughly negrofied "society" in which ball-bouncers are worshipped as gods.[35]

So we have moved from a culture in which bloomers were "*generally regarded as ridiculous*" to one in which they are compulsory; from one where shorts, *worn off the field*, are mocked as implicitly homosexual, to one where shorts *of any sort* are

---

[35] "The one-time Paradisiacal fields are completely exploited and plundered like a wheat-field in which a thievish horde of apes has taken up residence. Our bodies are infected with a mange which despite every kind of soap remains udumu-ized, pagutu-ized and baziat-ized [that is, made ape-like]. Never has human life been as miserable as it is today—despite all its technical advancements. Devilish human beasts oppress us from above, slaughtering millions of people in unconscionably murderous wars conducted for the enrichment of their personal money-bags. Savage human beasts undermine the pillars of culture from below. . . . What do you want with Hell in the Beyond?! Isn't the one we are living in now, and in which we are now burning, terrible enough?"—Dr. Jorg Lanz von Liebenfels, *Theozoology, or the Science of the Sodomite Apelings and the Divine Electron* (1905). Jorg is one of those "disreputable" sources of "Hitler's madness" we mentioned at the top; over the years, he has come to seem less and less "occult" and more and more prophetic.

mocked as being homo as such.

It's even gotten to the point where, clueless or impudent, Judaic curmudgeon Jim Kunstler—the Apocalyptic Grouch of the Capital District—finds it to be yet another problem . . . with the *goyim*:

> I went to a sporting goods chain store at the mall—where else?—seeking a new bathing suit (pardon the quaint locution). *The store was curiously named Dick's.* All they had were clown trunks. By this I mean a garment designed to hang somewhere around mid-calf, *instantly transforming a normally-proportioned adult male into a stock slapstick character: the oafish man-child.*
>
> This being a commodious warehouse-style store, there was rack upon rack of different brands of bathing suits, all cut in the same clown style. I chanced by one of the sparsely-deployed employees and inquired if they had any swimming togs in a shorter cut.
>
> "What you see is alls we got," he said.
>
> *Even the Speedo brand had gone clown — except for the bikini brief, which I wore back during 30 years of lap-swimming,* but which I deemed not quite okay for an elderly gentleman on the casual summer swim scene. So I left Dick's without a new suit, but not before having a completely unsatisfying conversation with one of the managers.
>
> "In the old days," I explained, "bathing suits were designed to minimize the amount of cloth one dragged around in the water. These clown trunks you sell not only make a person look ridiculous, but they must be an awful drag in the water."[36]

---

[36] The purpose of the clown shorts is to hide the laughable "white, white" body, hide all distinctions, and ape the styles of the manly Negro, not to prove useful in actually swimming, which Negroes abjure anyway. We might compare this to Oscar Wilde's explanation of his colorful outfit to Colorado miners: They learned that even his oft-ridiculed stage dress of black velvet jacket, lace cravat, silk knee breeches, and patent leather pumps could be understood in terms of pragmatics. As Wilde explained, "When a man is going to walk or row,

"That's what they send us," he said. "It's alls we got."[37]

(I can just hear MST3k's "comic redneck voice" delivering that line.)

Now, all this might be dismissed as "fashions just change" or "everything's relative" but as the latter phrase implies, that's a rather Lefty response, don't you think?

As MST3K demonstrates, this negrofication of our clothing cuts us off from our own white history—the "dead white men" are usually also wearing powdered wigs, silk stockings and . . . short pants; just a buncha fags, turn on the ball game.[38] Just as PC vocabulary makes crimethink impossible, so PC fashion makes even a decade in the past unusable. Consider, then, these comments on an episode of the '60s TV show, *The Outer Limits:* "Just found this on YouTube, there is an episode from *The Outer Limits* posted called 'Tourist Attraction.' Ralph Meeker is seen mostly in a t-shirt and black speedo. Won't see THAT on TV, except for Spanish telenovelas."[39] And these: "PE: I could have easily gone another 49 years without seeing Ralph Meeker in a speedo."[40] Though others disagree:[41] "Ralph Meeker is a God!

---

or perform feats which require a display of strength and muscle, the trousers are done away with and knee breeches are worn." See my "Wild Boys versus 'Hard Men'" in *The Homo & the Negro*.

[37] "We Are All Ninja Turtles Now," Clusterfuck Nation, July 7, 2014, http://kunstler.com/clusterfuck-nation/we-are-all-ninja-turtles-now/

[38] "During the revolution [Washington] surrounded himself with a group of young officers in a close-knit circle that was marked by affectionate bonds of unusual intensity; a group Washington himself referred to as his 'family'. . . trading stories with them while he cracked nuts by the fire." James Neill, *The Origin and Role of Same Sex Relations in Human Societies* (Jefferson, NC: McFarland, 2009), loc. 8563.

[39] As usual, Europe, especially the less "developed" parts, exist in a kind of time capsule. Thus, "ethnic" TV networks present us with men in tight pants and brief swimsuits, perfectly straight, while respectable female newscasters look like hookers. Alt-Rightists evince an affection for Eastern Europe as supposedly "preserved" by Communism, nurse man-crushes for Putin, and extol their "more feminine" women.

[40] http://wearecontrollingtransmission.blogspot.com/2011/

Us mere mortals should consider ourselves lucky that a man of his caliber would even be gracious enough to allow us to see him in all his speedo-wearing glory."[42]

Even the military itself has been affected; the uniform itself seems to have disappeared, replaced by the ubiquitous desert fatigues. Obviously providing not camouflage (like the impractical clown shorts), one wonders what it is intended to symbolize—submission to our desert overlords in Tel Aviv?

Needless to say, the whole outfit, including the ridiculous yellow suede boots (the most impractical footwear imaginable[43]), is greatly favored by the urban Negro. The only remaining touch of swank, as Watts would say, is the beret, which of course our manly, non-winning army boys consider to be "gay." As always, the choice remains: homo or negro.[44]

Back when America was winning wars, Gen. Patton designed a uniform for his boys: a green leather jumpsuit and gold helmet. The modern fatigues on the other hand, are indistinguishable from casual slob wear, such as the track suit. It is often worn, and not only by ex-servicemen, as street wear, while an old style uniform could only be worn as camp (or as

---

01/tourist-attraction.html?showComment=1294342596215%20
\%20c3385216412361453088

[41] Typically, the ordinary clothing of the past—boots, garters, foundation garments—becomes the fetishized clothing of "bad" girls and boys; hence, these comments from the "Speedo Fantasy Board."

[42] Another adds "I agree about Meeker—the only reason I ever go back to watch this episode. *I kept waiting for him to start slapping people around as was his habit when he played that certain P.I.*" He refers, of course, to Meeker's role in *Kiss Me, Deadly*, which we analyzed in "Mike Hammer, Occult Dick: Kiss Me Deadly as Lovecraftian Tale," in *The Eldritch Evola . . . & Others*.

[43] One of many flaws in *Agent for H.A.R.M.*—a third rate *Our Man Flint* that is filled with half-assed misunderstandings of what makes a spy movie cool, instead creating a "hero" that seems more like "your dad's golf buddy," as MST3k puts it—is that the titular agent spends the last third wearing a bright yellow cardigan.

[44] As detailed in my book, *The Homo & the Negro*, whose epigraph quotes the MC5: "You must choose, brothers and sisters, you must choose."

one of Kesey's "Merry Pranksters").

Speaking of street wear, even Ignatius Reilly's outlandish outfit is more of a uniform than this; he wears it constantly — one imagines it is seldom washed — and each element, from the duck hunting cap's earflaps to the ability of the baggy pants to retain warmth and bodily gases — is carefully designed within the rules of geometry and theology. Distinctive, informed with intelligence, practical — true Aryan attire.

No wonder, after the collapse of the Crusade for Moorish Dignity — negroes and uniforms, hence political movements, don't mix — Ignatius is "picked up" on the street, in pirate costume, by a French Quarter fag, whose coterie is subject to Ignatius' next attempt to recruit a paramilitary rebel force for theology and geometry.

Jonathan Bowden has suggested that the Right lives on in the unconscious. Perhaps we might amend that to say that the Right doesn't arise from the irrational Id (as the Frankfurt School would have it) but, though thoroughly rational, has been *exiled to* the irrational Id. Like many such exiled forces, it bides its time in the liminal wastelands. Perhaps its strongest camps are to be found among homosexuals and the devotees of S/M, being the last members of the Rainbow Coalition still allowed — for now — to exercise their love of uniforms and dressing up.[45]

But enough of these speculations. What are we to do? As Evola suggests, we must "ride the tiger." We must seize the opportunities we are given, play the hand we are dealt.

We have sunk so low that even what was once an ordinary business suit is seen as "over-dressed." Here, however, lies the

---

[45] As always, distinctions must be made. The "Chelsea Clone" look, like the concurrent UK Skinhead, was a uniform only in the negative sense we have been outlining here, an "anti-uniform" of drabness, if you will. This reflected the absorption of the homosexual into the Rainbow Coalition of Wreckers of Western Culture under the "gay" brand. Along these lines, we can understand Jack Donovan's contempt for "donning the clothing of masculine roles without making the required efforts." S/M still seems a bit *outré*, but we can imagine that the Left will come up with a nice, safe pseudo-oppositional identity for them; "nice S/M" being no more absurd than, say, "marriage equality."

key to getting up out of the abyss. If suits now look like uniforms, then suits can be our uniforms: we are the new Mad Men.[46]

The Talented 10th of the Negroes, though too small in numbers to affect their own culture, has already figured this out: the Fruit of Islam with their terrifying black suits, white shirts, and red bow ties.[47]

Or consider the Men in Black, originally the tormentors of UFOlogists, who have now spread throughout popular culture.

> Black suit. White shirt. Black tie. Sinister Shades. Ominous and overbearing manner. Speaking in code. No indication of emotions or a personality. Ostensibly some kind of covert operative, but very conspicuous. They are simultaneously imposing and nondescript, which fits their mission perfectly.[48]

We have plenty of actual New or Alt-Right role models — Gianfranco Fini, (president of Alleanza Nazionale), Gerolf Annemans, (Vlaams Belang), and good old Pym Fortuyn: all *successful* politicians; European, of course.[49] But apart from all the other advantages we hear about that third parties or nationalist movements have over there, I can't help but think that in today's world, the sharp suit, the true analogue of the fascist uniform,

---

[46] I discuss the counter-revolutionary potential of the "Mad *Männerbund*" in *The Homo & the Negro* and *End of an Era*.

[47] The "offstage narrator" in Tom Wolfe's "Radical Chic" (used to portray "the general mindset of the people through whose eyes you begin to see") articulates the moment when upper-class Whites moved their allegiance away from the Nation of Islam types and to the Black Panthers: "These are no civil-rights Negroes wearing gray suits three sizes too big — no more interminable Urban League banquets in hotel ballrooms where they try to alternate the blacks and whites around the tables as if they were stringing Arapaho beads — these are real men!" See the text with Wolfe's 2014 annotations here: http://niemanstoryboard.org/stories/annotation-tuesday-tom-wolfe-and-radical-chic/

[48] https://allthetropes.orain.org/wiki/The_Men_in_Black

[49] See footnote 36, on European "backwardness."

can't be ignored as a factor in electoral success.

> *Despite* being the symbolic presence of The Oppression of The Man, The Men in Black have *the mystique of being Badass and Cool, so heroes can be associated with them.* In those cases they are *merely protecting panicky Muggles by doing what's ultimately best.* [The essence of Fascism]
> Watch out for Conspiracy Redemption if they go too far, though.[50]

And "Conspiracy Redemption" occurs when, despite all the MSM propaganda the voters start saying, "Hey, wouldn't we actually be better off it B.I.G.O. really did take over?" Or to paraphrase Jef Costello, "Give me the lightning bolt and pass me the black Hugo Boss[51] suit, I want to join Thrush!"

Counter-Currents/*North American New Right*
November 26, 2014

---

[50] https://allthetropes.orain.org/wiki/The_Men_in_Black
[51] "Boss joined the Nazi Party in 1931, two years before Hitler came to power. By the third quarter of 1932, the all-black SS uniform (to replace the SA brown shirts) was designed by SS-Oberführer Prof. Karl Diebitsch and Walter Heck. Hugo Boss company produced these black uniforms along with the brown SA shirts and the black-and-brown uniforms of the Hitler Youth." (http://en.wikipedia.org/wiki/Hugo_Boss_%28fashion_designer%29#Support_of_Nazism)

INDEX

7/7 bombing, 202n60 9/11, 15n34, 67
10th Amendment, 93
120 Days of Sodom, 181n11 1930s, 220
1940s, 16, 30, 73n13
1950s, 31, 40, 73n13, 106, 110n7, 218, 220
1960s, 1, 16, 28, 37, 67, 91, 92, 105, 154, 180, 198n52, 216, 223
1970s, 1, 135n25, 180-81, 191, 196, 206, 220-21
1980s, 61, 197, 200n56, 220

A

"A Band Apart: Wulf Grimsson's *Loki's Way: The Path of the Sorcerer in the Age of Iron*," 17n3, 53n25, 121n3
A Family Affair, 26
A Room in Chelsea Square, 105-17
A Young Man's Fancy, 30-31
Abbey of Thelema, 197
Abin Sur, 4, 10
Abortion, 40n53
Abu-Ghraib, 67
Academic Marxism, 22
Achilles, 23n16
Adelman, Michele, 203
ADL, 19n9
Adventure Boys, 22-23
Advise and Consent (film), 168n12
After Strange Gods, 47ff.
Against Democracy and Equality: The European New Right, 84, 84n3
Age of the *Feuilleton*, 79
Agent for H.A.R.M., 224n43
Ah Pook is Here, 153n40
Ahnenerbe, 209n10
AIDS, 200
Alberich, 14, 202
Alcibiades, 27n26
Aldrich, Henry, 22
Alexandrovich, Grand Duke Sergei, 27n26
Alien Hand Syndrome, 172; see also Dr. Strangelove Syndrome

Alig, Michael, 179n3, 198, 200-204
Alinsky, Saul, 104
Alleanza Nazionale, 226
Alley Oop, 20
Allies, 159, 175, 177, 212n14
Altamont, 201n58
Alter, Alexandra, 89n6
Alt-Right, 17, 23, 59, 105-106, 223n39, 226
Altschul, Arthur Goodhart, 180, 193
Amazing Spider-Man #5, 2
Amazon.com, 3, 5, 24n19, 48n12, 50n35, 60, 75n19, 107n3, 110, 112, 121n3, 154, 205, 212n20
Ambisexuality, 24, 26, 35, 122n4, 144
America (novel), 50n19
American Idol, 75n20
American Medical Association, 43
American People, 37-38, 176, 220
Amis, Kingsley, 113n11
Amish, 213n21
Anarchists, 65
Anderson, Mark, 65n8
Andersson, Benny, 70
Androgyny, 12n29, 29
Androphilic, 122n4
Anglo-Catholicism, 47n8
Anglo-Saxons, 203n67, 214
Angry Years: A Literary Chronicle, The, 108n5
Angry Young Men, 108
Annemans, Gerolf, 226
Anti-archeofuturism, 201
Anti-utopia, 65-79
Apartment 3-G, 20
Appalachia, 180
Arab Street, 25
Arabic, 10
Arabs, 10n21, 25-27, 51n21, 106-107, 191
Arcadia, 20, 24-26, 31, 33, 41
Archeofuturism, 196, 200-201; see also Anti-archeofuturism
Aristocratic Radicalism, 186n22, 188n26

Aristokratia, 24n18, 132n17, 182n13, 186n22,
Aristotle, 181
Armstrong, Jack, 22
Artists of the Right, 17n4
Aryan, 2, 9-15, 16, 27n25, 29-30, 36, 40, 43, 50-56, 136n26, 170, 178, 179n5, 192, 196, 198-99, 203, 206, 225
Ashkenazi Jews, 213n21
Asimov, Isaac, 40
Assumption University, 47n8
Athens, 56, 197
Atkinson, William Walker, 114
Atlanta, 199
Atreides, Paul, 9n20
Atzmon, Gilad, 46
Auden, W. H., 109
Audrey, 145, 159
Aunt Alexandra, 92ff.
Auntie Mame, 110
Auschwitz, 212
Auster, Larry, 18n7
Australia, 220
Austria, 61
Austrian war bonds, 63
Austro-Hungarian Empire, 61, 63, 65n8
Austro-Hungarian foreign policy, 64
Avant-garde, 84, 101, 106, 128n13, 160n47, 178n1

B
B.I.G.O. (spy organization), 216, 227-28
B-52, 163, 166, 169, 171
Babbittiness, 93
Babylon, 181
"Babysitting Bachelor as Aryan Avatar: Clifton Webb in *Sitting Pretty*, The," 27n24, 30n31
Bach, Johann Sebastian, 124, 128
Bacon, Francis, 111
Bailey, Fenton, 178
Bangs, Lester, 161
Banville, John, 73n12
Barbato, Randy, 178
Barbusse, 113n11
Bardèche, Maurice, 154

Bare, Bobby, 180
Barton Fink Feeling, 19
Bathomet, 10n22
Batman, 6-8, 10
Battle of Flodden, 83
Battle of Versailles, 189
Baudelaire, 91n10
Bayard, Louis, 62n2 BCBG, 192
Beardsley, Aubrey, 65, 67n15
Beatles, 1
Beaton, Cecil, 111
Beatrice, 148
Beats, 106, 107
Beautiful Boy, The, 145n34
Beck, Glenn, 45n2
Becket, Samuel, 177n28
Behind the Veil of Vice: The Business and Culture of Sex in the Middle East, 107n2
Benoist, Alain de, 84, 86, 145n33
Beresford, J. D., 120n1
Bergdorf Goodman, 187, 191
Berlin, 60, 62
Bernhard, Sandra, 1n2
Best American Short Stories 1977, The, 49n17
Betjeman, John, 110
Beyond Theology: The Art of Godmanship, 91n10, 132n19, 133n21
B-films, 16
Big Board, The, 164, 169, 176
Big Chill, The, 86
Biggles, 33n38
Biggus Dickus, 19
Bildungsroman, 76
Billy Liar, 108
Biologic Adaptive, 147
Biological Determinism, 94, 98
Birth Control, 40n53
Bismarck, Otto, 79
Bitter Music: Collected Journals, Essays, Introductions, and Librettos, 144n31
Black, Jack, 5n11
Black comedy, 66, 105, 164n5; 175; see also Cockroach Culture
Black magic, 207
Black Panthers, 92n11
Black Shorts, 209-10, 215, 219

Index

Blackadder Goes Forth, 33n38
Blackshirts, 209
Blei, Franz, 62
Blood Brotherhood, 36n42, 54
Bloody Buggering Fools, 217n29
Bloomberg, Michael, 202n59
Blueshirts, 209
Blüher, Hans, 35n41
Bob (character in Young Man's Fancy), 30-31
Boggy Creek Monster, The, 220
Bolton, Kerry, 17n4, 182n13, 185-86, 191n33, 194n40, 197
Book of Kells, 77
Bookforum, 73n12
Boomer Beefcake and Bonding, 20n12
Borat, 179n4
Boss, Hugo, 227n51
Boston, 179n5
Bottom, 33n38
Botton, Alain de, 66
Bowden, Jonathan, 17n4, 225
Bowery Boys, The, 22
Bowie, David, 147n39
Bowles, Sally, 181
Boy (Tarzan's son), 22
Boy Scouts, 22, 35-36, 58
Boy's Own Mag, 147, 166
Boys in the Band, The, 114
Boys Next Door, 22
BRA (Black Run America), 18, 158
Bradley, John R., 25, 27n27, 177n3
Braine, John, 108
Brave New World, 150m 152
Breton, Andre, 45n2, 186
Brideshead Revisited: The Sacred & Profane Memories of Captain Charles Ryder, 25n23, 91n10
Bridge and Tunnel (social type), 201
Britain, 154, 208-09
British Union of Fascists, 207, 209, 215
British War Office, 64
Brod, Max, 62, 68, 196n47
Brodie, Jean, 80-87, 216n28
Bromance, 20, 31n34, 39-40
Brontë, Charlotte, 83
Brook Farm, 155n43
Brooks, Mel, 192

Brotherhood of British Freemen (B. B. F.), 217n29
Brown Shirts, 209, 227n51
Brown, Michael, 57n36
Bruno, 79
Buber, Martin, 196n47
Buddha, The, 95, 142
BUF, see British Union of Fascists
Bullock, Sandra, 88n1
Bunker, Archie, 56
Burpleson Air Force Base, 163-64, 171
Burroughs Ephemera 2: *Naked Lunch* Prospectus, 102n33
Burroughs, William, 17, 53, 57n34, 101-11, 144-45, 147, 150-52, 159, 203n63
Burrows, Stephen, 189
Bush/Obama Administration, 60
Buzz (young boy in *Mr. B Natural*), 29-30

C

Caesar, Julius, 22
Cairo, 111
Calloway, Cab, 1n1
Calpurnia, 97n24
Calvin, John, 85
Calvinism, 85
Camp, 107, 114, 224
Camp: The Lie That Tells the Truth, 114m13
Campbell, Martin, 1, 6
Campbell, Pete, 37
Camus, Albert, 73, 113n11
Canada, 18, 18n8, 49-50, 179, 187, 187n25, 197-99, 205, 205n71, 228
Capone, Alphonse, 37, 204
Capote, Truman, 89n8, 97n24, 102-103, 107n2, 135; see also Dill
Carlson, Jen, 103n36
Carmilla, 108
Carpenter, John, 97n20
Carradine, John, 88n3
Carson, Kim, 153n40
Carson, Rachel, 166n9
Carter, Dale, 176
Casino Royale (film), 6n12
Castalia, 76, 78-79
Castle of Fu Manchu, 207, 211

Catch-22, 105
Catcher in the Rye, The, 87n4
Cathedral of Light, 12
Catholicism, 45n2, 91
Catholics, 77, 82, 91n10
Céline, Louis-Ferdinand, 101
Center, The, 12, 132n17
Certificate of Relief, 205
Challenge of Aristocratic Radicalism, The, 188n26
Chambers, Whittaker, 91n10, 92n11, 106
Champetier, Charles, 84
Chanel, Coco, 178n1
Chavez, Hugo, 186, 188n26
Cheaper by the Dozen, 30n31
Chelsea Clone, 225n45
Chemical Muse, The, 205n70
Chess, 70
Chief, 148, 159
China, 189-91
Chinatown, 48n13
Chomsky, Noam, 59n41, 207n1
Choo, Jimmy, 192
Christian Socialism, 14
Church of the Holy Communion, 200
Church of the Sub-Genius, 10n21, 213n18
Churchill, Winston, 208, 212
Churchill's War: Triumph in Adversity, 208n6
Circumcision, 166n9
Cities of the Red Night, 153n40
Civil Rights Movement 1n1
Clarke, Alisdair, 35n41, 58n39
Class: A Guide Through the American Status System, 116
Cleveland, Pat, 183-84, 188n26, 190
Clinton, Hillary, 85-86
Clintons (Bill and Hillary), 92m11
Clockwork Orange, A, 147n39
Cloning, 61n34, 74, 77-79, 151
Clothes, 65n8, 137, 145-46, 157, 182, 190, 194n41, 197
Clusterfuck Nation, 223n37
CNN, 54n24, 100n30
Coast City, CA, 3
Cobble Stone Gardens, 153n40
Cockburn, Alexander, 166n9

Cockroach (Gregor Samsa's metamorphosis), 2n4
Cockroach Culture, 2-4, 5n11, 48n15
Coco Chanel and Igor Stravinsky, 178n1
Code of the Woosters, 209-11
Cohen, Sasha Baron, 179
Cohn, Roy, 91n10, 116
Coke Machine, 164-68
Cold War, 56, 96n17
Coleridge, Samuel Taylor, 108
Collective Consciousness, 98
Color Blindness, 94-98n25, 158
Colquhoun, 111
Comics, 1-2, 4-5, 9, 14-15, 17, 20-21
Coming Corporate State, The, 208n5
Coming Out (closet), 29, 114
Commie Conspiracy, 35n34, 167
Communism, 71, 153-54, 223n39
Comte, Auguste, 77
Conan the barbarian [sic] Twenty Stories, 23n15
Conan the Barbarian, 23n15
Concept, The Seriousness of, 17n5
Confederate battle flag, 93, 180
Confederate currency, 63
Conformity, 29, 50n19, 93, 214, 218
Conn Band Instruments, 30
Connolly, Cyril, 111, 119
Conservative Revolution, 187n24, 194n41
Conservative, The, 17ff.
Conspiracy Redemption, 227
Conspiracy theories, 59n41, 166-67
Continental Congress, The, 166
Coomaraswamy, Ananda K., 178m, 213n20
Cooper, Bert, 33-34
Copenhagen Interpretation, 77
Corben, Billy, 178
Core, Philip, 114m13
"Corner at the Center of the World, The," 132n17
Correct Sadist, The, 135n25
Correct Sadist 2: Dungeon Evidence, 135n25
Corvo, Baron: see Rolfe, Frederick
Barton, Benjamin, 100n30
Costanza, George, 1n2, 64
Costello, Jef, 8, 215-17, 227-28

Council of Elrond, 5
Counen, Jan, 178n1
Counter-Currents, iv, 17, 28, 170
Coward, Noël, 119
Cox, Brian, 112n10
Cozzens, James Gould, 105, 106n1
Creation (Biblical), 14, 166n9
Crisis of the Modern World, The, 27n27
Crosby, Bing, 36, 41
Cross-dressing, 20
Crossing the Border, 49n17
Crother, Bosley, 16n2
Crow; see Robot, Crow T.
Crowley, Aleister, 197
Crusade for Moorish Dignity. 225
Cthulhu, 10n21, 81
Cuba, 56
Cuckoo Strategy, 56
Cuesta, Michael, 112n10
Culture of Critique, 48n14
Culture-Alien, 32
Culture-Distorting, 42
Culture-Forming, 40, 58
"Curses, Cut-Ups, and Contraptions: The 'Disastrous Success' of William Burroughs' Magick." 101n31

D

D'Annunzio, Gabriele, 155n43
D'Oust, Maya, 11n27
Daily Telegraph, 110
Dandy, 31n26, 65n8
Danielou, Alain, 152n38, 178, 213n20
Dante, 148
Daphne of the Dunes, 130
Daredevil, 4
Dark Age, the, 136n26, 178; see also Kali Yuga
Das Glasperlenspiel, 75n18
Davenport, Iowa, 20
Davenport, William, 39n49
Davidson, Michael, 25n21
DC Comics, 1-7
DC Universe, 2
De Palma, Brian, 37n44, 53n25, 86n5, 122n6, 195n45, 204n67
DEA, 202m 204n65
Dead End Kids, The, 22

Dead Roads Trilogy, 147
Death Camps, 66n11
De-Ba'athification, 54n24
Decadence and Catholicism, 91n10
Deck, John Norbert, 126n8
Decline of the West, 182n14, 186n22
Deleuze, Gilles, 71n5, 78
Demian, 118n21, 120n2, 142n29, 175n22
Demian, Max, 118n21, 120n2, 175n22, 125n2
Democracy, 50n19, 216, 201n58
Denazification, 52n24
Dennis, Jeffrey P., 16-42
Derrida, Jacques, 71n5, 78
"Detroit City," 180
Detroit, 1, 58, 180, 188n26
Deuteronomy, 44
Devil Doll, 11n26
Devolution, 1m2
De-World, 75n17
Dialectic Couplet, 27n27
Dib, The, 145-46
Dick's Sportswear, 222
Dickens, Charles, 68
Diebitsch, *SS-Oberführer* Prof. Karl, 227n51
Dill, 89, 97n24
"Disco Inferno," 196
Disneyland, 1
Ditko, Steve, 3
"Dixie," 180
DIY culture, 66
Djerzinki, Michel, 73-79
Dobbs, J. R. "Bob," 213n12
Doctor Faustus: The Life of the German Composer Adrian Leverkühn as Told by a Friend, 79-80, 160
Donat, Robert, 36
Donner, Richard, 13
Donovan, Jack, 44n1, 58n39, 122n4, 225n45
Doomsday Machine, 172, 176
Doors, The, 159
Dover Books, 120
Doyle, Sir Arthur Conan, 108
Dr. Seuss, 154
Dr. Strangelove; or, How I learned to Stop Worrying and Love the Bomb,

105, 160n47, 162-77
Dr. Strangelove Syndrome, 172; see also Alien Hand Syndrome
Drag queens, 218n32
Draper, Donald, 34
Dru, Alexander, 47n8
Drugs, 52n22, 55, 111n9, 132n17, 153, 181, 182, 197-205
Dubois, W. E. B., 188n26
Duke, Daisy, 180
Duncan, Michael Clark, 4 *Dune* (novel), 139n27
Dune (film), 9n20, 10n22
DVD Verdict, 3

E

Earth, 3-14, 78, 172, 181, 201, 208
Eckhart, Dietrich, 62n3, 64n5
Ecsaine, 185
Ecstasy, 201
Edison Institute, The, 30
Edmonson, Adrian, 33n38
Effeminacy, 21, 26
Egodeath.com, 52n22
Eisenhower, Dwight David, 96, 176n24
Elders of Zion, 192
Eldritch Evola . . . & Others, The, 17n3, 19n11, 48n14, 65n10, 70n3, 76n21, 127n12, 132n17, 154n41, 213n20, 224n42
Elementary Particles, The, 70-79
Eleven (fictional magazine), 111
Eliot, T. S., 47-50, 59
Elizabeth II, 166
Elizabethan Golden Age, 50
Emerson, Ralph Waldo, 11, 188n26
Encounters at the End of the World, 193n36
End of an Era: Mad Men & the Ordeal of Civility, 37n43, 168n12, 213n21
"End, The," (song by The Doors), 159
Enemy of Europe, The, 28n28, 38n46, 40n54
Enlightenment, The, 135
Entheogen, 52n22
Episcopal Church, 45, 91n10, 197, 200
Ernst Jünger — Carl Schmitt: Briefe 1930–1983, 209n8

"Eternal Outsider: Veblen on the Gentleman and the Jew, The," 48n14, 65n10
Ethical Socialism, 113n12
Eton, 166
EU, 81
Eucharist, 52
Europe, 18n8, 28, 31-32, 61, 75-76, 81, 121, 207, 219n29
European New Right, 186
European Revolution of 1933, 202n60
Europeans, 28
Evergreen Review, 102n33
Evola, Baron Julius, 7n13, 7n15, 8, 10, 12, 16, 17, 19n11, 39-40, 45, 48, 54, 56, 65, 67-71, 76, 87, 113, 121-22, 127, 132, 152, 154, 173, 178, 188, 195, 200, 201n58, 213n20, 215, 224n42, 225
Evolution, 10, 22, 42, 57, 120n1, 121n2, 122, 125; see also Devolution
Ewell, Mayella, 98
Ewer, William Norman, 50n20
Excavating Kafka, 60-69, 196n47

F

Faber & Faber, 47n8
Fafner, 200-01
Fail Safe, 177, 177n28
Fairness, 99, 158
Family values, 8, 26, 30, 40, 42, 51, 53, 55-56
Fascism Viewed from the Right, 215n24
Fascism, 82, 84, 108n4, 154, 181, 187, 194n40, 211n13
Fascism, Sartorial, 207-27
Faulkner, William, 93
Faustianism, 43n, 179, 182, 184-85, 189, 194, 195n44
FBI, 202n60
Federal Court system, 179n6
Ferris, Carol, 3
Fez, 145
Fido, 129-30, 149, 160, 163
Final Frontier: The Rise and Fall of the American Rocket State, The, 176n24
Finch, Atticus, 89n7, 92-3, 95-100, 104
Finch, Jean Louise, 89-90, 94-101

Fini, Gianfranco, 226
Fink-Nottle, Gussie, 209
Finland, 83
Fish, Stanley, 68
Fitty, 1n2
Fiume, 155n43, 190n31
Flames, The, 120, 154n41-155
Flash Gordon, 6
Flash Mobs, 158n44
Flashheart, Squadron Commander the Lord, 33n38
Fleishman, Lisa, 203, 205n68
Florida, 199
Fluoridation, 166n9; see also Purity of Essence
Foetor Judaicus, 2
Folk music, 166n9
Fontana, Constance, 7n15, 67n15
Fontane Prize, 62
Footbags; see Hacky Sacks Footer bags, 210, 219-20
Foreign Affairs, 168
Forester, Dr., 211
Forrest, Nathan Bedford, 93
Forrester, Dr. Clayton, 207
Fortuyn, Pym, 226
Forward, The, 47
Foster, Meg, 193n37
Foucault, Michel, 71n5, 78
Foundation Trilogy, 40
Fr. Rolfe; see Rolfe, Frederick France and the French, 70, 73, 187, 189, 191, 208, 211
Francis, Coleman, 70, 88n3
Franco, Francisco, 80-82, 208, 212
Frankas, Jeff, 75n17
Frankfurt School, 35n41, 225
Franny and Zooey, 93
Franz Josef, Kaiser, 63-64
Frederick Rolfe, 91n10, 116n19; see also Corvo, Baron
Free Thought, 82
Freedom Rides, 99
Free-thinking Jews, 47-48
French culture, 71
French New Right, 84
Freud, Sigmund, 26, 32, 35
Freudianism, 27n24, 32
Friedberg, Eric, 203

From Krakow to Krypton: Jews and Comic Books, 5n10
Frowick, Roy Halston; see Halston
Führer, 80, 120n2, 173, 175n22, 217, 219n33
Führer Prinzip, 217
Fulford, James, 57n36
Functions, First, Second, Third, 54
Furlong, Paul, 40n53
Fussell, Paul, 115-16
Fustel de Coulanges, Numa Denis, 39n52
Future Histories, 74
Future Shock (club night), 201
Futurism, 181-86, 190n31, 191, 193, 194

G
Galadriel, 193n37
Galaxy (spy organization), 216
Galt's Gulch, 129
Game, 38, 171n18
Gandalf, 5
Gandhi, Mahatma, 208n7
Garden God, The, 108
Garrison, Jim, 208n4
Gaston de Blondeville, 108
Gatien, Peter, 178-206
Gawker, 100n30
Gay Fiction, 112
Gay Identity, 58
Gay Marriage, 42, 44n1; see also Marriage Equality
Gecko, Gordon, 61
Geeks of Doom, 5n11
Geisterkrieg, 186, 190n31
Geller, Jay, 2n3
Geller, Paris, 9n19
Gemeinschaft, 162
Genet, Jean, 62
George, Peter, 177n28
Gerald Sorme Trilogy, 108
Germany, 36n41, 50n24, 61, 79, 154-55, 158, 161, 188n26, 208
Giant Spider Invasion, The, 47n7
Gigi, 135
Gilman, Sander I., 68-69
Gilmore Girls, The, 9n19
Gilmore, Bob, 128n13

Giotto, 82
Girl in Lover's Lane, The, 30
Girl-craziness, 16, 20, 25-31, 40
Giuliani, Rudolph, 198, 202-205
Glass Bead Game, The, 75-79, 160
GMO foods, 166n9
Gnostics, 10n21
Go Set a Watchman, 88-104
God, Abrahamic, 10
Godwin, Joscelyn, 7n15, 67n15, 113n12
Godwin, William, 113n12
Godzilla, 15n34
Goebbels, Joseph, 66n11
Gold in the Furnace, 160n46
Gold shirts, 209
Goldman Sachs, 194
Golem, 32; American, 33
Golightly, Holly, 135
Good Thinkers, 83-84
Good War, The, 42; see also World War II
Goodfellas, 73
Goodrich, Thomas, 52n24
Gorey, Edward, 109, 110
Gothamist, 103n36
Gothic Novels, 107
Götterdämmerung, 159-60, 175, 196, 201
Govinda, 142n29
Graham, Will, 97n23
Grail, the, 10, 90n9
Grail: Two Studies, The, 90n9
Grant, Madison, 23
Gravity's Rainbow, 176
Great Recession, 194
Great War, see World War I
Green Hornet, The, 5n11
Green Lantern Corps, 4-6, 9, 12
Green Lantern mythos, 9
Green Lantern, The, 1-15
Green Lantern, The, 1-15, 127
Greenshirts, 209
Greer, Germaine, 145n34
Greyshirts, 209
Grimmson, Wulf, 17n3, 53-54n27, 121n3
Griswold, Clark, 218n32
Grossman, 193

Grove Press, 102n33
Guano, Col. "Bat," 26, 31n38, 164-68
Guard of Honor, 105
Guardian, The, 61n1, 71n11, 94-95, 98, 102n34
Guénon, René, 17, 27n27, 45n2, 72, 78n22, 136, 160n45, 195n42, 213n20, 214, 218n31
Guevara, Che, 80
Guild socialism, 50n20
Gulag, 60
Gurkha regiments, 187n25
Gysin, Brion, 152

H
H. P. Lovecraft: Against the World, Against Life, 70
Habsburgs, 61, 63, 64, 65n8
Hacky sacks, 185
Hadrian, 58n39
Hagel, Chuck, 43
Hakim Bey, 155n43, 190n31
Halakhah, 46n6
Haller, Harry, 13
Halley, Richard, 129
Halston, 136n26, 178-198, 200, 206
Halston Heritage, 192
Halstonettes, 188n6, 190; see also Ultraettes
Ham, 90n9
Hamilton, Andrew, 212n17
Hamlet, 179n3
Hammer, Mike, 220n42
Hammond, Hector, 1, 4, 14-15
Hampdenshire Wonder, The, 120n1
Hank, Jean Louis' intended, 93, 97n24
Hanson, Ellis, 91n10
Hardy, Andy, 16, 21n13, 22, 26, 32-33, 37, 42
Hardy, Judge, 26
Harlan, Brian, 128n14
Harlan, Viet, 206
Harper's, 64n4
Harris, Oliver, 102n33, 103n36
"Having race," 188n26
Hawes, James, 60-69, 196n47
Hawthorne, Derek, 8
"He Writes! You Read! *They Live*!,"

97n20
Heck, Walter, 227n51
Hegel, G. W. F., 11, 17n5
Hegel: Texts and Commentary, 17n5
Heine, Heinrich, 62
Heinlein, Robert, 120
Hellstorm: The Death of Nazi Germany, 1944–1947, 52n24
Helm, Matt, 216
He-Man Woman Haters Club, 16
Hepburn, Audrey, 135
Hermetic Quest, 9
Hermetic Tradition: Symbols & Teachings of the Royal Art, The, 12n28
Hero myth, 6, 15n34
Herzog, Werner, 193n36
Hesse, Hermann, 13, 75n20, 78-79, 142n29, 175n22
Hetero-mania, 21, 26
Heterosexuality, Premature, 35, 37
Hickman, Craig, 72n10
Hierarchy, 53-54, 71, 201n57, 213n25
High Church, 90
High Noon, 175n23
Hilberry College, 49n17
Hilco Consumer Capital, 192
Hill country of Alabama, 90n9
Hillman, D. C. A., 205n70
Himmler, Heinrich, 13, 56n31, 209n10
Hinduism, 11
Hine, Phil, 148n36
Hiss, Alger (traitor and spy), 92n11, 166n9
Hitchens, Christopher, 208n7
Hitler, Adolf, 28, 39n51, 66n11, 79-80, 82, 159, 161, 176, 194n40, 207-208, 227n51,
Hitler Youth, 227n51
Hitler's Mentor, 62n3
Hodgson, Joel, 29-30, 207
Hoffman, Michael A., II, 19n9, 48n12, 52n22
Hoffman, Michael, 52n22, 197n50, 199n54, 205n70
Holbeyfield, James, 181n36, 193n36
Hollander, Xaviera, 135n25
Hollywood nihilists, 39
Hollywood Raja: The Life and Times of Louis B. Mayer, 16n2
Hollywood, 2, 5n11, 16n2, 19, 39, 42, 216
Holocaust, 60-66, 177, 212
Holocaustianity, 60-66
Homer, 196n48, 199n55
Homintern, 109
Homo & the Negro, The, 17n3, 37n44, 44, 58n39, 86n5, 97n20, 107n2, 121n3, 122n6, 204n67, 211n13, 214
Homoeroticism, 21, 28, 36, 171
Homophobia, 27n27, 52, 56n32, 107, 112
Homo-romance, 21, 23-25, 31, 33-35, 40n53, 41
Homosexual, The, 19, 27, 34, 36, 58, 225n45
Homosexuality and Male Bonding in Pre-Nazi Germany: The Youth Movement, the Gay Movement, and Male Bonding before Hitler's Rise, 35m47
Hoover, J. Edgar, 106
Hopkins, Anthony, 112n10
Hopkins, Bill, 108n4
Horizon, 111
Horizontality, 55n29
Horning, Rob, 72n9
Horton, Scott, 64n4
Houellebecq, Michel, 65n9, 70-79
Hour of Decision, The, 188n26
How Proust Can Change Your Life, 66
How to Stay Well, 43n56
Howard, Robert E., 17n4
Huffington Post, 166n9
Hugo Boss (company), 227n51
Humanitarian interventionism, 86
Hungry Ghosts: Seven Allusive Comedies, The, 49n17
Hurry on Down, 108
Huston, Anjelica, 136n26, 193n37
Huxley, Aldous, 150, 209n9, 217n29
Huysmans, J. K., 91n10, 135n25
Hypnotism, 207

I
ICA, 111
Iliad, 199n55

IMDb (Internet Movie Database), 13, 30n32, 162n1, 168n13, 169, 206
Imperium, 27n24
In Cold Blood, 102-103
In My Own Way, 91n10, 134n22
Incredibly Strange Creature: Or Why I stopped Living and Became a Mixed-up Zombie, The, 160n47, 177n28
Incredibly Strange Creatures Who Stopped Living and Became Mixed-Up Zombies, The, 160n47, 177n28
Individualism, 50n19, 71, 82, 84, 153, 186, 214
Indo-Europeans, 91n90
Inspector Lee, 102, 103n36
Internet Movie Database, see IMDb
Introduction to Magic: Rituals and Practical Techniques for the Magus, 201n58
Iran, 28n27
Iranians, 28n27
Iraq War II, 52n24
Irish Catholics, 91n10
Iron Man, 6
IronFanofSteelofThunder, 7
Irving, David, 208n6
Islam, 71, 107n3, 120n2, 154, 197, 226
Island, 150, 152
Israel, 5n10
Ivry, Benjamin, 47n9

J
J. C. Penny, 191, 192n35, 194n41
Jackie 60 (club), 198
Jackson, James, 87
Jacob, Alexander, 90n9
Jam Handy (industrial film company), 28
James, Clive, 209n9
James, Henry, 50
Jannings, Emil, 208
Japan, 184
Jazz, 128
Jeeves and Wooster, 210, 215
Jefferson, Thomas, 188n26
Jeffersonian Democrat, 96
Jeffery, Ben, 72n10
Jellaba, 145

Jenks, Jorian, 208n5
Jerusalem, 56, 212n17
Jewish Guru Figure, 49n17
Jewish History, Jewish Religion: The Weight of Three Thousand Years, 51n21
Jews, 2n3, 5n10, 44, 46-51, 53, 56, 63, 68-69, 81, 87-88n4, 110n4, 155, 212-13n21; see also Jews; Judaics; The Tribe
JFK (film), 208n4
JHVH, 10n21, 98
JHVH-1, 10n21
Joel, Billy, 181
Joel: see Hodgson, Joel
John Birch Society, 92n11
John Carter, 4n8
Johnson, Greg, vi, 35n35, 39n48, 43, 46n4, 95n16, 97n23, 98n27, 132n19, 154n42, 178n1-2, 187n24, 191n32, 194n41, 195n42, 206n75, 207
Johnston, Ben, 128n13
Jordan, Hal, 1-2, 8
Jordan, Michael, 221
Jor-El, 207
Jowitt, Earl, 92n11
Joyce, James, 74
Joyce, William, 211
Judaic Cultural Supremacy, 60
Judaic Culture, 1
Judaics, 1, 43, 44, 155, 202n59, 203; see also Jews; The Tribe
Judeo-Christian, 35, 53n26, 55
Judy (character in "Young Man's Fancy"), 30-31
Jünger, Ernst, 209n8
Jungle Book, The, 23n15

K
K., Joseph, 155
Kafka, Franz, 48n15, 60-69, 196
Kafka's Clothes: Ornament and Aestheticism in the Habsburg Fin de Siècle, 65n8
Kali Yuga, 122n5, 160; see also Dark Age
Kaplan, Arnie, 5n10
Kaufmann, Walter, 17n5

Index

Kazakhstan, 196n47
Keith Waterhouse, 108
Kemi, 146
Kennedy, Hubert, 35n47
Kennedy, Jackie, 187, 208n4
Kennedy, Joe, 49n17
Kennedy, John F., 34n39, 176, 208n4
Kentucky, 179n6
Kerouac, Jack, 106, 125n25
Kersey, Paul, 18, 96n18-19, 163n4
Kershaw, Kris, 199n53
Kesey, Ken, 225
Kick Ass, 4n8
Kilbride, Percy, 11
Killowog, 4
King, Martin Luther, 18, 96
King's Speech, The, 4
Kinnear, Greg, 15n34
Kipling, Elsie, 212n17
Kipling, Rudolph, 212n17
Kipling, Rudyard, 23n15
Kiss Me Deadly, 19n11, 224n42,
Kissoff, Premier, 168, 171
Klansman, 95
Klinger, Leslie, 48n13
Klondike (card game), 116n18
Klugman, Jack, 88n4
K-Myth, 60-66
Knecht, Joseph, 76-79
Knife-fights, 36
Knock-out game, 158n44
Koch, Ed, 202-03
Kojecky, Roger, 48n12
Kong, Major, 163-64, 169n16
Kopff, E. Christian, 56n31, 215n24
Kovalesti, Serge F., 89n6
Kraft durch Freude, 177
Krautrock, 33n38
Kubrick, Stanley, 162, 175, 177n28
Kunstler, James, 222-23

L
L.I.E., 112n10
L'Arco e la Clava, 16
Lacan, Jacques, 71n5, 78
Lady Gaga, 146
Lamentations of Dr. Faustus, The, 79
Lane (Franny's obtuse boyfriend), 93
Lane, Lois, 13

Lang, Fritz, 206
Lanz von Liebenfels, Dr. Jorg, 57n37
Larson, Christian, 42
Last and First Men, 120
Last Exit to Brooklyn, 110
Last Laugh, The, 208
Laughter, 61, 141, 143, 149-50, 164n5
Lawrence, D. H., 8, 108n4
Lawyers, 99-100; see also Scumbags;
    Shysters
Le Fanu, Joseph, 108
Leap, The, 108n4
Leavis, F. R., 113
Lebensraum, 55n29
Lecktor, Dr. Hannibal; see Lecter, Dr.
    Hannibal
Lecter, Dr. Hannibal, 11n23, 93n14,
    112-13, 180n8
Lee, Bill, 101-102
Lee, Harper, 88-103
Lee, Stan, 1
Left Bank, 73m13
Left, 42, 52n23, 58, 81, 106, 166n9-167,
    194, 202n59, 211n13, 216, 225n45
Leisure, 40n54m 47n9
Leisure, the Basis of Culture, 47n8
Lem, Stanislav, 120
Leonardo da Vinci, 82
Leper Colony, The (bomber), 168, 172
Lesbians, 145; unconscious, 81, 84, 86
Levi, Dolly, 193n37
Lewis, Wyndham, 49n17
Liberal Media, 58
Liberal Society, 71, 78
Liberalism, 67, 71, 84, 87, 96, 154
Life Essence, 171
Ligotti, Thomas, 70n4
Limelight (club), 197m 199, 201-202,
    206
Limelight (film), 136n26, 178-79, 197-
    206
Lipstick Boys, The, 108n6
Little Bo Peep, 29
Little Rascals, 16n1
Lively, Blake, 1, 3
Liza with a 'Z'; see Minelli, Liza,
Lo, 125, 130-31, 150, 156
Loki, 179n3, 200
Loki's Way, 17n3, 53n25, 54m27,

121n3
London, 11n26, 202n60
Lord Michael, 201, 204
Lord of the Rings (film), 5
Los Angeles, 79, 160n47
Lost Boys, 22-23
Loughlin, Sean, 54n24
Lovecraft, H. P., 17, 48n13, 50, 68, 70, 73n13
Lovecraftian, 5, 21, 108, 220n42
Lower East Side, 48n13
Lucifer, 10, 12; see also Prince of the Air; Satan
Lumpenproletariat, 83
Lynch, Trevor, 167, 178n1; see also *Trevor Lynch's White Nationalist Guide to the Movies*; *Son of Trevor Lynch's White Nationalist Guide to the Movies*
Lynskey, Anna, 71n6

M

Ma and Pa Kettle (film series), 11
MacBryde, 111
MacCool, Glynns, 102n34
MacDonald, Kevin, vi, 23n16, 48n14, 49n17, 58n40, 206n75
Mackenzie, Suzie, 72n11
MacLaren-Ross, Julian, 110
MAD (Mutual Assured Destruction), 175
"Mad *Männerbund*," 227n46
Mad Men, 34, 37, 109, 168n12, 226
Mad Men, Season 1, "Nixon vs. Kennedy," 34n39
Magic, 101n31, 104, 132, 142, 155n43, 191, 201n58, 207, 213n21
Magical Universe of William Burroughs, The, 101n31, 104n38
Magister Ludi, 75n18
Magnate, Mr., 127, 131
Magnus Hirschfeld, 26, 35
Malka, Ben, 192
Mamet, David, 209n11
Man Who Disappeared (America), The, 50n19
Mandrake, Group Captain Lionel, 31n34, 163-71
Manhunter, 11n23, 97n23, 112n10,

125, 132n18, 169n17
Mann, Thomas, 79-80, 160, 207n2
Männerbund, 12, 16-17, 21, 29, 35n41, 36-40, 53-54, 121-22
Manning, Michael, 12n29
Man-o-sphere, 22n14, 38
Manson, Charles, 41
Mao Tse Tung, 80
Marchand, Philip, 50n18
Maria (*Metropolis*), 172
Marinetti, Filippo, 186, 189
Mario and the Magician," 207n2
Markham, Sean, 202, 204
Marriage equality, 99, 225n45; see also Gay Marriage
Mars, 116n18
Marshall McLuhan: The Medium and the Messenger: A Biography, 50n18
Marvel Comics, 1-3
Marx Brothers, 203
Marxism, 45n2
Masculine principle, 38
Masculinists, 35n41, 199n45
Master Musicians of Joujouka, 152
Master race, 56n31
Mathematics, 51n21, 75, 79
Matheson, Richard, 31n33
Matrix, The, 97n20
Maurras, Charles, 47
Mayall, Rik, 33n38
Maycomb, 94
Mayer, Louis B., 16
MC5, 224n42
McCain, John, 18n7
McCarthy, Joseph, 91n10
McGeary, Thomas, 144n31
McLuhan, Marshall, 49-51
McWhist, 147
Mechling, Jay, 21n13
Meeker, Ralph, 223-24
Meister Eckhart, 91n10
Mellon, Tamara, 192
Men Among the Ruins, 8n18, 39n50, 54n28, 122n5
Men in Black, 226-27
Mencken, H. L., 87
Merry pranksters, 225
Meru, Sky Marshal Tehat, 163n4
Metapolitics, 186

Methodist-Presbyterianism, 85
Metroland, Margo, 89, 92n11, 98
Metropolis (film), 172
Metrosexual, 65n8, 113
MGM, 26
Michelangelo, 58n39
Michigan, 179n6
Midtown New York, 183
"Mike Hammer, Occult Dick: *Kiss Me Deadly* as Lovecraftian Tale," 19n11, 224n43
Mind Science; see New Thought
Minelli, Liza, 176, 181, 184, 190, 196n46
Mineshaft Gap, 162, 176n24
Mineshafts, 170n17, 173, 176; see also *Gemeinschaft*
Minton, 111
Miscellanea (Guénon), 45n2
Missile Gap, 176n24
Mitzvot, 46n6
Modernism, 66, 101
Modernity, 18n8, 55n29, 70, 84
Mona Lisa, 148
Monophonic, 128, 130
Montgomery Ward Catalogues, 101
Monty Python, 19
Moore, Michael, 179
Morgenthau (Manhattan DA), 204
Morrison, Temura, 4
Morte d'Urban, 91n10
Mosley, Sir Oswald, 207, 209, 212, 215
Mother (club), 198
Mowgli, 23n15
Moynihan, Michael, 201n58
Mr. B Natural, 29-30
Mr. Chips, 36
Mr. Scoutmaster, 36, 41
MST3k (Mystery Science Theater 3000), 11n26, 29-31, 47n7, 70, 74n14, 88n3, 180n9, 198n52, 207, 211, 218, 223, 224n43
Muffley, President Merkin, 166, 171, 173-74, 176
Mulford, Prentice, 126-27, 141n28
Mullins, Eustace, 92n11
Murnau, F. W., 208
Murphy, Timothy J., 145n33-150,
153m40, 159-60, 164n5
Muscular Christianity, 22
Music and the Power of Sound: The Influence of Tuning and Interval on Consciousness, 152n38
Music of the Twentieth-Century Avant-Garde: A Biocritical Sourcebook, 128n13
Music, traditional, 152
Mussolini, Benito, 80, 82, 191n11, 208, 212
Mystery Cults, 200, 201n58
Mystery Men (film), 15n34

N
NAACP, 94, 96
Naked Jockstrap Wrestling, 30
Naked Lunch, 100-101, 203n63
Napoleonic civil emancipation, 51
Nation of Islam, 154, 226n47
National Book Award, 62, 91n10, 106
National Film Board of Canada, 179
National Socialists (NS), 154-55, 158, 161, 188n26, 208
Nature, Contemplation, and the One: A Study in the Philosophy of Plotinus, 126n8
Nazi Survival Myth, 177n29
Nazis, so-called, see National Socialists, NS Germany
Nazism, 161, 227n51
Negroes, 1n1, 40, 40n54, 44, 90n9, 96, 137, 218, 225; see also Talented Tenth
Negrofication, 18, 40n54, 218-23; see also *The Homo and the Negro*
Neill, James, 24, 26, 34-37, 107n3, 121n4, 135n25, 144, 223n38
Nelson, Michael (pseudonym), 105, 111
Nemesis, 10n21, 200-201
Neo-Cons, 54, 202-03
Neo-Platonism, 42, 114
New Annotated Lovecraft, The, 48n13
New Jersey, 90n9, 91n10, 203
New Left, 59, 111n7, 154
New Left Review, 208n7
New Right vs. Old Right & Other Essays, 31n35, 43n57

New School for Social Research, 209n10
New Thought, 11, 42, 114, 126, 127
New Thought: A Practical American Spirituality, 11n25
New York Newspapers, 92n12, 96n19
New York Post, 92n12
New York Times, 89n6
New Yorker (social type), 197, 206n73
New Yorker, 74, 91n10
Ng-Gunko, 125, 135, 137, 144-46, 154
Nibelunglied, 14
Nietzsche, Friedrich, 35, 67-71, 79, 160-61, 186, 188n26-189n28
Night Train to Mundo Fine, 88n3
Nihilism, 67
Ninth Symphony (Beethoven), 79
Nixon, Richard Milhous, 34n39, 189
Noah, 90n9
Noble savages, 87
Noël Coward Reader, The, 106, 107n2
Nolan, Christopher, 8n16
Nolan, Hamilton, 100n30
North Africa, 152
North American heartland, 179
North American New Right, 178n2, 187n24, 195n44, 215n26,
North American New Right, 186
North, The, 90, 92n11,
Northern California, 196, 198
Nostradamus, 61
"Notes on *The New Annotated Lovecraft*," 48n13
Notes on the Third Reich, 56n31, 215n24
Nova Express, 101n31-103n36, 153m39
Nova Express: The Restored Text, 102n33, 103n36
Nova Trilogy, 102
Nowicki, Andy, 38n48, 171n18
NS (National Socialist) Germany, 155, 158, 188n26, 208
Nuisance abatement, 202
Nuremberg defense, 202n60
Nuremberg Rally, 12

O
O. Henry Award, 49n17
O'Malley, Father, 36, 41
Oa, 4-5, 9, 12
Oates, Joyce Carol, 49n17
Obama, Barack Hussein, 18n7
Objectivist, The, 217
Occidental Observer, The, 57n33, 59, 59n40
Occultism, 45n2
Odd John, 31n34, 105, 120-61, 162-77
"Of Costner, Corpses, and Conception: Mother's Day Meditations on *The Untouchables* and *The Big Chill*," 86n5
Ohio, 179n6
Okamoto, Dr. Miyoshi, 184
Old Sarge, 148
Old Testament, 19n9, 48n12
Olde Tyme Liberalism, 96
Oliver, Revilo P., 27n24
Olsen, Jimmy, 37n45
Olsen, Peggy, 37
Olympic Towers, 183m 197
"One Night in Bangkok," 70
One Voice: A Reconciliation of Harry Partch's Disparate Theories, 128n14
One-eyed God: Odin and the (Indo-)Germanic Männerbünde, The, 199n53
Open borders, 202n59
Orbach, Jerry, 193
Order (Elite), 7, 12, 56n31, 76
Orphan, 4
Orthodox and ultra-Orthodox Judaism, 46n6
Orwell, George, 68
Oscar™, 80
Other, The, 2n5, 20
Our Gang, 16n1
Our Man Flint, 217, 224n43
"Our Wagner, Only Better: Harry Partch, The Wild Boy of American Music," 75n21, 127n12
Out Our Way, 20
Outer Boroughs, 201
Outer Limits, The, 223
Outside the Law School Scam, 88m2
Outsider, The, 113n11

Oven State, 176
Owellian, 60

P
Packard, Vance, 116
Paglia, Camille, 145n34
Pals, 36, 40
Pamela, 109
Pangborn, Franklin, 27
Parallax, 4, 10, 12-13
Parenti, Michael, 59n41
Parfrey, Adam, 11n27
Parker, Sarah Jessica, 192-93
Parmenides, 77
Parrott, Matt, 17n6
Partch, Harry, 75n21, 127-30, 144, 152, 160n47
Party Monster, 178-79, 198, 201n57, 206n73
Pasolini, 181n11
Passing of the Great Race, The, 23n16
Pater, Walter, 91n10, 129n16
Path of Cinnabar, The, 45n2, 67n15, 113n12
Patroclus, 23n16
PC, 27n27, 33n38, 34, 71, 84-87, 105-107, 154, 223,
Peanuts, 20
Pearse, Padraig, 108
Peart, Neil, 199
Peck, Gregory, 88n4
Pelosi, Nancy, 85
Pency Prep., 87n4
Penthouse Letters, 135n25
People of the Body: Jews and Judaism from an Embodied Perspective, 2n3
Permanent War, 31
Persia and Persians, 25n21, 23n27
Pesci, Joe, 73
Pet Shop Boys, 113n11
Peter Pan, 29
Petras, James, 59n41
Phantom of the Opera, The (cultural meme) 112m10
Pharisees, 42, 44-59
"Phil and Will: Awakening Through Repetition in *Groundhog Day*, *Point of Terror*, and *Manhunter*, Part 2," 97n23

Phipps, Alexander, 30-31
Phonies, 87n4
Picasso, Pablo, 111
Pickens, "Slim," 163n2
Pieper, Josef, 40n54, 47n8
Pillbox hat, 187, 190
Pink Swastika, The, 32n38,
Pipes of Pan, 152
Pirate Utopias, 155n43
Plato, 11, 55, 58n39, 78
Playboy, 49n16, 163n3, 168
Playboy Editorial Award, 49n17
Playboy Stories: The Best of Forty Years of Short Fiction 2, 49n17
Plotinus, 11, 126n8
Point Counter Point, 217n29
Polygamy, 20, 29
Pontiac Firebird, 180
Pop, Iggy, 1
Population crisis, 40n53, 56n31
Porn, 60-67n15, 180, 188n26, 220
Port of Saints, 147, 153n40
Post-Modernism, 195n42
Potter, Harry, 81
Pound, Ezra, 211
Power, Susan, 86
Powers, J. P., 91n10
Prague, 60-61, 63-64
Preston, Keith, 84
Priapism, 46
Primary Colors, 111
Prime of Miss Jean Brodie (book), 80-87, 216n28; (film), 80, 81
Prince of the Air, 191n34; see also Lucifer; Satan
Prince Valiant, 20
Proclamation of London of the European Liberation Front, The, 32n36
Progress (cultural meme), 27n24, 66n12, 55n29, 96
Prohibition, 49n17
Projection (Judaic psychological technique), 204
Propaganda, 28, 42, 64, 154, 156, 186, 216n27, 227
Proust, Marcel, 62, 64
Prussian Socialism, 113n12
Psychoanalysis, 26, 45n2
Psychology, 26, 42, 116n19

Psychomania, 7n13, 10-12
Public schools (British-style), 36, 111, 165, 167
Public sector, 87
Pulitzer Prize, 90
Pulp fiction (genre), 16
Punch, 110
Purdah, 25n21
Purity of essence, 166n9; see also Fluoridation
Putin, Vladimir, 27n26, 223n39
Pynchon, Thomas, 176

Q
Quality of life enforcement, 202
Quality, 214, 218-19
Queer, 105, 114-15, 120, 122-25, 128, 135n25, 144-45, 152, 162
Quest for Corvo: An Experiment in Biography, The, 116n19

R
Ra's al Ghul, 10n22
Race realism, 95n16, 98n27
Racism, 89-99, 154, 158
Radcliffe, Ann, 108
Radical chic, 226n47
Rainbow coalition of wreckers of civilization, 58, 106, 225
Ralph Adams Cram: Boston Bohemia, 1881–1900, 91n10
Rand, Ayn, 34, 217
Rätsch, Christian, 52n22
Raven, Alexander, 208n5
Ravers, 201
Red Alert, 177n28
Red Army, 66n11
Red Zone Cuba; see *Night Train to Mundo Fine*
Redwoods, 196, 198
Reed, Douglas, 19n9
Reed, Jeremy, 108
Reed, Lou, 161
Reich, Wilhelm, 83
Reid, Forrest, 108
Reign of Quantity and the Signs of the Times, The, 78n22, 195n42, 214n22
Reilly, Ignatius, 225
Religion, Abrahamic, 10-11

Renaissance, The, 55n29
Reproductive Strategy, 40n54
Republican Party, 18n7
Revenge of the Creature, The, 220
Review of James Neill's "The Origins and Role of Same-Sex Relations in Human Societies," 24n19, 121n3
Revolt Against Civilization, The, 23n16
Revolt Against the Modern World, 10n22, 39n52
Reynolds, Ryan, 3
Rice, Condoleezza, 86
Rice, Tim, 70
Richardson, Samuel, 109
Richthoven, Baron von, 33n38
Ride the Tiger: A Survival Manual for Aristocrats of the Soul, 7n15, 67n15, 71, 225
Ridenhour, Jameson, 108
Riefenstahl, Leni, 219n33
Ring, The (*Green Lantern*), 3-15
Ripper, General "Jack" D., 31m34, 163-71
Risus sardonicus, 164n5
Robertson, Ritchie, 50n19
Rivendell, 5
Robber Barons, 14
Robin Hood, 4n8
Robinson, Tom, 98
Robot, Crow T., 29-30
Rock, Chris, 211n13, 215n24
Rocket State, 176
Rogan, Seth, 5n11
Roger, Bunny, 27n26
Rolling Stone (magazine), 145, 147n39
Rolls Royce, 196
Roman Empire, 187n25
Romeo and Juliet, 109
Romeos, 36
Romney, Mitt, 45n2
Room at the Top, 108
Rootless cosmopolitans, 15
Rosenberg, Alfred, 66n11
Rosenkrantz and Guildenstern are Dead, 179n3
Rostkowski, Mark, 24n18
Roth, Tim, 15n35
Rottwang (*Metropolis*), 172
Round the Red Lamp, 108

Royal Military College of Canada, 187n25
Rucci, Ralph, 182-83, 195
Rumsfeld, Donald, 54n24
Rush (rock band), 199
Rush, Geoffrey, 4
Russell, Ken, 206
Russia, 56, 153
Russian Ambassador, 163, 170, 175, 177
Russian novelists, 116n18

S
S. Fisher Co., 60
S/M, 225
SA, 227n51
Saarsgard, Peter, 1, 4, 13
Sabu, 22
Sadducees, 44
Sade, D. A. F., Marquis de, 181n11
Sailer, Steve, 48, 57n36, 93, 103n37, 218
Saint Laurent, Yves, 189
Salazar, António de Oliveira, 208
Salinger, J. D., 91n10
Sallis, Ted, 5n10, 195n44
Salo, 181n11
Salon, 62n2
Salt Lake City, 56, 57
Salvation Army, 218n32
Samsa, Gregor, 2n4, 62
Samson, Brock, 207
San Francisco, 196
Sanctuary cities, 99
Santa Cruz islanders, 39n49
Sante, Luc, 153n40
Sartre, Jean-Paul, 113m11
Satan, 158; see also Lucifer; Prince of the Air
Satanic, 161, 197
Saturday Night Fever, 201
Savage, The, 150
Savitri Devi, 157, 160, 177
Schoenberg, Arnold, 160n47
Schopenhauer, Arthur, 2n3
Schrodeder, Leopold von, 9Cn9
Schuon, Frithjof, 47n8
Science of Getting Rich, 11
Science, 51n21, 55n29, 76, 78-79, 85, 185
Scotland, 124, 142
Scout; see Jean Louise Finch
Scumbags, 99-100; see also Lawyers
Seagram, Joseph, 49n17
Seattle World's Fair, 219n33
Second Foundation, 40
Secret Source, The, 11n27
Secret, The (Oprah's), 11, 14
Seinfeld, 64n6
Self Condemned, 49n17
Sellers, Peter, 163n2, 166
Sellers, Terence, 135n25
Servo, Tom, 29-30
Sexology, 26
Sexual Personae, 145n34
Sexual Revolution, 71, 220
Shahak, Israel, 51n21
Shahîn, 130, 147
Shakespeare, 50
Shamans and shamanism, 53-54, 123-25, 132, 204n67
Shand-Tucci, Douglass, 91n10
Shaw, Clay, 208n4
Sherlock Holmes, 4n8
Shiva, 10
Shorts (male), 73, 209-10, 212, 215, 219, 221-22, 224
Shylocks, 205
Shysters, 99-100; see also Lawyers
Silver Age of Comics, 3
Silver Shirts, 209
Silverman, Sarah, 1n2
Simpson, Mark, 220-21
Sinclair, David, 147n39
Sinestro, 1, 4, 5, 15
Sirius, 120
Sitsky, Larry, 128n13
Sitting Pretty, 27n25
Skerl, Jeanette, 148
Skinhead, 41, 85, 225n45
Skydivers, The, 70
Smiles, smiling, 4n8, 36, 123, 139-44, 148, 151, 159, 164n5
Smirnov, Yaakov, 8n16
Smith, Maggie, 80, 81
Smokey and the Bandit, 180
SNL, 19n9, 135n24
Sobran, Joe, 48n11

Soccer rioters, 201
Social and Political Thought of Julius Evola, 40n53
Social Darwinists, 14
Social Gospel, 14
Social Republic, 181n11
Socrates, 197
Solar vs. Telluric, 214
Some Boys, 25n21
Son of Trevor Lynch's White Nationalist Guide to the Movies, 178n1
Soul of Man Under Socialism, The, 113n12
South Africans, 154, 209
South, The, 90, 94, 104, 109, 199
Southern Baptist, 90
Southern Way of Life, 93
Soviet Union, 8n16, 154
Spain, 81-82
Spanish Civil War, 80
Spark, Muriel, 80, 83-84
Sparta, 51n21
Spawn, 13n31
Speedo (swimwear), 220-24
Speedophobia, 220-21
Spellman, John Cardinal, 91n10, 106
Spender, Stephen, 111
Spengler, Oswald, 182, 184-86, 188n26, 189n29, 191, 194
Sphinx, 142
Spider Baby, 131, 141
Spider Man 2-3
Spode, Roderick, 7th Earl of Sidcup, known as Spode or Lord Sidcup, 209-10
Spring Comes Again, 208n5
Squirm, 180n9
SS (*Schutzstaffel*), 56n31, 80, 82, 122n5, 190n31, 227n51
St. James, James, 201n57
St. Patrick's Cathedral, 184, 197
Stach, Reiner, 63
Stalky & Co., 147, 166
Stapledon, Olaf, 105, 120-21, 153, 155, 161
Star Wars II: Attack of the Clones, 4
Star Wars, 6
Starfighters, The, 198n52
Starling, Clarice, 93

Starship Troopers (film), 13n31, 163n4
Staten Island, 201, 204
STDs, 36
Steckler, Ray Dennis, 136-37, 160n47
Steppenwolf (novel), 13
Sterzinger, Ann, 75n17
Stirnerites, 35n41
Stoddard, Lothrop, 23
Stoker, Bram, 108
Stone, Oliver, 208n4
Strange Case of Alger, The, 92n11
Strangelove, Dr. (Merkwürdigliebe), 162, 172n19, 173-74, 177
Stravinsky, Igor, 178n1
Strong, Mark, 1, 4
Stucco, Guido, 201n58
Studio 54, 179n5, 181, 199-200
Stuff Black People Don't Like, 40n54, 96n18, 158n44, 163n4
Sturgeon, Theodore, 120
Stymie, 16
Sublimation, 35
Sudler-Smith, Whitney, 178-80, 192-194n41
Sunić, Tomislav, 84n3
Superdickery, 37n45
Superman, 2, 37n45
Supreme Court, 93
Supreme Identity: An Essay on Oriental Metaphysic and the Christian Religion, The, 47n8
Sutherland, Douglas, 116
Sutherland, Graham, 111
Swan, Curt, 3
Switzerland, 79, 116n18
SWPL, 28
Symons, A. J. A., 116n19
Syphilis, 79, 160

T
T. S. Eliot's Social Criticism, 48n12
Talented tenth, 188n26, 226
Talkative Corpse, The, 75n17
Talley, Andre Leon, 180m 182, 188n26, 190
Talmud, 19n9, 46n6, 48n12, 51n21, 193
Tantric Yoga, 46, 200
Tarantino, Quentin, 61

Index

Tatara, Paul, 13n31
Taunton, Gwendolyn von, 39n51, 40n53, 186n22, 188n26
Taylor, Alan, 80
Taylor, Jared, 23n16
Tchaikovsky, Peter, 58n39
Team spirit, 84
Teenage pregnancy, 36
Teenagers from Outer Space, 78n23
Teeth, 138, 142, 145
Telepathy, 124-25, 148-49
Templars, 20n22
Temporary Autonomous Zones, 190n31
Teutonic Knights, 33n38
Thanksgiving, 106
Thatcher, Margaret, 39
Theozoology, or the Science of the Sodomite Apelings and the Divine Electron, 57n37
They Live, 97, 137
Third Eye, 10
Third Reich, 56n31, 176, 215n24
Third World, 34n39
Thongs, 73
Those Who Can See, 97n20
Thought Vibration: Or, The Law of Attraction in the Thought World, 115n19
Thoughts are Things, 126-27, 141n28, 143n30
Three Stooges, 230
Thrush (spy organization), 223
Thurmm, Nathan, 19n9
Times Square Station, 218n32
Tío Mate, 148
To Kill a Mockingbird, 88-104
Tobias, N. A., 188n26
Tokyo, 15n34
Tolerance, 95-96
Tomar Re, 4, 12
Tocqueville, Alexis de, 50
Torah, 46n6
Toray Industries, 184
Toronto, 49, 205
Totalitarian Humanitarianism, 84, 86
Towards the White Republic, 42n35,
Town, The, 3
Townsend, Peter, 47n8

Tractate Bikkurim, 46n6
"Tradition, 'Traditionalism,' and Really Existing Homosexuality," 25n22
Tradition, 24n18, 25, 32, 45n2, 178, 213-15
Tradition, Aryan, 10n22
Tradition, Christian, 52
Tradition, Hermetic, 12n28, 120n2
Tradition, Primordial, 11
Traditional clothing, 213ff.
Traditional Muslim society, 24-5
Traditional theory of music, 129, 152
Traditionalism, 7, 47n8, 114
Tragic City: Birmingham 1963-2013, The, 96n18
Trampps, The, 196
Transcendent Unity of Religion, The, 47n8
Trevelyan, Raleigh, 27n26
Trevor Lynch's White Nationalist Guide to the Movies, 206n75
Trial, The, 61
Trials of Roderick Spode ("The Human Ant"), 209n11
Tribe, The, 5n10, 63-64, 180-81; see also Jews; Judaics
Tribeca Film Festival, 192
Triumph of the Will, 12
Tropic Thunder, 193
True Right, 17n3, 18n8
Trusts (business), 14
Tsomotre, 129-30
Turgidson, General "Buck," 162-76
TV Tropes, 164
Twain, Mark, 100, 106
Twelve Angry Men, 87n4, 88
Twilight Zone, 31n33
TYR II, 52n2

U

UFOlogy, 207
Ultraettes, 190; see also Halstonettes
Ultrasuede (material), 184-85,
Ultrasuede: The Life of Halston, 136n26, 178-97
Ulysses, 74
UN General Assembly, 5
UN Security Council, 5

Uncle Jack, 90, 95, 98-99n28
Undersea Kingdom, The, 220
Uniforms, 184, 190n31, 208-209, 215n28-17, 225-27
Unpleasantness at the Bellona Club, The, 167n11
Untermenschen, 9, 40n58
Untouchables, The (film), 37n44, 53n25, 86n5, 122n6, 195n45, 204n67
Unz Review, 103n37
Upper West Side Jews, 87n4
Upstairs Downstairs, 112
Ur Group, 201n58
Utopia, 54, 71, 129, 143-44, 150, 152, 159, 162, 167, 170, 172, 175-77, 216; see also Anti-Utopia; Utopia, Queer, 144, 162

V
V-2, 176
Valancourt Books, 104, 107, 109
Valhalla, 14m 201
Vatican II, 91n10
Vaughan, 111
Veblen, Thorstein, 48n14, 65n10
Venner, Dominique, 196n48, 199n55
Venture Bros, The, 207
Verlaine, Paul, 91n10
Verticality, 55n29
Vienna Circle, 77
Viet Nam, 56
Vigilantism, 7
Viking heritage, 47n7
Violent Years, The, 31
Virginia, 47
Visconti, Luigi, 83
Vlaams Belang, 226
Vogue, 180, 182
Voltaire, 87
Vreeland, Diana, 196

W
Wagner, Richard, 75n21, 127n12, 213n20
Wain, John, 108
Wales, 69
Wandervogel, 35n41
War Room, 163-77

Warhol, Andy, 186-87, 198, 200
WASPs, 22
Watchmen, 88
Watson, Peter, 111
Wattles, Wallace D., 11
Watts, Alan, 45, 47n8, 51, 91, 132-34, 213n21, 224
Waugh, Evelyn, 25n23
We Boys Together: Teenagers in Love before Girl-Craziness, 16, 21-25
Weaving (symbolism), 76-77
Weaving, Hugo, 5
Webb, Clifton, 27, 30n31, 41
Weber, Mark, 208n6
Weimar, 181
Weininger, Otto, 67n15
Weinstein, Harvey, 192-93, 196n47
Welch, Robert, 92n11
West Virginia, 179n6
What to Do on a Date, 28-29
Where the Wild Boys Are, 17n3
White America, 40, 44n1, 93, 158
White culture, 22
White guilt, 158
White man, 23, 40n54, 97n23, 157, 179
White Nationalists, 17n6, 44, 46, 54n26, 178n1, 216n75
White trash, 93n14, 99, 180n8
Whitopia, 44, 57
Why You Should Read Kafka Before You Waste Your Life; see *Excavating Kafka*
Wild Boy, 16-17, 27n26, 75n21, 127n12, 144, 146, 148, 153, 222n36
"Wild Boys vs. 'Hard Men,'" 27n26
Wild Boys: A Book of the Dead, The, 47n4, 57n34, 120, 144-45, 148-49, 153n40, 159
Wild Cherry, 179n5
Wilde, Oscar, 67n15, 91n10, 107, 113, 113n12, 114, 116n18, 222n36
Wilhelmine Germany, 79
Will, The, 10-15
Willoughby, 94, 101-102
Wilson, Colin, 108-109, 113n11
Wilson, Darren, 57n36
Wimsey, Lord Peter, 167n11
Winthrop, 20
Wisdom, 90n9, 199

Wising Up the Marks: The Amodern William Burroughs, 145m33
Wizard of Id, The, 20
Wodehouse, P. G., 209-12
Wolfe, Tom, 226n 47
Women's Wear Daily, 189, 190
Wood, Edward D., Jr., 31, 193n37
Woodstock, 201n58
Wooster, Bertie, 209-10, 214-15
Word Virus: The William S. Burroughs Reader, 57n34, 111n9
Workers' Accident Insurance Institute, 62
World Trade Center, 183
World War I, 33n38, 61
World War II, 21, 26, 31, 33n38, 175, 216
Worstward Ho, 177n27
Wotan, 179n3, 198-203
Wright, Jeremiah, 18n7
Wyndham, John, 120
Wynne, Frank, 70

X
X, Malcolm, 92n11

Y
Yeats, William Butler, 108, 127n12
Yiddish, 14, 63, 65n10
Yiddish Theatre, 65n10
Yockey, Francis Parker, 27n24, 28, 32, 37, 40, 113n12
Young Adult Books, 87n4
Yuppies, 14m 61, 63, 66

Z
Zebra Killer, 92n11
Zeitblom, Serenus, 160-61
Zimbu, 148n36, 151
Zivilisation, 195
Žižek, Slavoj, 113n12
Zoe, Rachel, 192-93
Zombies, 67, 160n47
Zooey, 91n10
Zorn, Fritz, 116n18

About the Author

James J. O'Meara was born in Detroit, educated in Canada, and now lives in an abandoned glove factory in America's Rust Belt. He is the author of *The Homo & the Negro: Masculinist Meditations on Politics & Popular Culture*, ed. Greg Johnson (San Francisco: Counter-Currents, 2012); *A Review of James Neill's "The Origins and Role of Same-Sex Relations in Human Societies"* (Amazon.com: Kindle Editions, 2013); *The Eldritch Evola . . . & Others: Traditionalist Meditations on Literature, Art, & Culture*, ed. Greg Johnson (San Francisco: Counter-Currents, 2014); and *End of an Era:* Mad Men *& the Ordeal of Civility* (San Francisco: Counter-Currents, 2015). His articles and reviews have also been published by Counter-Currents/*North American New Right*, *The Occidental Observer*, *Alexandria*, *FringeWare Review*, *Aristokratia*, and *Judaic Book News*.